THE
RECURRING
SILENT SPRING

Pergamon Titles of Related Interest

Spallone, Steinberg MADE TO ORDER: The Myth of Reproductive and Genetic Progress

Related Journals
(Free sample copies available upon request)

REPRODUCTIVE AND GENETIC ENGINEERING: Journal of International Feminist Analysis
WOMEN'S STUDIES INTERNATIONAL FORUM

The ATHENE Series

General Editors
Gloria Bowles
Renate Klein
Janice Raymond

Consulting Editor
Dale Spender

The Athene Series assumes that all those who are concerned with formulating explanations of the way the world works need to know and appreciate the significance of basic feminist principles.

The growth of feminist research has challenged almost all aspects of social organization in our culture. The Athene Series focuses on the construction of knowledge and the exclusion of women from the process—both as theorists and subjects of study—and offers innovative studies that challenge established theories and research.

On Athene—When Metis, goddess of wisdom who presided over all knowledge was pregnant with Athene, she was swallowed up by Zeus who then gave birth to Athene from his head. The original Athene is thus the parthenogenetic daughter of a strong mother and as the feminist myth goes, at the "third birth" of Athene she stops being Zeus' obedient mouthpiece and returns to her real source: the science and wisdom of womankind.

H. PATRICIA HYNES

THE
RECURRING
SILENT SPRING

PERGAMON PRESS
New York   Oxford   Beijing   Frankfurt   São Paulo   Sydney

Pergamon Press Offices:

U.S.A.	Pergamon Press, Inc., Maxwell House, Fairview Park, Elmsford, New York 10523, U.S.A.
U.K.	Pergamon Press plc, Headington Hill Hall, Oxford OX3 0BW, England
PEOPLE'S REPUBLIC OF CHINA	Pergamon Press, Qianmen Hotel, Beijing, People's Republic of China
FEDERAL REPUBLIC OF GERMANY	Pergamon Press GmbH, Hammerweg 6, D-6242 Kronberg, Federal Republic of Germany
BRAZIL	Pergamon Editora Ltda, Rua Eça de Queiros, 346, CEP 04011, São Paulo, Brazil
AUSTRALIA	Pergamon Press Australia Pty Ltd., P.O. Box 544, Potts Point, NSW 2011, Australia
JAPAN	Pergamon Press, 8th Floor, Matsuoka Central Building, 1-7-1 Nishishinjuku, Shinjuku-ku, Tokyo 160, Japan
CANADA	Pergamon Press Canada Ltd., Suite 271, 253 College Street, Toronto, Ontario M5T 1R5, Canada

First edition 1989

Library of Congress Cataloging in Publication Data

Hynes, H. Patricia.
   The recurring silent spring / by H. Patricia Hynes. -- 1st ed.
     p.   cm. -- (The Athene series)
   ISBN 0-08-037117-5 :   ISBN 0-08-037116-7 (pbk.) :

   1. Carson, Rachel, 1907-1964. Silent spring. 2. Carson, Rachel, 1907-1964. 3. Ecologists--United States--Biography. I. Title. II. Series.
QH545.P4H96   1988
574'.092'4--dc19
[B]   88-29049
                                      CIP

Printed in the United States of America

∞™ The paper used in this publication meets the minimum requirements of American National Standard for Information Sciences -- Permanence of Paper for Printed Library Materials, ANSI Z39.48-1984

DEDICATION

For Jan Raymond
whose love and intelligence affect,
move, and stir me to full power

Love-thou art high-
I cannot climb thee-
But, were it Two-
Who knows but we-
Taking turns-at the Chimborazo-
Ducal-at last-stand up by thee-

Love-thou are deep-
I cannot cross thee-
But, were there Two
Instead of One-
Rower, and Yacht-some sovereign Summer-
Who knows-but we'd reach the Sun?

Emily Dickinson
The Complete Poems of Emily Dickinson

CONTENTS

ACKNOWLEDGMENTS

I began this book while working in the Environmental Protection Agency and continued writing it while being Chief of Environmental Management at the Massachusetts Port Authority. In both public agencies I had many colleagues who listened with great interest and enthusiasm to incipient ideas which subsequently formed the analysis of this book. Of those, I am particularly grateful to Sally Edwards, Susan Santos, Clara Chow, Barbara McCallister, Gerry Levy, Charles Bering, Robin Ellis, Bob Reyes and Norm Faramelli for their sustained collegial support. EPA head librarian Peg Nelson and Massport technical services librarian Natalie Ridge gave me invaluable and rapid assistance with scientific literature, government documents, and film. Dr. Donna Bedard of the General Electric Company generously provided me with reports of her work on PCB biodegradation. Roberto de la Cruz, the New England Regional Representative of the United Farm Workers of America, AFL-CIO, reconstructed the history of farmworker activism against pesticides. Dr. David Ferro and Mr. William Coli of the University of Massachusetts, Amherst, discussed the concepts of integrated pest management (IPM) and provided me with technical reports on the current Massachusetts program. Vital conversations with Shirley Briggs, Executive Director of the Rachel Carson Council, confirmed my understanding of Rachel Carson as a woman who lived at "the broad margins of life."

I am grateful to the Athene Series editors, Gloria Bowles, Renate Klein, and Janice Raymond and Acquisitions Editor, Terri Ezekiel, for their great interest in publishing this book and for a smooth and rapid publication process. My agent Charlotte Cecil Raymond kept track of me as I toured Europe on a German Marshall Fund Fellowship while she finessed publication details. Alice Hanley Raymond was an excellent proofreader whose presence made that job enjoyable.

My family being large and rambling, it is easy to thank them collectively for an intangible past which set roots deep in me. Some of those roots fed this book, among them my mother's belief that education and a sense of spirituality were the most important things she could give her children. I especially thank my sisters, Marge and Mary, for their specific engagement in my work and in whom I have become; and I bless my brother Michael for his benefaction.

Many friends have followed my life as I began and completed this book. To Barbara Hanley, Jill Mayer, and Sister Dorothy Hennessy, I say how glad I am that we remain in each other's lives. Gena Corea, Kathy Barry, and Andrea Dworkin are dear friends whose radical, passionate work for women always inspires my own. There are those friends whose good company, conversation, and correspondence has offered respite from long days of writing: Kathy Alexander, Denice Yanni, Fern Johnson, Marlene Fine, Georgina Kish, Linda Scaparotti, Nellie Kanno, Alix Dobkin, Judy Luce, Gloria Brown, Susan Brindle, Susan Yarbrough, Susanne Kappeler, and Ann Frazier. From afar, Marille Herrmann has stayed close to my work; and we have shared the rigors of being feminists in science. Eileen Barrett asked when this book would be written, two years before I started. She has been a friend whose life of the mind always stirs my own.

INTRODUCTION

Writing a book on Rachel Carson and *Silent Spring* has been both easy and difficult. The ease lay in the double-edged blow of Carson's work. *Silent Spring* struck unerringly, like lightning, at the heart of the pollution crisis: man beating nature into submission with pesticides, as she saw it. The pesticide industry, skilled in the metaphor and habit of war on insects, turned the force of their armaments against her book. They tried to stop its publication; they produced parodies of it; they withdrew advertising and financial support from journals and media programs which favorably reviewed the book. One corporate scientist dedicated all his waking hours to crusading against the book and for pesticides. He charged that *Silent Spring* was "littered with crass assumptions" and would cause famine and death.[1]

Concurrently with the industrial whiplash, *Silent Spring* was compared to *Uncle Tom's Cabin*,[2] as another book written by a woman which

---

1. On learning that he died of a bee sting, I remembered two cartoons published after *Silent Spring* which depict the insects' affection for Rachel Carson. A grasshopper prays, "God bless Momma and Poppa . . . and Rachel Carson." In the second butterflies, ladybugs, wasps, and bees gather wildflowers and carry them to Rachel Carson's grave. It would seem that nature knows best. See Brooks 1972.
2. Harriet Beecher Stowe wrote *Uncle Tom's Cabin* prior to the American Civil War "from a passionate reaction against the recorded sadisms of slavery." Like *Silent Spring* this book became an immediate national sensation, described by Henry James as "less a book than a state of vision, of feeling and of consciousness." Another parallel between the two women's work is the sexualization of male contempt for them. Carson, as we shall see, was scornfully called "a spinster" who should have no concern for genetics; Stowe was "abused as a sexually driven nigger lover." Finally, both women so threatened the systems they challenged that extensive campaigns were launched to undermine their work. Within three years of its publication some thirty anti-Uncle Tom novels appeared. See Cross, 1973, pp. 393–402.

would substantially alter the course of American history. Almost immediately it was translated into every language of the industrial world. After the immense success of *The Sea Around Us*, Shirley Briggs, a close friend, had painted Carson as her readers imagined: an amazon standing tall and strong before a wild sea, vigilant to protect the earth. With *Silent Spring*, Carson would shake and awaken the world. Within a few years of its publication in 1962, every country in which *Silent Spring* was widely read was holding hearings on environmental legislation. By 1967 the Environmental Defense Fund had formed and was developing the legal grounds on which to have DDT banned. In April 1970, Earth Day was celebrated. *Silent Spring*'s cracking open of the world made the effort of writing this book easy.

The difficulty arose when some of those closest to her work resisted any new biographical work on Carson. They contend that she was private, so there is not much to know or tell about her person; that her life was her work, so people should read her work rather than probe her life; that enough has been written about her by those who knew her and, furthermore, that the definitive work on her already exists, Paul Brooks' *The House of Life*. In addition, some of her personal papers no longer exist; they were destroyed immediately after she died. The letters to Dorothy Freeman, the only other person besides her mother to whom Carson "gave herself completely," as Paul Brooks wrote, are currently unavailable. These letters were written just before and during the years in which Carson researched and wrote *Silent Spring*.

Both realities, that *Silent Spring* is the most vital and controversial book ever written on the environment, and that obstacles lie en route to writing about Carson, have shaped the direction and proportion of my work, while they have not dictated it. Much as a pearl originates with a grain of sand, after which its luster, color, and proportion are shaped by the circumstantial ecology of the oyster, so this book had its own originating grain: one not unlike *Silent Spring*'s.

In her Acknowledgements, Rachel Carson explains why she undertook *Silent Spring*. "In a letter written in January 1958, Olga Owens Huckins told me of her own bitter experience of a small world made lifeless. . . . I then realized I must write this book" (Carson 1962, Acknowledgements). My own book originated from a similar place: my shock at the kill-potential of technology and the many "silent springs" throughout the planet; my anger at living in a world in which nature and women are presumed to exist for the use and convenience of men, so that the destruction of nature and violence against women are interconnected, increasingly technologized, and infect all corners of the earth. This book originated, as did Carson's, from looking at what she called "so much death." Like her, I wrote from a deep desire for all of this to change.

I reread *Silent Spring* in early 1984 while working as a senior engineer in the United States Environmental Protection Agency's (EPA) hazardous waste program. EPA was emerging from a crisis in its loss of environmental mission, instigated by the Reagan Administration and carried out by his appointees, including EPA Administrator Anne Gorsuch. I was struck that the staff of a government agency clung so tightly to its mission "to protect the environment." That reading of *Silent Spring* and the stubborn remnant of idealism in EPA led me to all of the biography on Carson and the analytic work on *Silent Spring*. I found what Steven Fox did when he began researching what would become *John Muir and His Legacy: The History of the American Conservation Movement* (Fox 1981), only the order differed. Fox started with studying the American conservation movement and discovered its originating force, John Muir. I started with Carson, and an intuition of her influence on EPA, and found the second wave of American environmentalism. Like his work, mine contains the elements of biography, history, and analysis. He developed these in sequence; mine are interwoven. Fox found authorized biographies, uncritical studies, subsequent picture books, and juvenile biographies based on the original biographies, most written without access to Muir's papers. He had access to the papers and wanted to write a "fresh picture of the man." I found authorized biographies written with access to most of Carson's papers, derivative works, juvenile biographies, vignettes, and Fox's own chapter on Carson within the work on Muir. I found an increasingly stereotyped, one-dimensional, "unmarried" woman—Fox is as culpable as the others in constructing her thus—and wanted to write a fresh picture of the woman.

Silent Spring altered a balance of power in the world. No one since would be able to sell pollution as the necessary underside of progress so easily or uncritically. I have thought long and hard about this because it is so rare—a few times a century—that a woman's mind finds such full expression and full effect. Was it a readiness in the world for the message? Yes and no, or better, not just that. Six months before *Silent Spring*, Murray Bookchin, under the pen name of Lewis Herber, published *Our Synthetic Environment*, a book which covered the same ground as *Silent Spring*, and also wider territory. Bookchin wrote that the pollution of the natural world, environmentally induced illness, and the centralization of life in cities devoid of nature, result from modern society's domination of nature and alienation from it. In the introduction to a 1974 edition, he reviewed and updated this work, and compared its impact to that of *Silent Spring*. Asking why Carson's work catalyzed the industrial world and his did not, he concluded that the world was "captivated by the superb prose of *Silent Spring*, while his work had a small, specialized audience . . . the technically trained" (Bookchin 1974). Ironically, of the

two she was the technically trained scientist; and her work had more
scientific rigor than his. Without offering the respect for Carson's work
that Bookchin did, industry also charged that the "poetic nature
writing" allured readers and made for soft science. Was her power primarily in her prose? Bookchin is a very good writer; she was a gifted
one. He "told"; she "showed." One finishes his book with the facts in
hand; one reads her book armed with them. Mediated by prose, the
difference is more than one of writing style; it is the difference between
rational and passionate thinking. In his work we are critical onlookers.
She wrote with a "feeling mind and thinking heart."[3] In her work we
enter into the problem.

Carson brought to her work a pragmatic, worldly critique of government, one benefit of 14 years of working for the federal government in
the Fish and Wildlife Service. The book was activist, not just expository;
it was written to reform, not just to have a forum. She pinned down the
loopholes in federal environmental regulation, exposed the manipulation of data to cover up pesticide hazards, and identified conflicts of
interest in government regulation of pesticides. The reforms she called
for in the book and afterwards in Congressional hearings were grounded
and actionable. There was somewhere to go with her work: she called it
"the other road, the one less traveled by."

Carson wrote from the inside of science out. This is critical for me and
is ingrained in the writing of this book. In the latter part of the nineteenth century and early twentieth century, the era in which Carson was
born, a woman scientist was a contradiction in terms. As middle- and
upper-middle-class American women began campaigning to enter the
science departments of male universities, professional men propounded
unscientific and self-serving myths of women's lesser mental ability and
stamina to do science, based on the demands and limitations of female
biology. Women were seen as best doing soft, noncompetitive, "wom-
anly" activities which left their energy intact for reproduction. Science
was tough, rational, competitive, and "masculine"; it would siphon off a
woman's reproductive energy.[4] Maria Mitchell, the astronomer and most
prominent American woman scientist of the nineteenth century, made

3. Paraphrased from Janice Raymond 1979: "to feel with all my intellect and think with all
my heart."
4. The biologically determinist arguments were aimed at middle-class white women who
wanted access to universities to study science. The theories of rigorous work damaging
reproductive organs were not applied to nineteenth-century working-class women who
worked factory jobs which were more physically demanding than studying, nor to black
women who labored in plantation fields, often gave birth there, and were expected to

an astute observation in her 1875 Presidential address to the Association for the Advancement of Women. "In my younger days, when I was pained by the half-educated, loose, and inaccurate ways which we all had, I used to say, 'How much women need exact science.' But since I have known some workers in science who were not always true to the teachings of nature, who have loved self more than science, I have now said, 'How much science needs women'" (Rossiter 1982, p. 14). Looking from the inside of science, she captured a fundamental struggle of women in science, to pierce the mystique of male ability and female inability woven like a tight integument around science. Piercing it, she saw, as Carson would, the lie within.

The challenge for women scientists of the nineteenth and early twentieth centuries was how to get into science departments, how to get educated, and then how to get professional work. Male strategies, as Margaret Rossiter documents, first kept women science students out of their universities altogether and then out of their graduate departments, once women had gained access to the undergraduate level. Then male science faculties refused to employ women scientists, even if they had to educate them. Finally, they adamantly opposed advancing or promoting any but the most extraordinary (Rossiter 1982). At the turn of the century, Ellen Swallow, a precursor of Carson in environmental work, suffered every element of this defeatist strategy. Swallow's entire adult life was a series of crusades to prevail against the obstacles put in her way by the Massachusetts Institute of Technology (MIT), first to matriculate in the chemistry department, then to be admitted to the Ph.D program, and finally to be given a tenured faculty position. The Ph.D and tenured position were never granted her, although MIT recognized and used her brilliance by retaining her as an instructor for 25 years. Her most notable work—the founding of the interdisciplinary science of ecology—was delegitimated and rejected by the scientific aristocracy of MIT, as unpedigreed, insufficiently specialized, and too much a field of women. In the latter part of her life she took the same science to the audience more receptive to her—women in the home—calling it domestic science or home economics. This reduction of environmental science and engi-

---

provide new generations of slaves. Clearly the biological theories of women's inferiority were constructed as women's demands to enter men's world began to threaten male dominance. See Birke 1986, p. 27. Ruth Bleier summarizes the intent of biological theories about women's intellectual inferiority which have arisen with the first and second waves of feminism as "a necessary part of the system and set of conventions by which all-male science faculties justify their continuing exclusion of women as colleagues" (Bleier 1986, p. 11).

neering into home economics was a trivial end to work which had enormous potential for the environmentally unregulated industrial world at the beginning of the twentieth century.[5] In turning to a female audience and a "feminine" field, Swallow actually was diverted to servicing men. She became another in that history of talented women who work through men or for men because there is no other forum for their work. The woman who started the first laboratory for women at MIT finished her life professionalizing housekeeping, cooking, and child care.

Until Rachel Carson, historians could dedicate only a few pages in the annals of the American ecology movement and the history of environmental science to the contributions of women. This was not for lack of women or their contributions but because most lived and worked as assistants to and in the shadow of "great" men. In his biography of John Muir, Stephen Fox wrote of Marion Randall Parsons, one of the prominent women in American conservation, "[She] worked closely with Muir in his last years going out to Martinez . . . to feed him and serve as his secretary" (Fox 1981, p. 342). At the beginning of Muir's career another woman, Jeanne Carr, a botanist, served as sister, mother, colleague, encouraging him to write, sharing her botanical findings with him, and introducing him to prominent men. "Under her tutelage," the isolated, unsure of himself, at times misanthropic Muir, "bloomed and thrived" (Fox 1981, pp. 45–46). Rachel Carson has shattered, I hope, the tradition of women in the conservation and environmental movement functioning as the supporters and helpmates of the heroic male leaders. This role has rendered the majority of women invisible, understated, or mute to history, while it has allowed men to shape the analysis and values of environmentalism. On her own authority as scientist and prominent naturalist writer, Carson challenged the directions, the priorities, and the values of the science–industry–government complex which was spawning increasingly destructive technologies.

When Carson began researching *Silent Spring* in 1958, she had already recognized that an analysis of science and its technologies was critically needed at a new level of meaning. The atomic bomb had been exploded on Japan; the sea was the dumping ground for waste from nuclear pow-

---

5. Swallow placed all of her trust in the liberating and uplifting power of scientific knowledge, as if knowledge of the chemistry of cooking and contaminants in the home would be as empowering as scientific expertise in municipal water pollution and water distribution systems, or in the chemistry of hazardous waste; and as if science used uncritically does not serve to sustain and reinforce the prevailing social and political structure of a society. Her attempts to educate women in domestic science and to "uplift" the quality of domestic life did, in fact, support "sexual romanticism" and played into the condescension and classicist elitism of the early twentieth century home economics movement.

er and weapons production; chemical pesticides were being aerially sprayed throughout the United States. She summed it up as a shift in the balance of power between men and nature, wrought by technology developed for World War II and afterwards billed as mid-twentieth century progress to legitimate its postwar use in society.

> Man's attitude toward nature is today critically important, simply because of his new found power to destroy it . . . I clearly remember that in the days before Hiroshima I used to wonder whether nature . . . actually needed protection from man. Surely the sea was inviolate and forever beyond man's power to change it. Surely the vast cycles by which water is drawn up into the clouds to return again to the earth could never be touched. And just as surely the vast tides of life—the migrating birds— would continue to ebb and flow over the continents, marking the passage of the seasons.
>
> But I was wrong. Even these things, that seemed to belong to the eternal verities, are not only threatened but have already felt the destroying hand of man.
>
> Today we use the sea as a dumping ground for radioactive wastes, which then enter the vast and uncontrollable movements of ocean water through the deep basins, to turn up no one knows where . . .
>
> The once beneficent rains are now an instrument to bring down from the atmosphere the deadly products of nuclear explosions. Water, perhaps our most precious natural resource, is used and misused at a reckless rate. Our streams are fouled with an incredible assortment of wastes—domestic, chemical, radioactive, so that our planet, though dominated by seas that envelop three-fourths of its surface, is rapidly becoming a thirsty world.
>
> We now wage war on other organisms, turning against them all the terrible armaments of modern chemistry, and we assume a right to push whole species over the brink of extinction . . . (Carson, July 1962).

Little more than a century ago, women began the struggle to be admitted to science institutions and to prove that women can think technically at least as well as men. Little more than 25 years ago, a scientifically trained woman indicted science for the destructive pathway it has taken. In the latter part of the twentieth century a feminist in science faces a more complex and more ominous reality. All of the hazards to nature and to life that Carson described are magnified. Science is increasingly less connected to nature and more synthetic in its activity. Yet its newest frontiers are the oldest ones: ecosystems, with the application of engineered microorganisms; and the bodies of women, with the new reproductive technologies. The underlying assumption of these technologies is the same: women and nature exist for the use and convenience of men. As such, they can be playgrounds and expendable frontiers for "technically sweet" (Oppenheimer's description of the atomic bomb project) science tinkering. Both technologies are justified as urgently needed, altruistic technical "fixes" for the problems of increasing human infertility and increasing world hunger due to nature's insufficient fertility. The underlying environmental, occupational, and sociopolitical causes of both problems are barely examined. The risks to ecosystems are downplayed as "science fiction" and as underestimating nature's complex ability to absorb mutated organisms. But environmentalists have been able to forestall the commercial application of engineered organisms into the environment. This initial success was due to the legal structure of environmental protection which was urged and inspired by *Silent Spring*.[6] Women have not fared as well. The risks to women, individually and as a class, of the hormones, drugs, medical procedures, and total medicalization of their lives, are overlooked as public policy centers on the ethics of commercialization of, and research on, embryos. In many countries experimentation on embryos is limited to the first 14 days of life. In those same countries experimentation on women with risk-laden drugs and medical procedures is not limited or forestalled. Nature and embryos, it seems, are better protected than women from invasive and potentially dangerous technologies.

The assumption that women and nature exist for the use and convenience of men has generated technologies undreamed of when Carson wrote *Silent Spring*. Carson broke ground for ecology and ecological activism in a science world she saw as increasingly hostile to nature. What then is the ground for feminism to break in science, a world equally hostile to women, but unchecked by a consciousness of women's integrity? This question flows under this entire book and surfaces in the final chapter.

This book is more biographical of *Silent Spring* than of Rachel Carson. There is only one chapter about Carson herself. The others analyze the science of *Silent Spring* and its subsequent political and ethical impact on the world. This is a proportion I believe Carson would like, because she

---

6. Throughout much of the 1980s, field tests of genetically engineered bacteria, planned by major industries, universities, and new biotech research groups, have been blocked by environmentalists using repeated lawsuits and court petitions. For example, in 1983 a research team at the University of California, funded by Advanced Genetic Sciences, planned to introduce an "ice-minus" bacteria, a bacteria from which a gene that codes for ice formation on plants was removed, on a potato crop. The National Institutes of Health approved the field test. A coalition of environmentalists obtained a court injunction against the field test on the grounds that the group had not complied with the 1969 National Environmental Protection Act which requires an environmental impact statement for the whole release program as well as for the individual projects. Although Advanced Genetic Sciences did win a court challenge to spray genetically altered bacteria on strawberry plants in 1987, environmentalists have used the structure of environmental protection to stall experiments on the environment and to raise public consciousness about the risks of releasing genetically engineered organisms into nature. Nature has that much standing in environmental law. Would that women had equal standing in civil rights law.

conserved her personal self for her friends and preferred to be known by the rest of the world for her work. However, it is ample space in which to deconstruct the image of Carson created by a first generation of male biographers and reproduced by a recent second generation of them: that of a withdrawn, often lonely woman who lived a full professional life because her books were world-acclaimed, but an unfulfilled existence because she never married. My hope is that it enables her, as she expressed to Dorothy Freeman not long before she died, to live on through her work in the minds of those who would not know her.

The chapters are organized around the basic questions one asks of an inspired work which fueled the modern environmental movement. Why did Carson write *Silent Spring*? How did she make hydrocarbons compelling? *Silent Spring* crystallized an "ethic of the environment" which inspired grassroots environmentalism, the "deep ecology" movement, and the creation of the Environmental Protection Agency (EPA) and its state counterparts; it influenced the ecofeminist movement and feminist scientists. Where is that "ethic of the environment" felt and lived today? What is the net effect of institutionalizing a passion for the environment into a profession, environmental engineering, and a public agency with the mission to protect the environment, such as the Environmental Protection Agency? Were Carson writing today, what crisis in nature would she single out, as she did with pesticides, as paradigmatic of the others? Given the dominance of war-related and death-related technology today, would Carson still find as much value in science as she did in her last chapter, "The other road"? With the full benefit of the past two decades of feminism, how would Carson analyze the relationship of men and women to nature? Where would she direct her critique, what connections would she make between pollution and other oppression, most specifically the oppression of women? Or, turning the question of Carson writing today into one of my reading her work today, what do we learn from a feminist reading of Carson and *Silent Spring*?[7]

Chapter 1 has many purposes, but the main aim is to tell the story of how Carson came to write *Silent Spring*. The foreground is the time, the place, the state of the industrial world, the circumstances that started her writing. The background is an entire life of women who enabled her to achieve her full powers through believing in her and teaching her, through friendship and collegial respect, and through sharing her passion for nature.

---

7. Eileen Barrett suggested turning the question of how Carson would be writing today into my undertaking a feminist reading of *Silent Spring*. Conversation, May 1987.

Carson did not initially set out to write *Silent Spring*; in some respect she was chosen. A letter from a friend, Olga Owens Huckins, begged for help to stop the government from spraying DDT and killing wildlife. This began the chain of events which culminated in Carson's deciding to write a short work on pesticides. What she found in her research— widespread fish kills, death of wildlife, the portent of widespread cancer, government cover-up, partnerships of academic science and in- dustry, and silence from the medical profession—convinced her that she must construct an "unshakeable foundation" to withstand the storm the book would cause. She wrote to convey what she saw, that it was now possible for man to destroy the entire world, and pesticides were "one part of a sorry whole—the reckless pollution of our living world with harmful and dangerous substances" (Brooks 1972, p. 310). When she finished, she hoped that this book, which looked at so much death, would ultimately be a book about life.

In every meaning of the word "life," it was. The book was "an ani- mating force, a source of vitality, it transcended death." It "brought to life" in that it caused the world "to regain consciousness"; it "put spirit into the world." It was written "for dear life," that is, "desperately, ur- gently" and "for life . . . so as to save one's life." It was "true to life," in the sense of "not deviating from reality, faithfully representing real life." Finally in the original meaning of the word "life," to stick, to adhere, and continue (American Heritage Dictionary 1981), it was, as she had hoped, a book about life. *Silent Spring* has stuck in the consciousness of the world and continued to be the most influential book written on the environment. Its continuity has extended not only forward but also back through Carson's life. *Silent Spring* was the full blaze of the 17-year-old whose essay on herself disclosed the sparks: "Sometimes I lose sight of my goal, then again it flashes into view, filling me with a new determina- tion to keep the 'vision splendid' before my eyes."

Rachel Carson's first friend was her mother, Maria Carson, a woman remembered by Carson's friends for her love of books and nature. They enjoyed a lifelong bond constructed of the mutual love of ideas, Maria's constant support of Rachel's work, their shared raising of Carson's nieces and then a grand-nephew, and last, a mutual commitment to the purpose of *Silent Spring*. In her biography of the writer and activist Josephine Herbst, Elinor Langer wrote, "The legacy of her mother's belief in her was the greatest resource that Josie had" (Langer 1983, p. 29). This was also true for Carson, at least initially, until surpassed by her own belief in herself. With this friendship Carson's affection for women took root and grew into the rich, discerning capacity for friendship with women which marked her life.

Chapter 1 places the influence women had on Carson (her mother first and then her biology professor at Pennsylvania College for Women) within the tradition of women for whom women are first in their lives. Passionate friendship among women makes women visible and vital to each other (see Raymond 1986), and it has functioned as a strategy for power as Margaret Rossiter has documented (Rossiter 1982). This is precisely what the male biographers of Carson have misunderstood, ignored, and in some cases denigrated.

Raymond (1986) presents communities of women—nuns, the marriage resisters in the Kwantung area of China, the Beguines of Europe—who chose to live lifelong with women and who found love where their work was. On many levels this was true for Carson. Her vital love of nature, which led her to study science and later to write three books on the sea, besides *Silent Spring*, formed a universe within which she had rich, intellectual, and intimate friendships with women. It is most likely a consequence of this integral world of friendship and shared ideals, that while her scientific and literary colleagues were mainly men and men have written her biographies, women have championed, sustained, and carried on her work.

For example, Marie Rodell was Carson's literary agent, a choice Carson made carefully after several interviews. "Thus began a partnership and intimate friendship," wrote Paul Brooks, "that endured for the rest of Rachel Carson's life, and—as the monumental and detailed correspondence between them shows—became a leading factor in her subsequent success" (Brooks 1972, p. 112). Shirley Briggs worked with Rachel Carson in the Fish and Wildlife Service as an artist and illustrator in the mid-forties. They took many field trips together, Carson taking notes on wildlife and vegetation, Briggs doing illustrations, and were close friends for nearly two decades. When Carson died, Briggs continued the effort of education about the hazards of pesticides and vigilance over government policy on pesticides which *Silent Spring* began. With other friends of Carson she founded the Rachel Carson Trust for the Living Environment, now the Rachel Carson Council. Since 1965 she has served as Executive Director of this international resource center and clearinghouse on pesticides. After Carson's death, the journalist and author Ann Cottrell Free was responsible for getting the Department of Interior to name their new Maine coast wildlife reserve the Rachel Carson National Wildlife Refuge.

On another level, there are women like myself who did not know Carson but who are aroused, not by the force of her personality but rather by the passion and ethical authority of her work. Everywhere I have spoken on *Silent Spring*, in the United States, in Japan, and in Europe, women have told me they can remember when they read *Silent Spring* and how they felt. All conveyed that they were moved at a level rarely reached. This cracking open and going deep into the world, which Carson achieved in *Silent Spring*, created possibilities for women who came after her, whether they knew her or not. Since the publication of *Silent Spring* in 1962, women have emerged as the most insistent, sane, and recalcitrant voices in their societies, singly and collectively, to protest the war on nature and what Carson called "the folly and the madness of a world in which half of mankind is busily preparing to destroy the other half and to reduce our whole planet to radioactive ashes in the doing" (Carson July 1962, p. 5). This book is written to ennoble that fact and to plumb its depths.

Chapter 1 debunks the myth that Carson was a woman rich in work, but less than rich—impoverished even—in love. Her work was an expression of her love and she found love where her work was. Chapter 2, "*Silent Spring* revisited," begins her work.

There are three concepts at the core of *Silent Spring*. In nature, nothing exists alone. A chemical poison sprayed on a potato field is taken into the potato skin. Some residue washes through the soil into groundwater and is drawn to a drinking water well where it is pumped to the kitchen tap. Other residue is eroded with soil into a nearby stream and ingested by insect larvae which are eaten by a fish. The fish is eaten by a bird, another fish, a wetland animal or a human being. The second concept follows from the first. With the intensive use of pesticides since the end of World War II, the whole world is being poisoned along with the insects. For example, DDT is found in the polar ice caps, in the milk of mammals, in sperm, in food, and as recently as May 1987, in the upper sediments of Boston Harbor. Lastly, Carson advocates that we take "the road less travelled," a science and technology based on a reverence for life even where we must struggle against it.[8]

The subject of *Silent Spring* is pesticides; specifically, the chlorinated hydrocarbons DDT, aldrin, and dieldrin; and the organic phosphates, such as parathion and malathion. Pesticides were being sprayed lavishly across America in the late forties and fifties and promoted as the panacea for world famine and plague. Carson cut through the promotional veil to expose the hazards of modern pesticide use to nature and human beings.

In chapter 2, I present the major ideas of *Silent Spring* and analyze the work for its prophetic, consciousness-raising, political, and visionary qualities. The book begins with "A fable for tomorrow," two pages which

---

8. Carson (1962, p. 242) quoting from Dr C. J. Briejèr, a Dutch plant pathologist with whom she corresponded.

become the epicenter of controversy for industry and many scientists. A rural town is sprayed with a white granular powder. Farm animals, wildlife, fish, and human beings sicken and die; vegetation withers and browns. Spring is silenced. The critics called this scenario hysterical, exaggerated, and science fiction. The fable concluded: "A grim specter has crept upon us almost unnoticed, and this imagined tragedy may easily become a stark reality we all shall know" (Carson 1962, pp. 14–15).

In 1984, at the conceptual stages of this book, I met the type who ridiculed the fable. He was a chemical engineer from Rohm and Haas, a Philadelphia-based pharmaceutical corporation, traveling on the train I was taking from Belgium to a conference in Holland. His reaction to the mention of Rachel Carson was to laugh and say, "Everybody knows she exaggerated." Where had the events of the fable ever happened, her critics had asked. She replied that there was no one place where it all happened; but each element of the catastrophe had happened in many places. The fable was a warning of what could happen. Since I started writing this book in 1985 there have been at least three publicized "silent springs," in Bhopal, Chernobyl, and the Rhine River, two of which involved pesticides. Many of the major ecological disasters of the past two decades have occurred in the manufacture, storage, use, and disposal of pesticides or chemical compounds with deadly biocidal components.

On July 10, 1976 a chemical reaction went out of control in a trichlorophenol plant and a cloud of powdery crystals containing almost pure dioxin fell on the town of Seveso, Italy. Children ran to play in it because it looked like snowflakes (a chilling resemblance to the "white granular powder" which had "fallen like snow" in Carson's fable). Four days later plants and flowers began to wither and brown; animals, birds, and fish were sick and dying. It was eight days before local doctors were alerted to the chemical fallout. Hundreds of people were hospitalized; the land became uninhabitable. Pregnant women lived a nightmare filled with the fear of a deformed child, the humiliation of standing before a bureaucratic civil process established to evaluate their requests for an abortion, and the condemnation of the Catholic Church who called them selfish and evil for not wanting to look after deformed children.

On the night of December 2, 1985, a catastrophe with no parallel in industrial history occurred. It has been called "the Hiroshima of the chemical industry." The Union Carbide Company operated a plant in Bhopal, India to formulate a range of pesticides and herbicides derived from a carbaryl base. A runaway reaction occurred in a large storage tank of methyl isocyanate (MIC) and released most of the contents. The MIC facility was located adjacent to a residential neighborhood. The company did not inform the authorities immediately; for two hours after the leak, no one was evacuated. As a result, at least 2,000 people died and 200,000 were injured, of whom 30,000 to 50,000 are too ill ever to return to their jobs.

In the fall of 1986, a chemical storage area in Basel, Switzerland, caught fire. Firemen flooded the factory with water; a dike was breached and 10–30 tons of pesticides, fungicides, and other agricultural chemicals poured into the Rhine River. Fish, "normally resistant"eels, and insects were killed. "The Rhine seems 'dead' for 100–200 kilometers downstream of Basal," reported *Nature* (Rich 1986).

There are the less dramatic, less publicized "silent springs," with no explosion, no toxic cloud, only the quiet seep of farm chemicals into aquifers. In the rural American farming town of Whately, Massachusetts, the private wells of farmers have been replaced with a municipal water supply because the pesticides they sprayed on their tobacco and potato fields, EDB and TEMIK, washed into groundwater and were drawn into their wells. In the case of drinking water contamination from pesticides used in agriculture, the major issue for the EPA hazardous waste Superfund program is a programmatic one: how to declare farmland or contaminated sole source aquifers beneath them as Superfund sites. Traditionally, Superfund sites are defined as waste disposal sites which cause endangerment to human health and the environment. The contamination in Whately resulted from "normal" agricultural practice—use of pesticides on crops and soil—not from indiscriminate and environmentally unsound waste disposal. This bureaucratic dilemma points up the problem Carson exposed and explained 25 years earlier, one which EPA has ignored by centering most resources and publicity on hazardous waste disposal sites. With pesticides, use is disposal into the ecosystem. "Are we not poisoning ourselves along with the insects?" Carson had asked of intensive chemical agriculture.

In order to persuade her readers that this manner of killing weeds and insects could kill us along with them, Carson educated them in what may be the finest example of "science for the people." Her chapter titles show her method: "Elixirs of death," "Surface waters and underground streams," "Realms of the soil," "Earth's green mantle," "And no birds sing," "Rivers of death," "Indiscriminately from the skies," and "The human price." In these chapters she instructed her readers in the chemistry of organic pesticides, the science of ecology, and the theories of how cancer develops and the potential environmental sources of cancer, in prose that "broke through the dullness barrier in science writing" (Sterling 1970, p. 112). So thorough is her research that *Silent Spring* has served as a fundamental text on ecology—neither outdated nor inaccurate—which need only be amplified with the subsequent development of ecological methods of pest control, such as integrated pest management, and recent research on environmental toxicology which was spurred on by her work.

Carson attacked the worldview that nature is a warehouse where men pick and choose what they want and discard the rest. The habit of dominance and conquest, she said, drives man's intensive use of chemicals to eliminate the parts of nature which interfere with his progress. She showed that war on people and war on nature employ the same weapons: nerve gases developed for World War II were used as pesticides in agriculture after the war. Likewise, herbicides developed for agriculture before the Vietnam War were used as defoliants in that war. The destruction of people and nature with chemical poisons constitutes the same failure to solve problems other than by force. Carson's work restated the complexity of being both part of nature and separate from it in an industrial society. It politicized pollution by asking the political questions. Who creates it? Who protects it? Who profits from it? Who supports it? How do they mystify it as the price of progress and disconnect it from all other acts of violence? Who are its victims? These questions and their answers are common knowledge today because environmental issues now have a political base. Thirty years ago, as she began writing *Silent Spring*, people were less able to critique "a better life through chemistry" and "progress is our most important product," the public relations slogans which buttressed the expanding chemical industry in the fifties and enabled it to recycle war technologies into peacetime uses.

At this same time, the post-World War II transition was being picked apart by another woman in a parallel work. Betty Friedan exposed the pseudo-progress and pseudo-existence of the college-educated, middle-class American housewife in the fifties (Friedan 1963). The "happy housewife" propaganda of the post-World War II women's magazines was intended, in part, to recycle women out of the wartime industrial effort back into the home. At home, using their talent on creative housekeeping and child care, women would give the workplace back to men and live in the world vicariously through their husbands. Friedan gave reality and language to women who could not name their own desperate discontent with small, unworldly, powerless lives. During the same years that Rachel Carson was amassing the analytic tools and the language for a world which had become uneasy with, but was unable to critique, "the better life through chemicals" mystique, Friedan wrote *The Feminine Mystique*. Both fed streams of thought which would fill a common reservoir.

In her final chapter, "The other road," Carson calls us to chart a new course in the science and technologies we develop to live in this world, a course based on an "understanding of the living organisms they seek to control and of the whole fabric of life to which these organisms belong" (Carson 1962, p. 244). She amassed numerous studies and experiments conducted worldwide since World War II simultaneous with the expanded use of chemical pesticides, to demonstrate the potential for methods of insect control based on two fundamental approaches. One is an array of techniques which target the crop-destroying or disease-causing insect and affect that insect population only. These include male sterilization, synthesizing insect repellents or attractants, and fatal bacterial infections such as *Bacillus thuringiensis*, which are harmless to all but their intended targets; and the release of natural insect parasites and predators. The second approach encompasses the entire web of life rather than the individual insect species. Here Carson cites the Canadian and European science of "forest hygiene" where "birds, ants, forest spiders, and soil bacteria are as much a part of the forest as trees" (Carson 1962, p. 258). Carson scanned the world for scientific work which manifests an understanding that we share our earth with other creatures. She saw those efforts and that spirit toward nature as the world's only hope for human coexistence with nature. *Silent Spring* concludes as it began, with the prophetic warning that when man uses science as a weapon against a part of nature, he uses it against the entire earth.

Early in 1959 Rachel Carson wrote to Clarence Cottam, a respected wildlife management expert and her former director at the Fish and Wildlife Service, that she knew her book's critique of chemical pesticide use would be explosive. "I feel it is far wiser to keep my own counsel insofar as I can until I am ready to launch my attack as a whole," she wrote (Graham 1970, p. 39). Frank Graham, Jr. said of Carson working on *Silent Spring*, "She knew that by taking up her pen to write honestly about this problem, she had plunged into a sort of war" (Graham 1970, pp. 39–40).

Chapter 3, "The world aroused," chronicles and analyzes the vortex of industrial and government reaction to *Silent Spring*. Industry set in motion a many-pronged offensive against the book. The government's response was a mix of defensive potshots from smarting government workers and an outbreak of self-scrutiny and deliberation which resulted in a code of environmental law and the Environmental Protection Agency.

Industry attacked before the book was published. After the serialized version appeared in *The New Yorker* in summer 1962, the Velsicol Chemical Corporation sent a five-page letter to the publisher, Houghton Mifflin, recommending the book not be published because of misinformation about certain chemicals which that company manufactured. The

Monsanto Chemical Company commissioned a parody to be written entitled "The desolate year," and rushed the galley sheets to newspaper editors and book reviewers throughout the country to beat *Silent Spring*'s publication date. Certain companies allegedly threatened to withdraw advertising from garden magazines and newspapers that favorably reviewed or cited *Silent Spring*. The National Agricultural Chemicals Association doubled its public relations budget and distributed enormous numbers of critical reviews of *Silent Spring*. The theme was the same one used by the American Cyanamid Company's Robert White-Stevens, the indefatigable champion of pesticides. A world without pesticides is doomed to pestilence and famine. An organization called the Nutrition Foundation, whose purpose was to support research in the science of nutrition, assembled a "Fact Kit" on *Silent Spring*. It consisted of a defense of chemical pesticides, several critical reviews of *Silent Spring*, and a letter from the Foundation stressing the "independence" of the critics. CBS scheduled a documentary to be aired on April 3, 1963 entitled, "The *Silent Spring* of Rachel Carson." In it Eric Sevareid summarized the major points of the book and interviewed Rachel Carson; Dr Luther Terry, the Surgeon General; Orville Freeman, Secretary of Agriculture; George Larric, Commissioner of the Food and Drug Administration; John Buckley of the Interior Department; and Robert White-Stevens of American Cyanamid. More than 1,000 letters came in to CBS insisting that the show not be aired. Three of the show's five industrial sponsors withdrew sponsorship just prior to April 3.

Industry played to the remnants of McCarthyism in American government and public. They charged that *Silent Spring* was dangerous for the United States because it was part of a Communist plot to ruin American agriculture, industry, and the economy, and to render this country defenseless before the East. It was dangerous for the world, they forecast, because pesticides were the cutting edge of progress and to ban them would return the world to the dark ages of pestilence and famine. Technology's march of progress was captured in the General Electric Company's fifties slogan, "Progress is our most important product." Interestingly this slogan has given way in the eighties to "We bring good things to life," just as chemical pesticides have taken backseat to engineered microorganisms in agriculture and the new reproductive technologies have emerged as the cutting edge of biomedical science. Like chemical pesticides in the fifties, these technologies are heralded as bringing new control over unreliable nature. The professions which stand to profit from them, the biochemical and biomedical, gloss over the risks and low success rates. National commissions and agencies responsible for developing policy and regulation—the American Fertility Society, the National Institutes of Health (NIH), and EPA, for example—discuss the technolo-

gies with the same spirited enthusiasm that the US Department of Agri-
culture (USDA) showed for the new chemical pesticides in the fifties.
And the American Fertility Society suffers the same conflict of interest
USDA did in approving and regulating pesticides: the biomedical profes-
sion as self-policing policymakers. I will return to these parallels in
Chapter 5.

Some reviewers said Carson was not a scientist so the book wasn't
scientific. (She had a masters' degree from Johns Hopkins University in
marine biology.) Others said that even if she were a scientist, the book
was emotional and science isn't emotional, so the book was unscientific.
Some did not read the book but criticized it anyway; while others distorted her critique of pesticides and critiqued her for their own distortion. For example, Norman Borlaug, the "Father of the Green Revolution," and White-Stevens, the corporate pesticide crusader, said that
Carson called for a ban on all chemical pesticides. They went on to
portray the horrors of a world without pesticides and to blame Carson
for those potential horrors. A close reading of *Silent Spring* shows she
was against the modern chemical method of washing whole towns and
the countryside with pesticides. She argued for selective spraying when
chemicals were necessary. She asserted that biological/ecological controls had not been researched and used as seriously as chemical ones,
and that they ought to be favored.

Industry and government aimed to discredit the book by discrediting
the woman in ways that men have traditionally used against women
who oppose them. The critics sexualized their contempt for her. One
said he "thought she was a spinster, what's she so worried about genetics for?"[9] How odd that Carson, the socially valueless spinster, the
single woman who is dried up, barren, and heartless would be concerned about human beings. Others, drawing from the same stereotype,
associated her with the eccentric, out-of-it, pain-in-the-neck lady in ga-
loshes who wages irrelevant campaigns for trees and birds. Edwin Diamond, a former editor of *Newsweek*, accused Carson of worrying about
cats' deaths from DDT while not caring about the 10,000 people who die
daily throughout the world from malnutrition and starvation. They

---

9. Graham 1970, pp. 59–60. Carson's detractors used the word *spinster* with the contempt
and pity that, Mary Daly writes, has been "a powerful weapon of intimidation and decep-
tion, driving women . . . into marriage." Daly reclaims the spinster by amplifying the
word's original etymology: "a woman whose occupation it is to spin." The spinster "is
derided because she is free and therefore feared." She spins her webs of ideas "with
intensified integrity." In the best sense (the Dalyan one), Carson was a spinster, fearlessly
constructing a web of ideas which would shake the world with their intensity and integrity.
See Daly 1978, pp. 392–400.

called Carson dangerous, irrational, and hysterical. The historian of science Carolyn Merchant observed that modern science arose to bring order to disorderly nature as the witch burnings were taking place. She wrote of this connection, "Disorderly woman, like chaotic nature, needed to be controlled" (Merchant 1980, p. 127). In the mid-twentieth century the chemical industry alleged that their pesticides would rescue the world from the precariousness and chaos of nature. Like the witch of medieval Europe, Carson was blamed for the violence of nature, the destruction of crops and the death of children which her call to curb the use of pesticides would cause.

The spinster comment was made by a member of the Federal Pest Control Board. Those public officials who were stung by her critique of government's ignorance of pesticides, collusion in their use, and cover-up of their hazard, used the same ammunition as industry. Simultaneously, however, *Silent Spring* "lit a fire," as one news commentator put it, under other parts of government.

President John Kennedy read *The New Yorker* version of *Silent Spring*. Jacqueline Kennedy met with Carson and others to discuss the pesticide problem.[10] In late summer 1962 Kennedy requested that the President's Science Advisory Committee (PSAC) study the pesticide problem and make recommendations for pesticide use and regulation in the United States. The PSAC report, entitled *The Use of Pesticides*, was issued in May 1963. The report acknowledged that DDT and other persistent compounds have been found worldwide in the tissue of humans and throughout the environment. It chronicled extensive damage to fish, birds, and other wildlife because of pesticide spraying. The recommendations to the President, specifically regarding reform of pesticide law and stricter enforcement, were consonant with those of Carson in *Silent Spring* and in subsequent testimony in Congressional hearings. "Elimination of the use of persistent toxic pesticides should be the goal," it concluded (Graham 1970, p. 84).

The report became a watershed for many reviewers who, before the report, had criticized *Silent Spring* and after its publication changed their tune. From Holland a scientist wrote Carson that the PSAC report was a potent weapon for quelling the storm brewing there in the chemical industry and chemical-minded scientists' circles. At this same time, Senator Abraham Ribicoff decided that a broadgauge Congressional review of all federal environmental programs was needed. He chaired the study

10. Carson remarked afterwards that she was impressed with Jacqueline Kennedy's intelligence, given the media portrayal of her as White House decorator.

which would be known as "The Ribicoff Report," a report which had the same confirming effect of Carson's work as the PSAC report.

Silent Spring caused a ferment in government during the sixties, resulting in Executive and Congressional scrutiny of the weaknesses in environmental protection. Carson is a powerful example of what one individual can do in the world, with or without a political base. The critique of individual action as "individualistic" and inferior to collective, political process (as if one always precludes the other) is irrelevant here. While she consulted with hundreds of scientists throughout the world, her analysis and politicizing of pollution was a singular, original contribution which had no prior guarantee of support from any group. It was a work which generated enormous discussion and debate in society and which created a base on which to build a movement. But it preceded and stirred a movement; it did not come from it, nor did it wait for it. Fifteen years in government gave her a political realism, so she was able to put her finger on the weaknesses in existing laws and the obstacles to strong enforcement of them. Simultaneously, her depth and idealism, for which her prose was a perfect vehicle, gave a loftiness to the Congressional committee hearings, the committee reports, and their recommendations. And it had consequence.

On December 2, 1970 the newly formed Environmental Protection Agency opened in a tiny suite of offices at 20th and L Streets in northwest Washington. President Nixon had been convinced that it was necessary to establish an independent agency located in the Executive Branch whose sole mission was to develop and enforce environmental regulations. "Independent" meant the agency would have no other jurisdiction or mission which could create a conflict of interest in regulating industry. On December 7, the first EPA Administrator, William Ruckelshaus, announced that he and EPA were starting with no obligation to promote or mediate the interests of industry. His and EPA's mission was the "development of an environmental ethic" (Lewis 1985, p. 9).

Chapter 4 is a critical examination of EPA, now generally regarded as the most prominent environmental agency in the world. By 1985, EPA's staff of nearly 15,000 held responsibility for protection of air, rivers and oceans, wetlands, regulation of new hazardous substances, pesticides, and hazardous waste and identification and clean-up of abandoned hazardous waste sites. The size of the agency, its status in the world, the scope of its mission, any and all of these make it a daunting task to measure the agency against its original standard, to develop an ethic of the environment. In Chapter 4, I use three issues to frame that analysis:

1. Do more regulations mean better environmental protection?
2. What is the net effect of environmental passion being professionalized and institutionalized?
3. Where ought EPA to be moving?

In probing the first issue I look at the meager accomplishments of the
pesticide program, examine the pesticide law and regulations for their
intentionality, and compare the unpopularity of pesticide enforcement to
the more heroic waste programs, such as Superfund. The question in
search of an answer here is how an environmental program, such as the
pesticides program, with the potential to minimize toxic substances, can
reduce to an understaffed, administrative, paperwork program which is
used more to stifle creative options than to foster them. The second issue
has to do with the institutional life of EPA. Does, for example, the life of
the institution compete with and displace the original mission and
ideals? Having gained a certain administrative maturity, has it lost touch
with the vitality of nature? Having embraced risk management and risk
communication as the way to make and sell environmental decisions,
has it lost touch with the importance of those human lives or particular
ecosystems lost because of "acceptable risk"? Does its apparent independence from industrial and political interest groups guarantee that
EPA is insulated from "plastic loyalties," Administration politics, and
conflicts of interest? Here I analyze the Anne Gorsuch Administration,
both for the losses to the environment and EPA's loss of integrity and,
ultimately, for the perverse misogyny of the outcome: the only Administration casualties were two women. The final issue has to do with where
EPA should be going, and in what direction it is moving.

In a recently published self-examination, *Unfinished Business* (EPA
1987), EPA admits to drifting backwards, following false signals, and
rushing off in wrong directions. The conclusion they and I came to inde-
pendently is that there are critical environmental problems which have no
better solution today than 15 years ago. The most egregious is the tens of
thousands of synthetic chemicals manufactured and in use everywhere,
the majority of which are insufficiently tested for toxicity. One essential
movement for EPA is back to its older, unfinished business: regulating
industry at the point of generating chemicals, not only or primarily at the
point of waste emissions. Within the unfinished business of limiting the
manufacture and use of toxic chemicals lies another: the international
traffic in pollution. Pesticides which are banned or restricted in the United
States, DDT for example, are manufactured in the United States, sold for
use in developing countries, and imported back in vegetables, fruits, and
meats. The other half of that "circle of poison" is exporting toxic chemicals

for use and consumption in other countries, as if *Silent Spring* had been written only for and about U.S. people and ecology.

Another consequence of EPA's failure to test the majority of toxic chemicals and pesticides is that the connection between these chemicals and human infertility, for example, while documented with a few chemicals, is largely unstudied and unknown. No one has yet estimated how much infertility is caused by exposure to toxic products, especially in those who manufacture, mix, apply, and use them. But it is well documented that some affect fertility and reproduction. Elkington (1985, pp. 48–64) cites research which indicates that American males today produce less than half of the sperm produced by the average male 50 years ago. The researchers strongly suspect the increased use of herbicides, pesticides, and a chemical flame retardant used in foam mattresses. All of these chemicals have been found in semen. Although it has been known that the exposure of fathers to certain chemicals can cause birth defects in embryos, and it is strongly suspected that toxic chemicals in semen can contaminate the uterine environment in women (Elkington 1985), the outfall of reproductive hazards has been against and upon women almost entirely. In the workplace fertile women are being defined as "hypersusceptible" and are being increasingly excluded from traditionally male jobs where they will be exposed to agents which harm both male and female reproductive systems. The Office of Technology Assessment report on reproductive hazards in the workplace states that it is women workers who are targeted by "fetal protection policies instituted by employers who fear future liability for offspring harmed by workplace exposures" (Office of Technology Assessment, 1986, p. 8). The response of the biomedical profession has been to ignore the environmental, occupational, and medical causes of infertility and rush toward technical fixes, such as superovulation and in vitro fertilization, which experiment with drugs, hormones, and risky procedures on women's bodies.

While EPA is not directly responsible for workplace discrimination against women because they are fertile and of childbearing age, or for regulating the new reproductive technologies, its negligence with respect to the environmental and chemical causes of infertility and reproductive toxicity has enormous consequences for women. Chemicals tested for carcinogenicity and effects on the embryo have rarely been tested for their effect on human fertility. Where chemicals have been found to cause infertility or pose reproductive hazards, this knowledge has been used against women. In the absence of a vigorous enforcement program to identify and ban or restrict chemicals which cause infertility, women are being excluded from jobs because they are "fertile" and a biomedical "revolution" is taking place on the bodies of women where they or their partner is infertile. Chapter 5 deals in depth with these consequences.

My purpose in this chapter is to hold EPA to the standard of passion and politic set by Rachel Carson in *Silent Spring*. There lie its moorings. Otherwise, disconnected from its original vitality, it will shift with the prevailing political winds and drift into being another faceless bureaucracy, composed of political appointees at the top, career bureaucrats in middle management, and frustrated environmentalists at the bottom. It will be more benign than others because of its mission; but it will feel no less banal.

"We stand now where two roads diverge," begins the concluding chapter of *Silent Spring*. One is a superhighway, deceptively smooth and fast, but "at its end lies disaster." This is the course of filling the world with poisonous chemicals in order to save it from insects. The other, "the one 'less traveled by,' offers our last, our only chance to reach a destination that assures the preservation of our earth." This latter, Carson wrote, is the path of biology, based on an understanding of insects as living organisms and of the whole fabric of life to which they belong (Carson 1962, p. 244).

The era in which Carson wrote *Silent Spring*—when applied chemistry and physics generated new synthetic chemicals and the nuclear industry, while warnings of their risks came from biologists—is no longer. Biology has found its own forms of invasive technology and creates its own endangerments with the same disregard for the web of life of which Carson accused pesticide users. For example, companies such as DuPont and Ciba-Geigy which develop and market herbicides are developing crops which are genetically engineered to resist their brand of herbicides. The companies can thus expand their use of herbicides without destroying market crops. The most celebrated case concerns genetic engineering of bacteria which facilitate ice crystal formation on plants. The engineered bacteria lack the gene connected with ice formation activity. These bacteria will then be sprayed on plants susceptible to frost damage. The commercial expectation is higher crop yields.

Looking at the same world Carson did in writing *Silent Spring*—science applied to agriculture—it is apparent that the alleged promises, the potential problems, and the pretense of policy surrounding biotechnology in agriculture are an eighties counterpart of what Carson found in the fifties. The promises are higher crop yields for a world in which millions live hungry, malnourished, and at the edge of starvation. These are the altruistic underpinnings of agribusiness in search of new markets. Those who issue warnings about the unknown risks are called antiprogress, bureaucratic, and naive about science. The potential problems are the risks to soil, groundwater, the food chain, and farmworkers of increased herbicide use as herbicide-resistant crops are developed. Ecologically oriented research on herbicides indicates that, like pesticides, they exacerbate the problem they are designed to solve. Herbicides can make plants more susceptible to attack by insects and plant diseases. Scientists have pointed out that the potential risks of introducing bio-engineered plants and bacteria into the environment are that this will lead to gene transfer between plant species, accelerate herbicide resistance among plants, and that organisms released will grow, find susceptible hosts and survive in other than intended environments. As for policy, isn't it cause for concern that, in 1985, the National Institutes of Health, the agency responsible for overseeing genetic engineering research and enforcing research guidelines, had to be taken to court by a coalition of environmentalists to prevent the release of genetically engineered bacteria in the environment without an environmental impact assessment?

Carson's work gave us unambiguous analytic tools with which to critique and protest a world increasingly dominated by technologies which endanger ecosystems. But it is likely that she would look more critically at the uses of biology today than in 1960 and look in other places for an "understanding of . . . living organisms and the whole fabric of life to which they belong." In the 25 years since *Silent Spring* was published, another road has converged with the "one less traveled by" and it cuts deeper and wider. It is the course being sited by those who, like Carson, call for the preservation of nature to the highest degree possible and a transformation of science from its central paradigm of domination into one of reverence for life. We also see the urgency for a woman-centered assessment of science and technology based on women's right to personal and bodily integrity. Chapter 5 is about charting that road.

Carson concluded that the arrogant "control of nature" by science and technology was at the root of pollution and the silencing of spring. It is my conviction that one central paradigm of modern science—the domination of nature as if nature were female and science were male—is at the root of the control of nature and the control of those declared closer to nature by reason of their biology: women. The architect of modern science, Francis Bacon, exhorted science to wrest nature's secrets from her breasts, womb, and bowels. The keystone in his overarching program for science was to employ the metaphor of nature as a powerful, elusive, and difficult woman in a period of virulent woman-hating and control of women, the witch-burnings of Europe. The method of scientific information gathering was modeled on witch trials: interrogation, torture, and force (Merchant 1980, pp. 164–190).

Bacon's metaphor of nature as a woman to be raped into submission is not the first of its kind in the history of science. Myths from peoples throughout the world record men's theft of fire from women who first discovered it (Hynes 1982). Those myths are forerunners of modern science; Bacon's role in the history of western science was to centralize the rapist metaphor of nature as a woman to be subdued and to make it a controlling (though not exclusive) image of the spirit and method of science. The same mechanisms used by science to control nature are used to dominate women in science and by science. They are hierarchy of being, objectification, fragmentation, devitalizing and silencing, elimination of diversity, pitting the economy as the indicator of the "well-being of mankind" against the integrity and well-being of women and nature.

The control of women and nature has been fused and amplified in the place where men have located nature uniquely in women, women's fertility and reproduction. The new reproductive technologies represent the intersection of a most sophisticated control of women and nature. The fundamental law of ecology, that everything is interconnected, is violated here in the bodies and lives of women. For example, hormones are injected into a woman to make her ovaries superovulate without full knowledge of the long-term impacts on her body. The implications of starting down a pathway like the new reproductive technologies (e.g. the international traffic in women to form a breeder caste of poor and Third World women, sex predetermination in a world that prefers boy children, experimentation on human embryos, and genetic manipulation for eugenic purposes) have been only superficially discussed. Experience shows that developers of technology will use it with or without wisdom about consequences.

The implications for all women of these technologies, currently practiced on a few women, come clearer when we extrapolate from Carson's instruction about pollution. Pesticides sprayed on plants migrate into soil, groundwater, and rivers; they are carried by wind. They drift into the entire web of life to the surprise of scientists who developed them for "target" plants and organisms. While it is only a small number of women who are subjected to the technologies, all women are subjected to them in their supporting mythologies, their expanded use, and the probable increase of environmentally induced infertility. The technologies' benign portrayal in the media invigorates the myths of fulfillment and altruism through motherhood, biological or surrogate. The technologies are marketed to fertile as well as infertile women for convenience and as an expanded option. The talk of expanded options offered women by the technologies anaesthetizes women to the deeper questions of freedom of choice and motivation for choice. A healthy woman will become anachronistic, like industry says the "balance of nature" has. The argument that there is no longer such a thing as a balance in nature is used to justify or relativize activities which increase pollution. Like nature, woman in an industrial world will carry background pollution, "the poisoned womb," as John Elkington calls it, and routinely need biomedical intervention. The new reproductive technologies will thrive in all worlds, not just the white western ones, as infertility increases due to chemical manufacturing plants being located in "cheaper," developing countries, the increase in pesticide use there, and more frequent industrial accidents like Bhopal and Seveso. Clearly, women need an assessment of the complex impacts that the new reproductive technologies have on our lives no less urgently than an environmental impact study of releasing engineered bacteria into the environment is needed!

Silent Spring laid the groundwork for a nature-centered as well as a human health-centered system of environmental protection. Carson argued that people and nature have the right to exist unendangered from pollution, and should be enabled to do so. This can only be done by a regulatory framework which recognizes pollution as dangerous and wrong. Regulators must be free of ties to politicians and industry and of an inherent bias for new chemicals or technologies which engenders a nonchalance about their toxicity. Environmental protection must be grounded in the principles of ecology. Those were her arguments. Nothing comparable to this exists to protect women. Environmental agencies empowered to ban or restrict the manufacture and use of chemicals have neglected to assess the impact on fertility and reproduction of the majority of chemicals. Chemical industries have discriminated against women for the sake of the fetus and their own liability rather than lower exposure to chemicals in the workplace to a level safe for female and male workers and fetuses. This policy does not protect the fetus, nor women from damaged sperm, and from contaminants brought home on workclothes. The ethical questions raised about the new reproductive technologies have been centered on the embryo and "respect for human life," not the life of the woman. I will draw from the principles of environmental protection inspired by *Silent Spring* to make recommendations for policy on the new reproductive technologies and the protection of women in the workplace which is centered on women's right to self-defined, not fetal-defined, fertility-defined, nor male-defined, existence.

Earlier I asked the question whether Rachel Carson would make the connections between the domination of nature and domination of women by science were she living today. Then I reworked it into a more fruitful one: what can feminists learn from her work to deepen our own analysis of the masculinist ideology of science? This is not to avoid the question of Carson and feminism; rather I want to do more with it.

In letters to women Carson showed pride in being "the only" or "one of the only" or "the first" woman to succeed where few women had, as a graduate student and later in receiving honors for *Silent Spring*. But she denied being a feminist to *Life* magazine in 1963. "I'm not interested in things done by women or by men but in things done by people," she said (Gentle storm center 1963). Likewise, her contemporary Georgia O'Keeffe recoiled against being reviewed as "the greatest woman artist." Her reasons may explain Carson's distrust of being singled out as a woman scientist and woman writer. O'Keeffe knew that she was at least as good as her best male contemporaries, but they preserved themselves from comparison with a great woman by relegating her to the best of "the second sex." Both women were reviewed as "women," in the press. The outcome was that their work was psychologized as successful by male definitions of women. Carson was successful because her science was soft and popular and her writing was emotional. O'Keeffe's power was her explosion of pent-up female sexuality on canvas (Lisle 1986). Carson parts company with O'Keeffe in that she neither had nor sought a male mentor or facilitator of her work, and women were primary in her life. Carson's pride in herself as a woman who achieved "firsts"—the primary place of women in her life, her recognition of science's imperative to control nature and male scientists' passivity before this, her call for science to seek biophilic methods and solutions—all these conditions have ensured that her work and her manner of being a woman in science contributed substantially to the emerging feminism within science.

Whether Rachel Carson was or would be a feminist today is less important to me than the contagion of her work. I would modify her conclusion about the other road, the one "less traveled by." Widened and deepened by feminism, it offers our last, our only, chance to reach a destination that assures the preservation of earth and ourselves.

REFERENCES

American Heritage Dictionary of the English Language 1981. Boston, Massachusetts: Houghton Mifflin.

Birke, L. 1986. *Women, Feminism, and Biology: The Feminist Challenge*. New York: Methuen.

Bleier, R. 1986. *Feminist Approaches to Science*. Oxford and New York: Pergamon.

Bookchin, M. 1974. *Our Synthetic Environment*. New York: Harper Colophon.

Brooks, P. 1972. *The House of Life: Rachel Carson at Work*. Boston, Massachusetts: Houghton Mifflin.

Carson, R. 1962. *Silent Spring*. Greenwich, Connecticut: Fawcett Publications.

Carson, R. 1962. Of man and the stream of time. *Scripps College Bulletin*, July, 5–10.

Cross, B. 1973. Harriet Beecher Stowe, *Notable American Women 1607–1950*. T. James, J. Wilson James, and P. Boyer (eds.), pp. 393–402. Cambridge, Massachusetts: Belkap Press.

Daly, M. 1978. *Gyn/Ecology: The Metaethics of Radical Feminism.* Boston, Massachusetts: Beacon Press.

Elkington, J. 1985. *The Poisoned Womb: Human Reproduction in a Polluted World.* Harmondsworth, England and New York: Viking Press.

Environmental Protection Agency 1987. *Unfinished Business: A Comparative Assessment of Environmental Problems.*

Fox, S. 1981. *John Muir and His Legacy: The History of the American Conservation Movement.* Boston, Massachusetts: Little, Brown.

Friedan, B. 1963. *The Feminine Mystique.* New York: Dell.

Graham, F. Jr. 1970. *Since Silent Spring.* Greenwich, Connecticut: Fawcett Publications.

Hynes, H. P. 1982. Active women in passive '80. *Trivia,* 1(1). 71–74.

Langer, E. 1983. *Josephine Herbst: The Story She Could Never Tell.* New York: Warner Books.

Lewis, J. 1985. The birth of EPA. *EPA Journal,* 11(9), 9.

Lisle, L. 1986. *Portrait of an Artist: A Biography of Georgia O'Keeffe.* New York: Washington Square Press.

Merchant, C. 1980. *Death of Nature.* New York: Harper and Row.

Office of Technology Assessment 1986. *Reproductive Hazards in the Workplace,* Washington, D.C.

Raymond, J. G. 1979. *The Transsexual Empire: The Making of the She-Male.* Boston, Massachusetts: Beacon Press.

Raymond, J. G. 1986. *A Passion for Friends: Toward A Philosophy of Female Affection.* Boston, Massachusetts: Beacon Press.

Rich, V. 1986. *Nature,* **324**, 20 November, 201.

Rossiter, M. 1982. *Women Scientists in America: Struggles and Strategies to 1940.* Baltimore, Maryland: Johns Hopkins University Press.

Sterling, P. 1970. *Sea and Earth: The Life of Rachel Carson.* New York: Dell.

The gentle storm center. (1963, October 12). *Life,* p. 10.

THE BROAD MARGINS
OF LIFE

There was a unique difficulty in writing *Silent Spring*. It was how to make hydrocarbons compelling. Rachel Carson was world-acclaimed for her works on the sea when she submitted the manuscript of this book; but she awaited her editor's response with the tension of a new author. Her other books were trusted terrain. The sea—its genesis, its lure, and its life—had been the preoccupation of her precise, ardent mind for decades. The sea was her central character; she, its epic biographer.

Silent Spring was different. It was a laboriously constructed demonstration that widespread aerial spraying with toxic, persistent pesticides, such as DDT, aldrin, and dieldrin, which had increased more than fivefold from 1945 to 1960, constituted a post-World War II "peacetime" war on nature and human beings. It indicted government and research scientists who were lobbied and bought by the pesticide industry for collusion in the chemical assault on nature. It exhorted science to take a biophilic and ecological path: a reverence for life "even where we have to struggle against it" (Carson 1962, p. 243). It summoned government to regulate the manufacture and use of synthetic chemicals and to enforce environmental laws. *Silent Spring*, a chronicle of "man against the earth"—one of Carson's original titles for the book—was a worldly work of protest and reform.

It would anger, Carson was certain; but would it compel? The first of what would be millions of affirmations came from her editor at *The New Yorker*, which was to serialize the book before its publication. Once she received his response, she knew the book would accomplish what she longed for it to do. The next evening she wrote to Dorothy Freeman her feelings in finishing what would be the final book of her life:

After Roger [her nephew] was asleep, I took Jeffie [her cat] into the study and played the Beethoven violin concerto—one of my favorites, you know. And suddenly the tension of four years was broken and I let the tears come. I think I let you see last summer what my deeper feelings are about this when I said I could never again listen happily to a thrush song if I had not done all I could. And last night the thoughts of all the birds and other creatures and all the loveliness that is in nature came to me with such a surge of deep happiness, that now I had done what I could—I had been able to complete it—now it had its own life (Brooks 1972, pp. 271–272).

Rachel's friendship with Dorothy Freeman began during her first summer in Maine in 1953 and deepened with each successive year. The instant success of *The Sea Around Us*, which impelled the reissue of her first book, *Under the Sea Wind*, had enabled Carson to buy land in West Southport, Maine. There she built a one-story cottage on rocky headlands at the water's edge, close enough to hear the sibilant, lisping sounds of the incoming tide which she would recreate in her third book, *The Edge of the Sea*. A spruce and fir forest carpeted with ferns, lichens, and mosses enclosed the cottage on three sides. From her porch there was a half-dozen stone steps' descent to the wrack line of high tide and the same again to tide pools in rock crevices at low tide. The low-tide world—"when the ebb tide falls very early in the morning, and the world is full of salty smell, and the sound of water, and the softness of fog" (Brooks 1972, p. 159)—was the most exciting place for her. Here she could collect marine creatures to examine with a lens or under a microscope and, afterwards, scrupulously return them to their habitat. The world she evoked so powerfully for others, she finally lived within.

Dorothy Freeman's summer cottage on a north corner of the island was within walking distance. For ten consecutive summers they met for beach picnics, found wild haunts, lay on rocks and in sunny, grassy enclaves where they watched migrating birds, read to one another, and discussed progress on Carson's *The Edge of the Sea* and later *Silent Spring*. Dorothy led Rachel to that tiny "fairyland" tidepool which was memorialized in *The Edge of the Sea*. During their last summer in Maine together, Carson spoke intimately to her of death, when her own was impending, using the metaphor of Monarch butterflies whose migration they had watched together: "brightly fluttering bits of life . . . [on] the closing journey of their lives" (Brooks 1972, pp. 326–327). She would later be with Carson as she was dying.

Of Carson's many friends, it was Dorothy Freeman who knew most intimately the necessity of *Silent Spring*. Once Carson began her research on the synthetic chemical pesticides in use, no carefree love of the planet was possible any longer for her. This book, her friend understood, would be a moral and political weapon to save the earth from the metastasis of pollution. Yet in a certain sense, Carson did not elect to write

Silent Spring; she was chosen. After *The Edge of the Sea,* her next project was to be a global work on "man and ecology," for which she had amassed considerable literature on pesticides. However, a letter and inquiry from another friend, Olga Owens Huckins, changed this.

Olga Huckins, a writer for the former *Boston Post,* preserved a two-acre bird sanctuary behind her home in Duxbury, Massachusetts. In the summer of 1957 the state of Massachusetts aerially sprayed Plymouth County to kill mosquitoes breeding in marshes. The planes crisscrossed over the bird sanctuary, near the marshes, killing in their nonselective fashion insects, grasshoppers, bees, and songbirds. Huckins called the State and described the broadscale death she found in the bird sanctuary, only to be assured that their tests showed "the mixture used—fuel oil with DDT— . . . was entirely harmless" (Brooks 1972, p. 231). She chronicled the disaster in a letter to the *Boston Herald.* She called for a moratorium on aerial spraying until the immediate and long-term effects of pesticides on wildlife and human beings were known. She concluded: "Airspraying where it is not needed or not wanted is inhuman, undemocratic, and probably unconstitutional. For those who stand helplessly on this tortured earth, it is intolerable" (Brooks 1972, p. 232).

The State was proposing mass aerial spraying next, so Huckins sent a copy of her letter to Carson with an urgent inquiry about who in Washington could be consulted for help. Carson immediately urged her literary agent, Marie Rodell, to have one of her clients write an article on the subject. Within a few days she decided to do it herself and then sought an expression of interest from major magazines. At the same time a unique court case was in process. Citizens of Long Island were seeking a court injunction to prevent state and federal officials from spraying their land with DDT to control the gypsy moth. Seizing the event of this case to bring the dangers of aerial spraying with pesticides to the foreground of public awareness, Carson wrote E. B. White to suggest that he cover the trial for his magazine, *The New Yorker.* None of the magazines that Carson or her agent had contacted had showed interest in the proposed article; however, White suggested that Carson, rather than he, cover the trial for *The New Yorker.*

In the midst of finding someone to speak out, Carson saw that there would be no peace for herself if she kept silent. She "must write the book" (Brooks 1972, p. 233). She negotiated a long article for *The New Yorker* on pesticides, which she also intended to use as the core of a short book with the working title, *The Control of Nature.* Her intent was to finish this within a year and return to her expansive work on ecology.

As books will do, this one took on its own life: one that was larger and more labyrinthine than she originally conceived. Her research brought her face to face with a problem that was more egregious and more alarming than she had imagined. Not only did she "have to" write *Silent Spring*, but she would have to construct an "unshakeable foundation" against the storm of protest she realized it would provoke among the powerful promoters of pesticides. Four and one-half years later, after reading thousands of technical reports, after detailed consultations with hundreds of American and European scientists, through a "catalogue of illnesses" and the death of her mother, she would submit the manuscript of *Silent Spring* to her editor. Only then, when her anger at the "brutish senseless things" man perpetrated on nature had been given its most thorough documentation, could she think of "all the birds and other creatures and all the loveliness that is in nature with a surge of deep happiness" (Brooks 1972, p. 272).

Silent Spring was not original research, in the sense that Carson herself did not conduct field and laboratory studies to demonstrate her thesis that increased use of synthetic chemical pesticides was poisoning the entire ecosystem and creating worse insect problems than it purported to solve. Carson's material was the isolated threads of documented ecological horror—numerous and increasing wildlife kills due to pesticides—extant in the scientific literature, cited as findings of fact in the Long Island trial, and disclosed to her in correspondence with wildlife specialists. Her originality was two-fold. She synthesized these separate strands of studies and facts into a nearly flawless tapestry that portrayed the systematic violence against nature and against human beings, because we live in nature, perpetrated by those who declare parts of nature—insects and weeds—an enemy, and then wage chemical warfare on the entire ecosystem. Second, she infused the love of nature with a worldliness that ultimately aroused and quickened the modern environmental movement and impelled the government to regulatory action.

The evidence of the acute and chronic effects of pesticides existed by the time Carson began research on pesticides in 1958. Fish kills were so numerous that Congress ordered the Department of Interior to study the effects of pesticides on fish and wildlife. DDT had been in widespread use, aerially sprayed over farms, forests, lakes, and cities for 13 years. This was initially justified because of DDT's alleged spectacular success in stamping out insect-borne disease during World War II. But by 1946, studies documenting DDT as a threat to mammals, birds, and fish were published in scientific journals. DDT resistance among strains of flies and mosquitoes was apparent within a few years of its use. In 1952, because of insects' increasing resistance, the Department of Agriculture recommended that more frequent applications and greater quantities of insecticides were needed for adequate control.

As early as 1950 medical science had found that DDT accumulated in bodies, was passed on through milk by mothers to children, and possibly caused liver damage at levels considered "normal" in food. Two classic studies demonstrating the concentration and magnification of persistent pesticides in the food chain were published in 1957 and 1958. One studied western grebes at California's Clear Lake. Lake waters contained only residual quantities of the pesticide sprayed to control gnats closely related to mosquitoes. Microscopic plants and animals which filtered lake water for nutrients bioconcentrated pesticide residues at 20 times their concentration in lake water. Lake fish ate the aquatic plants and animals, magnifying the non-degrading pesticide by another factor of 10 to 100 times. Grebes, which ate the fish, died in large numbers. A year later a scientist of the Illinois Natural History Survey at Urbana published his study of the cycle of events which were causing large numbers of robins to die. Elm trees, which majestically lined so many American boulevards, were being sprayed with DDT to counter Dutch elm disease. The pesticide film on leaves was a source of DDT for earthworms. Earthworms were eaten by robins, which died in unprecedented numbers.[1]

Among the strands of published and acknowledged fact about the dangers of pesticides, Carson also found knotty contradictions. She observed to a friend that individual doctors and the medical literature might document the physical maladies caused by exposure to pesticides, but the American Medical Association and the Public Health Service were evasive when it came to taking a critical public stand. She cited the overt participation of science and government in the chemical industry's assault on nature and the fundamental conflict of interest inherent in government regulation of pesticides. During 1956 and 1957 the Department of Agriculture, the federal agency most responsible for regulation of pesticides, waged what she called an "all-out chemical war" on the gypsy moth by spraying DDT-in-fuel oil on millions of acres in the Northeast. Birds, fish, crabs, and "beneficial" insects were killed; milk and farm produce were contaminated above Food and Drug Administration (FDA) allowable levels. (The gypsy moth reappeared as soon as spraying stopped.) This was the "control program" for which the Long Island citizens sought a court injunction against government to prevent aerial spraying with DDT. The government's role in escalating pesticide use extended to the Long Island trial where Carson noted that government allied itself with industry defense "experts" and outnumbered those assembled by the plaintiffs.

Carson recognized another form of collusion in the escalating pollution of the natural world: professional men's silence before the wrong-

1. See Chapters 4 and 8 in *Silent Spring* for thorough documentation of ecological effects and implications for human health of the widespread use of DDT.

doing of science. "I am convinced," she wrote, " . . . that people, especially professional men, are uncomfortable about coming out against
something, especially if they haven't absolute proof that something is
wrong, but only a good suspicion. So they will go along with a program
about which they have private misgivings."[2] While Carson never developed this insight, she made it her mission to speak out. Not only did she
document the violence against nature, but she also named those who
were doing it, those who were profiting from it, and what techniques
they used to obscure the violence. Her straightforward account of those
in industry, government, and science who arrogantly, deceptively, and
profitably waged war on nature would, she knew, plunge herself into "a
sort of war" with them (Graham 1970, pp. 39–40). For this reason she
was careful not to disclose her work prior to publication, except to
trusted colleagues.

This book would differ from her previous ones. The difference was
not in the depth of research: there would be the same precise, rigorous
search for documentation, the same willingness to go where her research would take her. Again she would turn to the technical, scientific
literature, being one who fully understood the language but chose not to
use it. This mining of ideas she loved far more than the labor of turning
out a manuscript. *Silent Spring* brought new rigors, not in depth but in
breadth of research. Carson was a marine biologist by training, by intellectual passion, and by trade. Now she would have to master the literature of many other life sciences: entomology, toxicology, public health,
cell physiology, biochemistry, plant and soil sciences. Wrestling with the
final revisions of a chapter on chemical poisons, she expressed to a
friend how exacting was the work on this book.

> What lies underneath the most important part of this chapter is a whole
> field of the most technical and difficult biology—discoveries only recently

---

2. Brooks 1972, p. 241. Another form of this silence is the false split scientists make
between science for its own sake and its uses, as if one can do the former and ignore the
latter with impunity. For example, an American geneticist and Japanese biologist at the
University of Massachusetts, Amherst who are studying genetic mutations in descendants
of ferns irradiated by the atomic bomb in Nagasaki, insist that their work is apolitical and
for the interest of "pure science" only. Both scientists aver that the science of plant mutations, not the ethical question about the bomb, is what engages them. "Neither one of us is
interested in politics," one says, "except the politics of getting institutional support for our
research" (Wright 1985, pp. 30–34). Vera Kistiakowsky, physicist at MIT, feminist and
outspoken critic of the arms race, has also encountered the same passivity among her male
colleagues on the question of science collusion with the military. Commenting on the
reticence of many scientists to criticize military research and programs, she said that it may
not be so much from fear of retaliation as that it isn't "gentlemanly to take money and then
say bad things" (Marchant 1988, p. 41).

made. How to reveal enough to give understanding of the most serious effects of the chemicals without being technical, how to simplify without error—these have been problems of monumental proportion (Brooks 1972, p. 270).

Another major difference in this last of Carson's works from her others is its overt worldly nature. In her job as an aquatic biologist for the Fish and Wildlife Service during and after World War II, she had been aware of government plans to mine the oceans for minerals and energy resources once the land had been exhausted and that the sea was being reduced to a bottomless dumping ground for radioactive and hazardous waste. "My belief that we will become even more dependent upon the ocean as we destroy the land [is] really the theme of the book," she wrote of *The Sea Around Us* (Brooks 1972, p. 110). However, the preponderant purpose and effect of this work, like that of *The Edge of the Sea* after it and *Under the Sea Wind* before it, was not a worldly call to stop polluting the sea. Rather those books stirred people to love the sea because of its beauty for which she was their eyes, for its mystery of which she was the oracle, and for its cadence and sound for which she was its voice.

Silent Spring originated in Carson's recognition of the increasingly destructive uses of science and technology since World War II. The beauty of the living world she was trying to save was always uppermost; that is the person Carson was. But this book was undergirt and framed by anger at the senseless, brutish things which man was doing to nature. Outrage and "the unwelcomed awareness that it was now possible [for man] to destroy the physical world" (Brooks 1972, p. 10) had brought her forward to author *Silent Spring*.

Silent Spring was written with "two-sights seeing" (Raymond 1986).[3] Carson looked more closely into and was, simultaneously, more far-sighted about the widespread application of synthetic chemical compounds into the ecosystem, than were her critics. Looking backward and forward in time, she contrasted the "deliberate pace of nature" in shaping, directing, and diversifying the planet and its life forms over hundreds of millions of years with "the impetuous and heedless pace of men" in introducing annually thousands of new chemicals from laboratories into the marketplace and, ultimately, into the environment. Most often, these chemicals are used without complete certainty of their effect upon aquatic life if they find their way into the water cycle, or upon humans and wildlife if they enter the foodchain. Whether bacteria can

---

3. Raymond's vision of female friendship is based on "two-sights seeing: near- and far-sightedness." This is the essential tension of feminism, she writes, living in the world as men have fabricated it while creating the world as women imagine it to be. The concept of a dual vision was useful for developing the comprehensiveness of Carson's analysis.

biodegrade them and, if so, at what rate and into what by-products, are questions whose answers come, if at all, after the compound has contaminated the environment. Looking more closely than her critics at the web of life, Carson conveyed the awesome complexity of introducing biocides into a matrix where soil, water, plants, wildlife and humans are inextricably interconnected. We ignore at our own peril, she warned, the elementary principle captured by philosopher Wendell Berry, "Our land passes in and out of our bodies, just as our bodies pass in and out of our land . . . all who are living as neighbors here, human and plant and animal . . . cannot possibly flourish alone" (Berry 1977, p. 22).

In the chapter entitled "Elixirs of death," Carson compiled a litany of chemical pesticides, reciting their toxic properties. She critiqued the mindset which had declared "war on insects," as one of dominance; and she consciously connected these chemicals and that mindset with their militaristic progenitor, World War II. The chemicals had originally been developed for chemical warfare and tested for their biocidal potential on insects. After the war, excess planes and chemicals were recycled into so-called "peacetime" uses: a "chemical rain of death" on farmland, forests, and towns. Carson argued as a plaintiff conscious that her arguments against the defendants and apologists of "the war on insects" were overdue. After all, the industries' advertisements, the endorsement of the Department of Agriculture and many research scientists—the other side of the story—were well publicized and widely known. Published primarily in the wildlife biology and entomology literature and held as private suspicions among ecologists and biologists, Carson's findings and judgments had not yet been fully presented or defended in so public a forum until *Silent Spring*.

"For the first time in the history of the world," she wrote, "every human being is now subjected to contact with dangerous chemicals, from the moment of conception until death. In the less than two decades of their use, the synthetic pesticides have been so thoroughly distributed throughout the animate and inanimate world that they occur virtually everywhere" (Carson 1962, p. 24). These facts bore out the truth of Ellen Swallow's concept of ecology, pioneered 70 years earlier at the Massachusetts Institute of Technology (MIT): air, food, water, and human health are so interrelated that the science of ecology must comprehend hydrology; chemistry; public health; plant, marine, aquatic and wildlife biology; and environmental engineering (Hynes 1985). In that tradition of environmental analysis, *Silent Spring* brought together the findings of many scientific disciplines (for which critics labeled her work generalist, superficial, and unrigorous: the same tactic which had been used against Ellen Swallow at MIT to delegitimate her work) in order to warn the world about the dangers of the increasing use of synthetic chemicals as pesticides.

Using a parable at the opening of *Silent Spring*, Carson describes a rural town once fabled for its wildlife, which is sprayed with a white granular powder. Birds are heard no more; there are no fish to be caught; wildflowers, leaves, and thickets have browned; farm animals, adults, and children are dying. With this as backdrop she carried the private suspicions and knowledge of many biologists, ecologists, toxicologists, and birdwatchers into the public forum. The major points of *Silent Spring* are summarized accordingly.

1. Modern insecticides fall chiefly into two categories, chlorinated hydrocarbons and organic phosphates. They are easily manufactured because of their chemical simplicity; but the complexity of their metabolism and pathways in the environment and the human body is overlooked at worst and not fully known at best. Sprayed over farms, gardens, forests, and homes, they do not distinguish among their victims. "They should not be called insecticides, but biocides" (Carson 1962, p. 18).

"This industry is a child of the Second World War" (Carson 1962, p. 24).[4] The production of synthetic pesticides in the United States soared after World War II, increasing more than five-fold between 1947 and 1960, to about 650,000,000 pounds. Hundreds of new, synthetic chemicals are introduced annually into actual use in the United States. Synthetic chemicals have the potential to alter nature within a few decades, while nature has altered life over billions of years. The control of insects which destroy crops and cause disease must be done with methods which do not destroy the entire natural world along with the insects.

2. "In nature nothing exists alone" (Carson 1962, p. 55). When forests and crops are sprayed with pesticides, the spray enters into the entire ecosystem. It drifts and falls into lakes and rivers; in periods of high rains, it is carried by surface runoff to nearby streams; it filters through soil, enters groundwater which surfaces at rivers; it is discharged through stormwater sewer pipes and effluent pipes into receiving streams. These persistent organic compounds do not disappear. No longer detectable in the water column, they will be found in sediments, larvae, worms, fish, and people. They enter the food chain, passed on as one organism eats another. Chemicals which were dispersed in the environment in minute quantities become more concentrated in fish tissue, cow's milk, and human milk. The suggestion that herbicides, such as 2,4-D and 2,4,5-T, used to destroy unwanted weeds and plants, are not as harmful as pesticides because they are toxic only to plants, is dangerous. They may result in reproductive effects in animals and humans at levels much lower than those causing death.

---

4. Extending the concept of pesticides as a child of war is Wendell Berry's analysis of "food as weapon." Berry cites a Secretary of Agriculture who remarked that "food is a weapon" and a Secretary of Defense who spoke of "palatable levels of devastation." He writes, "Consider the associations that since ancient times clustered around food—associations of mutual care, generosity, neighborliness, festivity, communal joy, religious ceremony—and you will see that these two secretaries represent a cultural catastrophe. The concerns of farming and those of war, once thought to be diametrically opposed, have become identical. . . ." See Devall and Sessions 1985, pp. 150–151).

3. In theory the public is protected against unsafe residues of pesticides on food by the Food and Drug Administration (FDA), which determines and regulates the maximum residue of a pesticide which can remain on food sold in interstate commerce and not cause harm to public health. These maximum permissible limits are called "tolerances." This system provides paper security and promotes a completely unjustified impression that safe limits have been established and are being adhered to. The government should establish "0" tolerance for chlorinated organics and organophosphorus chemicals, and reduce the manufacture and use of toxic chemicals. The FDA should be given larger enforcement resources.

4. The US Department of Agriculture (USDA) is responsible for the registration of new agricultural pesticides and thus for protecting people and nature from dangerous chemical pesticides. In reality, USDA has functioned as the major federal promoter of chemical pesticides through a series of broad scale pest eradication programs such as the mass aerial spraying campaigns against the gypsy moth and the fire ant. In the case of the fire ant program, the mass aerial spraying of millions of acres with heptachlor and dieldrin was preceded by a publicity campaign in which USDA distorted the impact of the fire ant in order to justify the pest control program. In the campaign to manipulate perception, they made an insect which had been no more than a nuisance in Southern states into a menace to crop and livestock and human health. USDA showed complete ignorance of, or deliberate disregard for, the known toxicity of the poisons applied: both were many times more toxic than DDT. Subsequently, USDA cited the evidence of damage especially to domestic and wildlife from their eradication campaigns as exaggerated and misleading.

Much more money is being poured into research on chemical insecticides than into natural biological control studies. Major chemical companies subsidize research assistantships and university research programs, a fact which explains why certain outstanding entomologists are among the leading advocates of chemical control. Would they bite the hand that feeds them? "Knowing their bias, how much credence can we give to their protests that insecticides are harmless?" (Carson 1962, p. 229). Since natural biological controls do not promise the fortunes which allure companies and scientists alike, it is left to state and federal agencies to advocate for and find them, if at all.

5. People ought to have the civil right to live unendangered in their society. The application of poisons in their environment could justifiably be seen as a violation of that right.

6. The phenomenon of insect resistance to insecticides is not well understood. However, with intensive application of the persistent organic chemicals since World War II, the number of insect species resistant to chemicals began a meteoric rise. Before 1945 about a dozen species were known to have developed resistance to pre-DDT insecticides; whereas, by 1960, as many as 137 species were known to be resistant to the new organic chemicals. The government and industry response to resistance was to spray more intensively and more frequently, thus aggravating the very problem they alleged to solve, by creating "superbugs" and more resistant species.

There are ecologically sound alternatives to mass spraying of poisonous chemicals. All are biological solutions which derive from an understanding of the living organisms they seek to control, and of the whole fabric of life to which these organisms belong. These include, among others, sterilizing and releasing large numbers of male insects and the introduction of insect parasites and predators.

The "control of nature" is a phrase conceived in arrogance by men who expect that nature exists for their own convenience (Carson 1962, p. 261). Our aim should be to work with nature, not to use brute force, to reverence life, "even when we have to struggle against it" (Carson 1962, p. 243).

As Carson was speaking at Scripps Oceanographic Institute in California on "the fallacious idea of a world for man's use and convenience," the first of a three-part condensed version of *Silent Spring* was published by *The New Yorker* in June 1962. The first excerpt generated a tidal wave of letters to congressmen, newspapers, government agencies, and the author. It was the subject of over 50 newspaper editorials and some 20 columns. Seldom had *The New Yorker* received so much mail about something it published.

On publication day, September 27, advance sale of the book reached 40,000 copies, and some 150,000 copies were en route to Book of the Month Club. Candidates for public office wrote to Carson asking her to recommend a position on the pesticide issue. By the end of 1962, over 40 bills had been introduced in the various state legislatures to regulate pesticide use. The immediate success of *Silent Spring* with the layreader and public officials was solidified with positive reviews by prominent biologists and internationally known scientists. They included Robert Rudd, entomologist of the University of California; Loren Eiseley, anthropologist at the University of Pennsylvania; Sir Julian Huxley; and LaMont C. Cole, professor of ecology at Cornell. Carson particularly welcomed these reviews. She knew that her most formidable and virulent opposition would be scientists in the service of industry who were given the mission to poke holes in her science.

The reviews by Rudd and Eiseley praised her panoramic analysis of the escalating use of chemical pesticides. They also had high regard for the political and ethical urgency she brought to bear on the ecological crisis which was building. Rudd, whose own book *The Living Landscape* was a sequel to *Silent Spring*, concluded that *Silent Spring* "is a biological warning, social comment, and a moral reminder" (Graham 1970, p. 76). Loren Eiseley wrote, "It is a devastating, heavily documented, relentless attack upon human carelessness, greed, and responsibility" (Sterling 1970, p. 152). Ecologist William Vogt, who wrote the best-selling *Road to Survival*, predicted that "*Silent Spring* would do for the chemical pollution of our environment what Upton Sinclair's *The Jungle* did for the Pure Food and Drug Act in 1906" (Sterling 1970, p. 153).

LaMont C. Cole wrote what many have cited as the most valuable review of *Silent Spring* by a scientist. He took a microscope to the science of Carson's book. Finding only a few errors of fact (among the thousands of facts), he states that "errors are so infrequent, trivial, and irrelevant that it would be ungallant to dwell on them" (Cole 1962). He does disagree with three emphases in her work. Carson's concept of the "balance of nature" is obsolete among ecologists, he writes. Ecologists see nature as a dynamic system in constant motion where "a monkeywrench" of chemicals thrown in creates complications beyond those implied in a static system. Second, she shows preference for birds and animals over insects and does "not convey an appreciation of the really great difficulty of the general problem." Finally, Cole does not believe that chemicals are producing "superbugs," while he agrees insects develop resistance to insecticides (and thus begins the spiral of more intensive and more potent insecticide use). His review of the science of *Silent Spring* supports Carson's essential analysis of the crisis in the ecosystem while it disagrees with some of the points of her ecology. Cole opens his review by expressing gratitude that "this provocative book has been written" and concludes that the book will stimulate a "much-needed reappraisal of pesticide policies and practices" (Cole 1962).[5]

During 1963, in addition to the English-speaking world, *Silent Spring* was published in France, Germany, Italy, Denmark, Sweden, Norway, Finland, Holland, Spain, Brazil, Japan, Iceland, Portugal, and Israel. In all of these countries it provoked debate and laid the groundwork for later environmental legislation. The debate on pesticides in the House of Lords, London, took place in the spring of 1963. Nearly every speaker mentioned Rachel Carson and her book, an unprecedented event in Parliament.

The steady stream of awards Carson received matched the prominence she won in review, translation, and public testimony. In January 1963 she received the Albert Schweitzer Medal of the Animal Welfare League. The National Wildlife Federation selected her for their Conservationist of the Year award. Then followed the Frances Hutchinson Medal, the highest honor of the Garden Club of America, and the conservation award of the Izaac Walton League of America. In December 1963 she traveled to New York for what she described to a close writer

---

5. I recognize the value of this review for Carson at a time when she was under organized attack by industry. However, it is totally self-absorbed. Cole is preoccupied with his own theories, not her book; so that one does not get a full synopsis or discussion of *Silent Spring*. After all of his scientific fine-tuning of a few concepts of ecology, about which he thinks she was mistaken, or at best, developed simplistically, he does not conclude differently than she did about the phenomena she documented and its meaning.

friend, Lois Crisler, as "an extraordinary constellation of events" (Brooks 1972, pp. 321–322). First she would receive the Audubon Medal from the National Audubon Society, the first to a woman; and two days later the Cullum Medal of the American Geographical Society. Finally, the "most deeply satisfying thing that . . . happened in the honors department" (Brooks 1972, p. 322), she was elected to membership in the American Academy of Arts and Letters. The Academy citation read: "A scientist in the grand literary style of Galileo and Buffon, she has used her scientific knowledge and moral feeling to deepen our consciousness of living nature and to alert us to the calamitous possibility that our short-sighted technological conquests might destroy the very sources of our being" (Brooks 1972, p. 323). In editorial the *New York Times* proposed that Carson should receive the Nobel Prize, as did Paul H. Mueller, the Swiss chemist who developed DDT as a pesticide.

The surge of acclaim from the public, certain prominent scientists and public officials and distinguished professional societies was countered by an uproar in other parts of government, science, and corporate chemical and agricultural circles. The war Carson intuited would be waged on her book broke with the first excerpt in the *The New Yorker*. On August 2 the Velsicol Chemical Corporation sent a registered letter to Houghton Mifflin suggesting that the company reconsider its decision to publish *Silent Spring*. The letter cited "inaccurate and disparaging statements" about two chlorinated hydrocarbon pesticides, chlordane and heptachlor, both manufactured solely by Velsicol (Graham 1970, pp. 59–60). It allied Carson with "food faddists" and others manipulated by pernicious influences which attack the chemical industry for being grasping and immoral, but whose real intent in advocating a limit of the use of pesticides is to reduce the productivity of American and western European food supply to parity with Communist countries.

The attacks on *Silent Spring* were very often attacks on Carson. They associated her with Communists and "nature fanatics." They attributed idiosyncratic tendencies to her and made misogynist remarks about her person, personality, and lifestyle. She was portrayed as an eccentric spinster who liked birds better than children.[6] They charged that she was

---

6. "Strength in a woman is negative," one woman commented in analyzing the media's treatment of Nancy Reagan when it became obvious that she was directing Ronald Reagan on how to salvage his administration after news began breaking about the "Iranscam." Whether the "White House wives" have their own ideas, as did Eleanor Roosevelt and Rosalyn Carter, or act to protect their men in trouble, in the case of Nancy Reagan, they are meddlesome shrews. Women who don't show emotion or breakdown under duress, like Anne Gorsuch, are frigid—she was nicknamed "the Ice Queen." Women who are passionate about something other than men are eccentric spinsters.

unqualified to author the book. Some said she was not a scientist; others said that even if she were, her writing was too emotional to be objective. Her emotions blinded her to the progressive nature of chemical pesticides. In blocking progress, she was endangering the planet.

One of the best exposés of her critics' motives and devices is Carson's own, delivered in a speech to the Women's National Press Club on December 5, 1962. She traced the turbulent five-month history of contrasting response to *Silent Spring*: the "tidal wave" of letters to congressmen, newspapers, government agencies and herself; the chemical industry's outpouring of canned editorials, news releases, mailings, and negative reviews of the book—"heavy doses of tranquilizing information, designed to lull the public into the sleep from which *Silent Spring* had so rudely awakened it" (Brooks 1972, pp. 301–304). Industry's attack, she demonstrated, used all of the familiar, faulty devices. The first is to weaken the cause by discrediting the person who champions it: "So the masters of invective and insinuation have been busy: I am a 'bird lover—a cat lover—a fish lover,' a priestess of nature, a devotee of a mystical cult having to do with the laws of the universe which my critics consider themselves immune to." Another well-known, and much-used, device was to misrepresent her position and attack things she never said: "Anyone who has really read the book knows that I criticize the modern chemical method not because it controls harmful insects but because it controls them badly and inefficiently and creates many dangerous side effects in doing so."

Another piece in the pattern of attack was to treat *Silent Spring* as anachronistic and concentrate on soft-sell, soothing reassurances to the public. Carson described how defenders of the pesticide industry admitted that there was some truth to her book, but that these excesses were things of the past. She then listed seven news stories from the months just before and after her book was published to show the same deadly things were happening. Finally, there was the reviewer who was offended that Carson charged universities with colluding in the problem by taking grants from pesticide manufacturers to do research for them.

[T]he reviewer's . . . own university is among those receiving grants. Such a liaison between science and industry is a growing phenomenon, seen in other areas as well. The AMA, through its newspaper, has just referred physicians to a pesticide trade association for information to help them answer patients' questions about the effects of pesticides on man. I am sure physicians have a need for information on the subject. But I would like to see them referred to authoritative scientific or medical literature— not to a trade organization whose business it is to promote the sale of pesticides. We see scientific societies acknowledging as 'sustaining associates' a dozen or more grants of a related industry. When the scientific organization speaks, whose voice do we hear—that of science? or of the sustaining industry?

The text chosen for her speech was a newspaper article in which the reporter told her that no one he interviewed from the farm county bureau had read *Silent Spring*, but all had disapproved of it heartily.

Throughout the controversy which surrounded *Silent Spring* ("few volumes or their authors have been the subjects of such vituperative and prolonged attack" [Erlich 1979]), Carson's chief concern was that her book should have a lasting effect on government policy. In fact, this is a hallmark of the book's worldliness. She had written because she "felt bound by a solemn obligation" to do all she could, always keeping uppermost in her mind the beauty of the living world she was trying to save. Carson's achievement in this book, which guaranteed her work's endurance, was the fusion of her ethical passion for nature with a hard-eyed, political realism.

A survey of federal environmental history since *Silent Spring* reveals the extent to which environmental consciousness and policy in the United States were quickened, enlivened, and given direction by her work. Congressman John Lindsay of New York read the *The New Yorker* excerpts and had the concluding paragraphs of the first one entered into the *Congressional Record*. He wrote Carson that he wished that he could have inserted the entire article. In an August 1962 news conference, President Kennedy referred to the influence of "Miss Carson's book" when asked if federal agencies were looking into the dangerous long-term effects of DDT and other pesticides. Almost immediately he summoned his science advisor, Dr. Jerome Weisner, to establish a commission to study the problem of pesticides and prepare a report with recommendations concerning the use and regulation of pesticides in the United States. The study ensued during the next eight months, coincident with industry's and some scientists' campaign to discredit Carson's work. Carson testified before the committee in January 1963. The President's Science Advisory Committee (PSAC) report, entitled *The Use of Pesticides*, was issued on May 15, 1963. Most important among the report's recommendations was the endorsement of shifting emphasis away from broad-spectrum chemicals toward selectively toxic and nonpersistent chemicals, as well as biological methods of insect control based in insect ecology. The report acknowledged that fish and wildlife are as important in considering the harm of toxic chemicals, as are domestic animals and humans. Finally, it acknowledged that until the publication of *Silent Spring*, people were generally unaware of the toxicity of pesticides. That evening on CBS news, in reporting on the PSAC report, Eric Sevareid summed up her influence accordingly: "Miss Carson had two immediate aims. One was to alert the public; the second to build a fire under government. She accomplished the first months ago. Tonight's report by the Presidential panel is *prima facie* evidence that she has also accomplished the second" (Graham 1970, p. 85). In a May 19 feature article for the New York *Herald Tribune*, Carson praised the PSAC report for its recognition and candid disclosure of the hazards of pesticides (this part of the report reads like a synopsis of *Silent Spring*); but she pointed out the need for action.

> This excellent report alone does not solve our problem. It must now be translated into action. This is the task of government agencies which, given the will, could act quickly. It is also the task of the Congress and the state legislatures, where action will inevitably be slower. It is important to remember that pressures which opponents of reform know how to apply will continue unabated (Brooks 1972, pp. 306–307).

In the early spring of 1963, Senator Abraham Ribicoff of Connecticut wrote a constituent that, since reading Carson's book, he had concluded that "what is needed is a broad gauge Congressional review of all federal programs related to problems of environmental hazards, including pesticide control, air and water pollution, radiation and others" (Graham 1970, p. 81). He was appointed chair of the subcommittee established for that purpose. The Senate committee on environmental hazards began its hearings the day after *The Use of Pesticides* was released. On June 4 Rachel Carson testified before the committee. Her concise, actionable recommendations were anchored in her "unshakeable foundation" of research into government negligence and ignorance in the face of the chemical industry's saturating the environment with chemicals. She called for:

1. Recognition of the right of the individual to protection against poisons applied by others into the environment and the right to legal redress when that right is violated.
2. Restriction of the sale and use of pesticides to those capable of understanding the hazards.
3. Registration of pesticides not solely being the function of the Department of Agriculture.
4. Approval of new pesticides only if no existing chemical or other method exists.
5. Full support to research new methods of pest control in which chemicals will be minimized or entirely eliminated.

Two days later Carson appeared before the Senate Committee on Commerce to testify on behalf of two bills addressing the conflict of interest in the use and regulation of pesticides. Her recommendation for an independent agency at the Executive level, free from political control or influence by the chemical industry (as Congressionals were not) was clearly a cornerstone for the later creation of the Environmental Protection Agency.

> In the course of the more than five years I have now spent in intensive study of the pesticide problem, I have arrived at the conclusion that conflicts inherent in this problem can be resolved only by an independent board or commission to be set up at the level of the Executive offices. . . . As I visualized this Commission, none of its members would be drawn from Government departments. None would be drawn from the chemical industry. Conflict of interest should be eliminated completely . . .
>
> The Commission, I suggest, should be made up of citizens of high professional competence in such fields as medicine, genetics, biology, and conservation. It would represent the highest authority on problems arising from pest control problems, with power to resolve conflicts and make decisions on the basis of what the public interest as a whole demands (Brooks 1972, pp. 308–310).

After testifying, Carson left Washington for what would be her last summer in Maine. Throughout the writing of *Silent Spring* she had been increasingly plagued with a host of illnesses, including cancer. After its publication and extraordinary reception, she had written to Lois Crisler, "if only I could have reached this point 10 years ago! Now, when there is the opportunity to do so much, my body falters, and I know there is little time left" (Brooks 1972, p. 271).

That summer, unable to climb down the rocks from her house to the tidepools below, she did still enjoy many intimate walks in the woods and along the sea on West Southport with Dorothy Freeman. In September, at a rocky tip of the island, they watched the fall migration of Monarch butterflies. Later that afternoon, Rachel wrote Dorothy "a postscript to our morning at Newagen, something I think I can write better than I can say." She described the sky and wind, the surf, trees and gulls; the views of distant islands, and the migration of the Monarchs, "that unhurried drift of one small winged form after another, each drawn by some invisible force . . . for most this was the closing journey of their lives." The wholeness and completeness of the Monarch's brief, sufficient life became a metaphor for her own life, whose end was drawing near. "This is what those brightly fluttering bits of life taught me this morning. I found deep happiness in it—so, I hope may you. Thank you for this morning" (Brooks 1972, pp. 326–327).

In December Carson received the Audubon Medal, the Cullum Medal and election into the American Academy of Arts and Letters. She died the following spring, in April 1964, at the age of 56.

Had she lived, it is certain that Carson would have been called upon to give expert testimony in the hundreds of hearings on environmental regulation held in the remainder of that decade. For environmental history since the mid-sixties shows that her analysis, grounded in both a love of nature for its own sake and the conviction that human beings have an inviolable right to a healthful environment, worked as leaven raising ecological consciousness throughout American society and government. In every manifestation of the current environmental movement—Earth Day and the burst into being of grassroots environmentalism, ecofeminism and women's environmental activism, and the creation of the government's most vital agency, the Environmental Protection Agency—her influence is evident.

Dozens of environmental reform groups have sprung up, such as the Conservation Law Foundation, the Environmental Defense Fund, Natural Resources Defense Council, Friends of the Earth, and Greenpeace. They lobby for legislation, help write regulations, participate in the environmental impact study process for major projects, sue the government for not enforcing environmental regulations, sue polluters for violating environmental laws, do massive education and consciousness-raising through journals, books, and conferences, lobby and fund-raise to preserve land in the wild; and, most notably in the case of Greenpeace, take direct action to protect wildlife.

The history of the Environmental Defense Fund's founding and campaign against the use of DDT exemplifies the unity of ecological spirit and activism which *Silent Spring* embodied. In 1967, the Environmental Defense Fund (EDF) was launched, in one founder's estimate, "to build a body of case law to establish a citizen's right to a clean environment" (Dunlap 1981, p. 148). The right was not well established in law, but it was a concept articulated by Carson and germinating in public consciousness. In the series of court hearings and suits initiated by EDF to have DDT banned from use, the major points and arguments closely paralleled those of *Silent Spring*.

1. Ecology: Nature is an interconnected web of air, soil, water, and biological organisms.
2. DDT: Because of its physical and chemical properties, it persists and biomagnifies in nature. Putting it in one part of the ecosystem contaminates interrelated parts of the ecosystem.
3. Toxicology: There is extensive evidence of damage to wildlife, including birds, animals, and fish from DDT.
4. Humans: DDT has not been proven safe for humans. Unless it could be demonstrated that there were no unsafe biochemical or enzymatic changes in humans exposed to it, it is considered potentially hazardous.
5. Alternatives: DDT can and ought to be replaced with safer, more ecologically sound measures.

It took nearly three years of court proceedings, until 1972, for DDT to be banned by the newly created EPA. The decision was a substantial though partial victory on both material and symbolic grounds. DDT would be phased out of widespread use in the United States. (Later I will show that this ruling was considerably weaker than it should have been, in that it did not ban the manufacture of DDT for export to other countries and allowed for exemptions of emergency use in this country.) The victory on symbolic grounds was one of turning point. In the ruling against DDT, the post-World War II manifest destiny of the chemical industry was finally challenged. Thomas Dunlap, historian of science and public policy, has interpreted the entire process and outcome of putting DDT on trial as constituting an end to the "pre-*Silent Spring* era" in which "Americans assumed that science was good, that chemicals were necessary, that their use would be governed by experts, that these experts could be trusted, and that the side-effects of chemical use would be negligible" (Dunlap 1981, p. 235).[7] This ruling created the hope that if the "father of modern pesticides" could be defeated, so might "the sons" be.

While groups such as Environmental Defense Fund used the courts and press, operating as critical outsiders to government and corporations, the federal and state governments were undergoing a remarkable ferment within. It was presaged by actions like Congressman Lindsay's inserting *Silent Spring* into the *Congressional Record*. Between 1962 and 1980 more than a dozen federal laws and hundreds of state laws were promulgated to protect air, lakes, rivers, streams, wetlands, wildlife, groundwater, and oceans from pollution; to regulate the manufacture, use, and disposal of pesticides, toxic substances, and hazardous waste; and to identify and clean up all former hazardous waste dumpsites. A graph showing the exponential growth in federal environmental laws gives vivid testimony to the catalyst that *Silent Spring* was for public environmental policy.

In 1970 the Environmental Protection Agency (EPA) was created. Car-

---

7. Dunlap's history of the rise of DDT is a complex weave of the industry, agriculture, and government motives and role in turning agriculture into a chemical-intensive, unecological business. It serves as a good background to *Silent Spring*. His conclusion, after extensive coverage of the trial initiated by EDF to have DDT banned, is disappointing. The problem of DDT is not a scientific one, he writes. Because it is value-laden, it is a problem of public policy. However, science is value-laden. Its paradigms and sources of support, its interpretations and applications all take place within a system of belief and values. Thus we can speak of necrophilic and biophilic science or "the road not taken" as Carson did. In the case of the atomic bomb, some scientists, who worked on it and wanted to see it used, did influence policy on the use of the bomb. Therefore, I do think the ethical and social problems of DDT, nuclear power and weapons production, and recombinant DNA, to name three, are scientific ones as well as political ones.

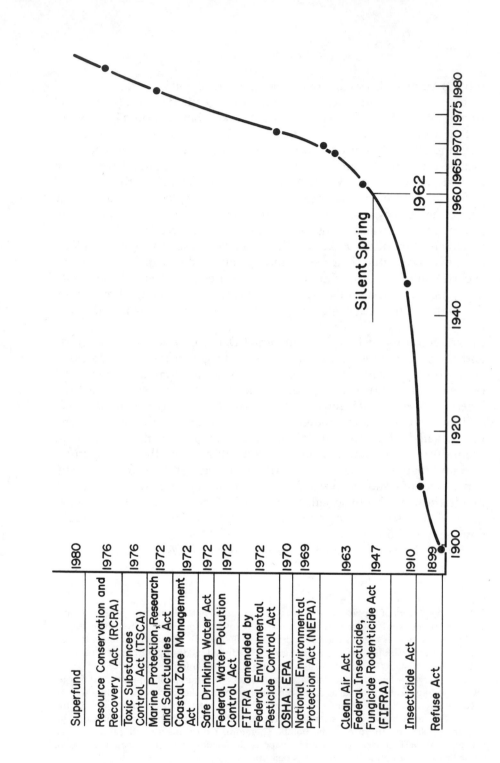

Superfund — 1980

Resource Conservation and
Recovery Act (RCRA) — 1976

Toxic Substances
Control Act (TSCA) — 1976

Marine Protection, Research
and Sanctuaries Act — 1972

Coastal Zone Management
Act — 1972

Safe Drinking Water Act — 1972

Federal Water Pollution
Control Act — 1972

FIFRA amended by
Federal Environmental
Pesticide Control Act — 1972

OSHA : EPA — 1970

National Environmental
Protection Act (NEPA) — 1969

Clean Air Act — 1963

Federal Insecticide,
Fungicide Rodenticide Act
(FIFRA) — 1947

Insecticide Act — 1910

Refuse Act — 1899

Silent Spring — 1962

1900 1920 1940 1960 1965 1970 1975 1980

son's conception of the environment as a single, interrelated web of soil, air, water, and all attendant creatures which rely upon these for life and well-being, resulted in a single federal agency whose sole purpose was the "protection, development, and enhancement of the total environment" (Lewis 1985, p. 9). Heretofore the protection of the environment had been parceled out among many agencies for whom it was usually a secondary mission, at best. Carson's exposure of the conflict of interest inherent in the Department of Agriculture regulating pesticides while promoting their use in farm policy and ignoring their effects upon wildlife, had effect. Jurisdiction over registration of pesticides was transferred from USDA to EPA, the agency charged solely with protection of wildlife and human health.

The first Administrator of EPA announced that he and EPA were starting with "no obligation to promote commerce or agriculture." Rather he envisioned the mission of EPA to be the "development of an environmental ethic" (Lewis 1985, p. 9). Carson's original and continuing influence on the Environmental Protection Agency was cited by an EPA journalist, on the 15th anniversary of the Agency in 1985, when he wrote that EPA is "the extended shadow of *Silent Spring*" (Lewis 1985, p. 6). Whether EPA has been true to the mission of developing "an environmental ethic," and whether it should aspire to being "the extended shadow" of *Silent Spring*—when shadows are merely faint representations—are issues critically examined later.

The stellar fact here is that, in a country renowned for two centuries of uncontrolled exploitation of natural resources, and an anthropocentric valuing of nature for its economic and recreational potential, a single woman's work has had such consequence.

- Nature now has standing in policy and law, for its own sake, not solely "for the use and convenience of man."
- Pollution has become a political issue. People now hold the conviction that we have a fundamental right to live unendangered from pollution.
- Carson brought together a love of nature and a concern for human beings in a complex unity, rarely if ever achieved in conservationist and humanist circles.

Finally, there is Rachel Carson's most unexamined stirring in the American society—her influence on women. This was captured in popular culture by a 1963 "Peanuts" cartoon. As Schroeder is playing the piano, Lucy is quoting Rachel Carson about when the moon came into existence. Exasperated, Charlie Brown yells, "Rachel Carson! Rachel Carson! Rachel Carson! You're always talking about Rachel Carson!" "We girls need our heroines," she retorts (Brooks 1972, pp. 238–239).

Here, as with grassroots environmentalism and environmental legislation, we can trace the exponential emergence of women in the seventies
and eighties, scientists and nonscientists, who take on governments and
corporate structures and their "strategic misrepresentation" of reality—
as Carson did—for the sake of saving the planet and our future from
environmental disaster.

Until *Silent Spring* women were a second sex in the conservation and
environmental movement. Stephen Fox's recent 400-page history of the
more than 100-year-old American conservation movement dedicates little
more than 10 pages to the contributions of women; half of those 10 pages
are about Carson. He writes in his section on women, "To approach any
reform movement only through its top leadership will obscure the full
story." He then quotes prominent men who aver that women have held up
half the sky in this movement, notably the wives of many of the men who
featured in his history. "Hazeldean Brant, Marcelline Krutch, Margaret
Murie, Avis DeVoto, and Anne Morrow Lindbergh all crucially reinforced
their husbands' conservation work." The references to women are frag-
mentary and "the full record is buried," he writes. "In any case they
deserve a large chapter in conservation history" (Fox 1981, pp. 341–345).
But it seems that he ignored his own *caveat* and obscured the full story by
not excavating the buried record of women. He presented the conservation
reform movement, in the 390 pages devoted to John Muir and dozens of
notable men, only through its top leadership.

Carson severed the tradition of only men having the big ideas and
setting the agenda in the environmental movement. Not being the wife
or the colleague of some great man, she was preserved from absorption
into a man's career. Her work cannot be collapsed into someone else's;
her full record cannot be buried. A broad-brush look at the history of
environmental activism before and after *Silent Spring* shows that her
work is a watershed for women in that movement.

Lois Gibbs exemplifies the remarkable phenomenon of the housewife
and mother turned environmental activist. Gibbs originally held the
traditional expectations prescribed in American society: women nurture
life in the domestic sphere, while men, as husbands and in government,
provide for the public sphere. A high-school graduate, she taught herself
environmental science in order to rescue her neighborhood, which had
fallen victim to hazardous waste dumping.

In 1978 Lois Gibbs, at 26, was elected president of the Love Canal
Homeowners' Association at the height of the neighborhood's protest
against the government's resistance to looking beyond the ring of homes
identified as affected by the dumping. Gibbs' own children were sick.
She and other mothers set out to establish unequivocally that the contaminants from Love Canal had travelled beyond where the agencies'

scientists and engineers had predicted. She devised an ingenious graphical/statistical method whereby she plotted sicknesses on a map of the neighborhood. Going door-to-door, she asked mothers if their children had suffered any unusual illness. Plotting the findings on a map, a triangle indicating epilepsy, a square indicating a birth defect, and so on, she discovered a clustering effect in which birth defects and disfigurements occurred in the areas of the neighborhood near former streambeds and swales which had been filled in prior to home construction, but where chemicals were now migrating.

When she presented her theory to the State Health Department, they discounted her findings as "useless housewife data." In her own words, "they treated me like an hysterical woman." So she and some volunteer scientists put the housewife data "in respectable scientific form, with all the pi-squareds and all that junk" (Hynes 1985). By February 1979 the State acknowledged the accuracy of the swale theory and eventually the government purchased all of the remaining homes in the Love Canal area.

Like most women in the Love Canal neighborhood, Lois Gibbs never went to college. She is self-educated in environmental chemistry, toxicology, and the rubrics of political organizing. Protesting, picketing, public speaking, and lobbying became a way of life for her during the years 1978–80. She and other residents even held EPA officials hostage in the Homeowners' Association office. She has since become a national symbol of what individual protest can accomplish at the highest levels of government. At present, she acts as consultant to public agencies and to citizens' groups throughout the country who wish to empower and organize themselves to effect state and federal clean-ups of hazardous waste sites.

Carson is a foresister also of scientists such as Dr Rosalie Bertell, a biostatistician who has done extensive research on the biological hazards of low-level radiation. She is now Director of Research at the International Institute of Concern for Public Health in Toronto, Canada and campaigns internationally against the dangers of nuclear technology. Bertell wrote that "a strong global rallying cry was heard in *Silent Spring* by Rachel Carson," and that women such as Dr Helen Caldicott of Australia (now of the USA); Petra Kelly, one of the founders of the Green Party in the Federal Republic of Germany; Solange Fernex of France; and Marie Therese Danielsson of French Polynesia have "elaborated and particularised" Carson's warning of the death of nature in the silencing of spring (Bertell 1986, p. 307).

Like Carson, there would be no peace for Bertell if she did not speak out. Recently she published *No Immediate Danger: Prognosis for a Radioactive World*. Her title is taken from the "mindless assurance which automatically follows every nuclear accident or radiation spill, namely, that

there is 'no immediate danger'" (Bertell 1986, p. viii). Bertell writes that
her most compelling reason for undertaking the task of explaining the
biological effects of exposure to ionizing radiation generated from the
entire nuclear industry—nuclear power plants, nuclear weapons production, the mining and milling of uranium for the industry, spills, leaks,
and waste stored or disposed into the environment—was the silence,
secrecy, and public ignorance about the hazards of nuclear technology.
She finds what Carson did in her research during the late fifties on the
ecological and biological dangers of pesticides. "Only [some] scientists
are fully aware of the subtle, cumulative nature of damage from low-level
radiation and the prolonged waiting time before such damage becomes
obvious in an individual, in her or his children," or in later generations
(Bertell 1986, p. vii).

In structure and in spirit Bertell's book is a sequel to *Silent Spring*. For
this reason alone it merits a close reading. Soon after *No Immediate
Danger* was published, a nuclear power plant exploded in Chernobyl. As
belts of radiation borne by winds encircled the Northern Hemisphere,
"world leaders" meeting in Japan collectively endorsed nuclear power
and made "gentlemen's agreements" to improve international reporting
of nuclear accidents. Bertell's analysis is as trenchant and as necessary as
Carson's was in 1962.

The nuclear technologies proliferate, Bertell demonstrates, because of
three fundamental "strategic misrepresentations." First, "atoms for
peace," the fifties government program to promote the nuclear industry,
would suggest that nuclear power plants generating electricity is a
"peaceful" use of the atom and is the primary purpose of the nuclear
industry. Thus, nuclear energy production is dissociated from nuclear
weapons production. Nuclear power plants become a symbol of
progress and peace, especially if the link between spent fuel rods from
power plants being processed for nuclear weapons production is ignored. Nuclear weapons production becomes a secret, military activity
which is never discussed and about which most citizens are ignorant.
These are the preconditions for people thinking that nuclear weapons
activity is minor, remote, and unobjectionable. The result: "a billion-
dollar weapon industry—unprecedented in war or in peacetime—was
woven into the fibre of the United States economy without most Americans being aware of it."[8] The infusion of money for nuclear technology
served weapons production as well as energy production; most nuclear
research serves dual purposes.

---

8. Bertell 1986, p. 169. See part three, pp. 157–174, for interrelationships between the
military and the peaceful atom.

The outcome of using a technology with roots in the atomic bomb and with ties to the military development of nuclear weapons is that "it has actually become necessary in many countries for armed guards to enforce national energy policy, sometimes violently, against the protests of unarmed citizens" (Bertell 1986, p. 13). Carson called turning plowshares into sprayguns and scorching the earth with pesticides a chemical war on nature. Bertell documents how the nuclear energy policy functions as a smokescreen for superpower military weapons production. She considers all nuclear technology, whether for weapons or for energy, the same—"the rule of the fist."

The second "strategic misrepresentation" is that the nuclear industry is a safe, low-risk industry. The silence and secrecy around casualties and victims of radiation from power and weapons production and testing has created the illusion that this is a safe technology. Bertell calculates that global victims of the radiation pollution related to nuclear weapons production, testing, use, and waste conservatively number 13 million. The current rate of weapons production globally (1985) generates between 7,000 and 15,000 victims yearly. The estimates include miners and nuclear workers whose radiation-related illnesses are not acknowledged by either government or industry. The victims suffer cancer, mild and severe congenital malformations, genetic damage in each generation until death of the family line. She concludes that the nuclear industry and the arms race is slowly depleting the human "store" of health. Carson asked if we are not poisoning ourselves along with the insects with the widespread use of toxic, persistent biocides. Bertell observes that in the race to test and manufacture weapons in order to protect ourselves from outside enemies, polluted air, food, and water become "enemies" within one's own country.

The third "strategic misrepresentation" is the use of "safety levels" of exposure to radiation in the nuclear industry. There is no safe level of exposure to low-level ionizing radiation. There is no level of ionizing radiation which does not damage cells, including ovum and sperm cells, and cause genetic damage, which may result in mild or severe cell mutations and cancer. "Permissible levels" of radiation are what Carson called, in writing of pesticides tolerances, a sanction for slow poisoning of people. These levels promulgated by government and the nuclear industry ignore the genetic damage from exposure to any level of ionizing radiation. And worse, they deceive people into thinking that, unless there is an accident, nuclear power and weapons generation and testing is safe.

A profound conflict of interest exists at the heart of standard setting by international and national agencies established to provide information and set radiation standards for nuclear technologies. The agencies consist of men who promote and support the technologies, a point Carson made so effectively about the Department of Agriculture regulating pesticides. For example, one of the two most prominent international agencies to which nations turn for guidance on nuclear radiation is the International Commission on Radiological Protection (ICRP). The ICRP, which is affiliated with the World Health Organization, has recommended the radiation standards and practices now generally accepted and implemented throughout the world. The members of ICRP are users of radiation and membership is self-perpetuating. Prospective members must be recommended by current ones or recommended by the International Congress on Radiology and approved by ICRP members. No scientists or physicians whose research and statements have challenged the commission's philosophy or recommendations sit on it. As for its record of protecting people from hazardous exposures to ionizing radiation, Bertell writes:

> In its functioning since 1950, the ICRP has never taken a public position in favor of protecting public health in any of the controversial radiation-related problems encountered: it has not taken a stand against above-ground nuclear weapons testing; it has not condemned radiation experiments on humans (prisoners, military personnel, and terminally ill patients); it has not called for a reduction of exposure of uranium miners to radon gas by increasing mine ventilation; it has not called for a reduction of medical uses of radiation for diagnostic purposes; it has not called for a reduction of exposure levels for nuclear workers as experience and research showed that their danger has been underestimated; it has not taken a position against the nuclear industry practice of allowing transient workers in the high-riskadiation exposure category to move from job to job without adequate control of cumulative exposures (Bertell 1986, p. 174).

Participation in radiation exposure setting has been dominated by colleagues from the military and civilian nuclear establishments and the medical radiological societies: people who have a vested interest in the use of radiation and who depreciate the risks of its use.

At the end of *Silent Spring*, Carson called for "the road not taken": biological solutions, not chemical fixes, for complex ecological problems. These solutions can only be developed with a "reverence for life even where we have to struggle against it." In conclusion to *No Immediate Danger*, Bertell calls for an end to seeking peace and economic prosperity through militaristic technologies. She looks to the women's movement and peace movement for a philosophy of existence on earth which would guide the development of peacetime economies and biophilic technologies.

In a plenitude of ways Rachel Carson has achieved the hope she expressed to Dorothy Freeman the year before she died: to live on in the minds of those who did not know her. For women like Dr Rosalie Bertell,

Carson's work is pioneering and paradigmatic. The problem she analyzed in *Silent Spring* was, in her own words, "one part of a sorry whole—the reckless pollution of our living world" (Brooks 1972, p. 310). For women like Lois Gibbs who fight the powers and principalities of governments and corporations to save some small corner of life on this planet, Carson is there as "one of the great fighters," as author Ann Cottrell Free called her.

Carson was moved to write *Silent Spring* because of a passionately written letter about one small corner of the world destroyed: a two-acre bird sanctuary. For women making the connections between the masculinist ravaging of nature and the rape of women, Carson was a forerunner. She saw the problem for nature: the arrogance of men who conceive of nature for their own use and convenience. We see it for women: a similar arrogance which assumes that women exist for the use and convenience of men. These connections will be discussed in depth later.

Rachel Carson's profound influence on women generates from the vitalism of her own work, but also from the primary and vital place that women held in her own life. This may explain the contagious quality of her work for women since. She was profoundly influenced by women and, in turn, she has done the same, living on in the minds of those who did not know her.

Rachel Carson's mother, Maria Carson, died in December 1958. Soon after, Carson wrote to Marjorie Spock, a friend she had met through the Long Island DDT trial:

> Some time I want to tell you more of her. Her love of life and of all living things was her outstanding quality, of which everyone speaks. More than anyone else I know, she embodied Albert Schweitzer's "reverence for life." And while gentle and compassionate, she could fight fiercely against anything she believed wrong, as in our present Crusade! Knowing how she felt about that will help me to return to it soon, and to carry it through to completion (Brooks 1972, p. 242).

Carson was referring to *Silent Spring*.

Mother and daughter lived together for nearly 50 years. Rachel dedicated her first book, *Under the Sea Wind*, to her mother. What Maria Carson was for her gifted daughter is best captured in a phrase developed by Nancy Richard, "the mother as mentor" (Richard 1982). The mentor, she explains, is a real, day-to-day model who begins with the student's dream as it is dreamed, sees her strengths, and gives practical day-to-day advice. The mother mentor "activates, shapes, and channels" the potential of her daughter, not necessarily formally but in the inherent structure of their relationship. She instructs; she directs her daughter protégée to other sources of education; and she is a practical example of living in the world with integrity. Richard writes that "it is the absence of the strong woman-centered woman, be it mother or mentor, that allows many a brilliant daughter to slip through the openings in the safety net we must construct between a young woman's dreams and her attempts at making them come true" (Richard 1982, p. 8).

Maria Carson had graduated from the Washington Female Seminary in 1887 with special honors in Latin and she was also a talented musician. She read to her three children each evening, but her love of books took root most firmly in her youngest child, Rachel. By the time Rachel was 10, she knew she wanted to be a writer and she had her first story published in a prominent children's magazine, *St. Nicholas*. A childhood friend's memory, as recounted by Philip Sterling, of her visits to the Carsons' home captures the day-to-day example of the life of the mind which Maria Carson offered to and enjoyed with her daughter.

> Charlotte Fisher, somewhat younger than Rachel, liked walking through the Carsons' woods on Sunday afternoons. Stopping at their house, she was always welcomed cordially. Over tea, cookies, and apples, there were lively conversations, usually led by Rachel's mother, about events and ideas of the time. All three were eager to tell each other about the books they had been reading. Springdale (Carson's hometown) had no public library then. Charlotte, who made frequent trips to a Pittsburgh library, brought back books for the Carsons and borrowed books from them. She remembered the relationship in later years as being based "not on dates or on being in the same crowd but as an intellectual kind of friendship with highly civilized people" (Sterling 1970, p. 38).

Being taken seriously by her mother—this was Maria Carson's tightly woven safety net around her brilliant daughter—Rachel took herself seriously. At 17, she declared to a schoolmate as they talked about entering university, "my major is going to be literature, not boys" (Sterling 1970, p. 40).[9]

---

9. I read Jean Strouse's (1980) biography of Alice James while writing this section and found myself comparing the diminished existence of James with the expansive existence of Carson, since both were recognized as brilliant and loved by their family. Like Virginia Woolf's sister of Shakespeare, Alice James was a woman with gifts equivalent to those of her brothers, William and Henry. But nothing was expected of her except her stimulating company. Her father mentored these two sons and expected greatness of them. She, the lifelong pet of her parents and brothers, was never challenged nor expected to express her talents in the world. So constricted, she lived caught in a cage of invalidism. Jean Strouse concludes that Alice James was significant, large, and unique within the "peculiar Jamesian" universe and that we "need not dwell on who she might have been." But this plays into the romance and mystique about "the Jamesian world," as if the affection of that unique family for her could be separated from how stifled she was physically and intellec-

Maria Carson had another profound effect upon her children; again it went deepest in her youngest child. She brought them close to nature and enabled them to feel it. She took her children on walks through the fields and woods of their land in southwest Pennsylvania near the Allegheny River. She never harmed spiders and insects she found in their house, but carried them outside. Rachel's brother was shamed into not hunting animals for sport by his mother's love of animals in the wild. She conveyed what Carson would later entitle a "sense of wonder" about nature, "a lifelong capacity to contemplate the beauty of the earth and find renewed excitement in living" (Carson 1965, pp. 88–89).

This love of nature went two ways in Rachel Carson. The first made her a biographer of nature, and the second compelled her to study science. The unity is rare. For most naturalists, modern science reifies nature and imposes answers on what they see. For most scientists, nature is a book of riddles and science is sophisticated detection work. Their interest is in the technique and solution, not in nature's vitalism.

A contemporary of Carson's, Dr Barbara McClintock, has best expressed the method of those rare few whose scientific work proceeds from a profound love of nature. McClintock received the Nobel Prize for her discovery of genetic transposition within a lifelong study of maize genetics. Asked by her biographer to explain how she could see under the microscope what had been thought unseeable, she called her method "a feeling for the organism" (Keller 1983). She looks for the difference rather than sameness in nature, for no two plants are alike and "you have to know that difference." She listens to her material and lets it speak for itself. Expressing the deep satisfaction of research which proceeds from a sense of intimate listening and watching, she said, "I know every plant in the field. I know them intimately and I find it a great pleasure to know them" (Keller 1983, p. 198). Her listening and looking from within the organism, as she put it, extended her ability to see under the microscope.

It was likewise with Carson. When she was asked how long she had worked on *The Sea Around Us*, her epic work on the sea, she replied that, in one sense, she had been writing it all of her life. Although she never

---

tually, and as if the James' family's peculiar mix of love and disregard for her can be seen apart from the social context of a world in which women are the second sex to men who "love" them. It is telling that, bound emotionally to the Jamesian world as Alice was, her last act was to entrust her diary not to her family but to her companion Katharine Loring who ensured that it was not edited, nor kept unpublished, nor destroyed, as her brothers wished. Henry James' comment on Alice James' diary captures the core truth of her life. 'The diary produces a unique and tragic impression of personal power venting itself on no opportunity."

saw the sea until after undergraduate school, she had been fascinated by it from earliest childhood and had read all of the classic sea literature. She told of a "memorable moment" as an undergraduate when a line from Tennyson's *Locksley Hall* "burned itself into [her] mind" (Brooks 1972, p. 18) and seemed to link her destiny with the sea.

For the mighty wind arises, roaring seaward, and I go.

This special blend of observational and cognitive, this listening to the material and letting it speak for itself, was Carson's way in nature. "The winds, the sea, and the morning tides are what they are," she said in accepting the National Book Award for *The Sea Around Us* in 1951. "If there is poetry in my book about the sea, it is not because I deliberately put it there, but because no one could truthfully write about the sea and leave out the poetry." The genius here is that she heard the poetry and could transcribe it.

For Carson, nature offered a renewed excitement, an inner contentment and the reserves of strength that would "endure as long as life lasts." Nature stirred in her a sense of the eternal and the transcendant. The tides, the beat of the surf; microscopic creatures pressing to gain a foothold on rocks and shifting beach to establish colonies; all of this awakened her sense of the mystery and meaning of life.

One of Carson's biographers suggests that throughout her life she was alone, "a loner," and lonely.[10] He is culpable in biography of the same fault McClintock says many scientists are guilty of in science: imposing an answer on what they see. In doing so, he missed a fundamental truth about Carson. Nature was a presence to Carson, so that alone in nature she was neither lonely nor alone. She wrote in *The Sense of Wonder*:

> What is the value of preserving and strengthening this sense of awe and wonder, this recognition of something beyond the boundaries of human existence? Is the exploration of the natural world just a pleasant way to pass the golden hours of childhood or is there something deeper?
>   I am sure there is something much deeper, something lasting and significant. Those who dwell, as scientists or laymen, among the beauties or

---

10. The biographer is Philip Sterling who blends facts of Carson's life with pop psychology to generate a version of an unmarried Carson who is often lonely and unhappy. This distortion of Carson, who never lived alone, but loved being alone in nature, is analyzed in more detail later in the chapter. Barbara McClintock had the good fortune to have a biographer, Evelyn Fox Keller, who let her speak for herself. Keller concluded that McClintock had lived most of her life alone, but that "no one who met her could doubt that it had been a full and satisfying life, a life well lived" (Keller 1983, p. 7).

mysteries of the earth are never alone or weary of life. Whatever the vexations or concerns of their personal lives, their thoughts can find paths that lead to inner contentment and to renewed excitement in living. Those who contemplate the beauty of the earth find reserves of strength that will endure as long as life lasts. There is symbolic as well as actual beauty in the migration of birds, the ebb and flow of tides, the folded bud ready for spring. There is something infinitely healing in the repeated refrains of nature—the assurance that dawn comes after the night and spring after the winter (Carson 1965, pp. 88–89).

The second path on which the love of nature took Carson was the study of science. In 1925 she entered the Pennsylvania College for Women (now Chatham College) in Pittsburgh, to study literature. In her sophomore year she enrolled in Biology 1 and 2 in order to meet her science credit requirements for graduation. Professor Mary Skinker, who taught biology, had a reputation for scholarship and impassioned teaching. After two semesters, Carson changed her major to biology, much to the consternation of her literature professors and the college administrators who thought that she was abandoning her future as a writer, that science was too rigorous a field for women, and that she was unduly influenced by Professor Skinker. She would later explain that this change did not mean that she liked literature less, but that biology gave her something to write about.

In studying biology Carson gained another mentor. With Skinker she discussed her plans for graduate school. They went on field trips to "see biology really happening." They wrote to each other during Carson's senior year when Skinker took a leave of absence to study for her PhD at Johns Hopkins University. Carson and some friends in biology formed a science club which they named Mu Sigma—M S in the Greek alphabet—for Mary Skinker.

Carson's enthusiasm for Skinker is charmingly expressed in a letter to Mary Frye, another science major and friend who admired Skinker and had collaborated in forming Mu Sigma. Frye is absent from school and has missed the prom.

> Yes I did have a glorious time. . . . It was so pretty. They had very dim lighting most of the time, and kept flashing green, lavender, and yellow lights across the room. A trifle hard on the eyes but indescribably pretty on the glass chandeliers and the mirror walls. . . . I had an awfully nice weekend. Miss Skinker was a perfect knockout at the prom. She wore peach-colored chiffon-velvet, with the skirt shirred just about 8 inches in front, and a rhinestone pin at the waist. Then she wore a choker necklace of rhinestones and two longer ones of tiny pearls (Sterling 1970, pp. 59–60).

Clearly her date paled by comparison with Mary Skinker!

In her senior year Rachel won a scholarship for graduate study in zoology at Johns Hopkins University. Skinker was no longer there,

having been forced to drop out because of illness. Before starting school
Carson vacationed with her at a mountain resort in Virginia. Although
there is no record of their correspondence after this point, the only other
reference to their friendship confirms its depth and longevity.

> Neither absence, distance, nor the urgency of her own affairs could di-
> minish her intense loyalty to friends. There was a day in 1950, for example,
> when Rachel got word that Mary Skinker was dying of cancer. She was
> pressed for time to finish *The Sea Around Us* and short of money, but she
> borrowed plane fare and flew to Chicago to be at Miss Skinker's bedside
> (Sterling 1970, p. 131).

The relationship between Mary Skinker and Rachel Carson was part
of a larger phenomenon among women scientists and their best female
students.[11] In the nineteenth and early twentieth centuries, the first
women faculty in science departments of women's colleges developed a
strategy for ensuring the success of their best students and the continua-
tion of their own work: the selection of bright protégées to succeed them
on the faculty. The "pioneer woman scientist" would encourage her
protégée and develop a close personal relationship. She would guide her
selection of a graduate school; correspond with her and oversee her
progress in graduate school; and, when she was finishing, arrange a

---

11. See Rossiter 1982, pp. 18–20. This book is a lode of facts on women scientists, their
contributions to science, the obstacles laid in their path by male scientists and institutions,
and the strategies these women devised to survive. While it documents the sexism of
science in its attempts to keep women out, the book is not a critique of patriarchal science
for its paradigms of control and conquest of nature. Also, Rossiter views the rich phenomenon of "protégée chains" and the fact that the majority of women scientists through 1940
did not marry through the lens of "heteroreality." (See Raymond 1986) Rossiter gives
excessive visibility and significance to married women scientists despite the fact that her
statistics show that a small fraction of women scientists were married in the period of her
investigation. One would have expected her to focus on the majority: single women.
Important questions to be asked might have been: What were the strategies such women
used to survive and succeed professionally? With whom did they collaborate? With whom
did they retire? Did they have female colleagues, friends, and/or lovers who affected their
professional lives? Instead, Rossiter devotes pages and statistical tables to documenting
who married whom of the small percent who were married and what sciences had what
percent of the female faculty who were married. In a table entitled "Notable Couples in
Science before 1940," Rossiter lists the married couples by the wife's field of science. It is
ironic to see Ruth Benedict and Margaret Mead listed with their respective husband scientists, but not with each other, though their relationship certainly lasted longer than Benedict's marriage to Stanley Benedict and even outlasted the total years of Mead's three
marriages. Rossiter's book does predate the 1984 biographies of Mead written by Mary
Catherine Bateson and Jane Howard, but certainly the information was known by many
before the actual publication of these two works and could have been investigated with the
careful and considered attention that Rossiter gives to the married scientists' relationships.

faculty position for her in the college's department. The student would join her mentor on the faculty, taking over some of her responsibilities and freeing her for other interests. When the senior faculty retired, the student would assume her position, select a protégée and continue the tradition of excellence. When the mentor died, often a science building or laboratory would be named after her; and her protégée, now chair of the department, would write the major obituary.

Some of these "protégée chains" lasted for several generations and developed traditions of academic excellence which distinguished the department nationally. For example, Susan Bowen and Cornelia Clapp originated a line of zoologists at Mount Holyoke from about 1870 until at least 1961. At Vassar, all the professors of astronomy were students and grandstudents of Maria Mitchell until 1932.

While details of Skinker's and Carson's relationship differ from the protégée chains, the core effect was the same. Skinker offered Carson a vital and never to be forgotten friendship, based on a mutual love of biology and a recognition and respect for each other's abilities. Janice Raymond cites the "professional lineage" of women professors and their protégée students as an example of the "lineage of women who have been and are primary to each other." She calls this lineage "a genealogy of female friendships" among women which are "momentous, prominent, remarkable, never to be forgotten, stirring, critical, vital and essential" (Raymond 1986, p. 35). Further developing the meaning of these friendships, she writes:

> Women who are primary to each other put each other first: first in the order of importance; first in the claims of attention, affection, and activity; first in not allowing men to interfere with or encroach on female friendship; first meaning first-rate, or that which shapes the finest fabric of female existence (Raymond 1986, p. 35).

This fundamental and radical valuing of women, this putting women first in her life, began with Carson's original friendship with her mother. What her "mother as mentor" gave to her daughter, in addition to a love of ideas and a feeling for nature, was a capacity for friendship with women. It is no wonder she would seek a rich friendship with Skinker. Carson's entire life was marked by creative and enduring friendships with women.

The influence which Maria Carson had on Rachel Carson, and the subsequent fullness of her life, is viewed very differently by Carson's male biographers and male acquaintances whom they quote. Obsessed with Carson's being unmarried, they paint her personality with a limited palette and portray a life without a man rather than a life with women.

Philip Sterling, who never knew Carson, tells us that she "came across as a soft-spoken, bright, fortyish lady, conservatively groomed, altogether personable, and entirely self-possessed" (Sterling 1970, p. 111). For effect, he contrasts the high drama of her literary life with the uneventful personal life of a "quiet little government employee who lived with her mother and kept a cat."[12] Later, talking of her new friendship with Dorothy and Stanley Freeman, whom she met in the early 1950s in West Southport, Maine, he calls her a "lifetime loner." The mutually creative friendship with Maria Carson, and the fact that they lived together and raised two nieces with whom Carson was very close—like sisters, one wrote later—doesn't count. Women together are women alone. Lifelong relationships with friends such as Marie Rodell, her literary agent, with whom she had voluminous correspondence and shared the details of her life, and Shirley Briggs, who since 1965 has directed the Rachel Carson Council to sustain the vision of *Silent Spring*, are invisible. These are relationships by default not by choice.

Continuing to portray her as dogged by the shadow of unhappiness, loneliness, and unfulfillment which lifts periodically, Sterling (1970) writes: "Rachel was happier this year than she had ever been in her not always happy life" (p. 129). The year was 1955. Let us look at the year and the circumstances of her life. Her third book, *The Edge of the Sea*, was just published and judged worthy to take a place beside her masterpiece of 1951, *The Sea Around Us*. This book was her first one written as a full-time writer. Carson had only recently achieved that for which she had yearned for years. "If I could just choose what seems to be the ideal existence, it would be just to exist by writing," she wrote in 1947 (Brooks 1972, p. 77). Carson had worked more than a decade and a half for the Fish and Wildlife Service, eventually becoming Editor in Chief, while writing *Under the Sea Wind* and *The Sea Around Us*. During that time she supported herself, her mother, and two nieces. If there is any truth to the observation that she was happier that year than previous ones, one need not look farther than the financial security she had achieved, which finally eased the relentless pace of working and writing, to explain happiness.

Sterling persists in pressing Carson's personality into his moldy stereotype: the lonely, bookish child who got stuck in a dull, quiet life with her mother and never married. "[Life] . . . had not been easy . . .

---

12. Shirley Briggs (1970, p. 9) wrote that between the calculated attempts of some of the pesticide industry spokesmen to create a peculiar caricature of her, and some better-intentioned efforts of others to picture her as an odd and humorless recluse, who Carson really was is erased.

[Carson] would have raised her thin, delicately arched eyebrows at the suggestion that life had in any way shortchanged her. True, she was unmarried. She confided to a friend that she would have liked to marry. Yet she never spoke of any one man she might have chosen. . . . She did nothing . . . to encourage anyone's romantic interest in her" (Sterling 1970, p. 130). Fishing for larger than personal reasons, since it is not to be believed that a woman might choose not to marry, he posits a "hardship" theory and a "surplus" theory. In the thirties men could not afford to marry; in the forties there was a surplus of women because of the war.

Borrowing generously from Sterling, Stephen Fox portrays Carson as an isolated, overprotected child. He too theorizes why she didn't marry, blaming overly tight family ties which trapped her: "these family loves and responsibilities exacted a price in isolation from the outside world. Carson would have liked to marry, she confided to a friend [cited from Sterling], but apparently was inhibited by the familial cocoon" (Fox 1981, p. 81).

Paul Brooks, Carson's editor from Houghton Mifflin and a personal friend, has written what is considered the definitive biography of her. The heart of his material is Carson at work. He lets her speak for herself by using generous sections of her work and staying close to letters and speeches as a way to fill in the details of her life and give a sense of her person. He, too, however, brings the same prejudice to his biography as does Sterling: not marrying, Carson lacked a fullness to her life. He adds a new theory: her mother kept her from it.

> Maria Carson was undoubtedly the strongest single influence in her daughter's life. Her love of nature went along with a love of books, and she fostered Rachel's literary ambitions from the start. When the daughter became famous, the mother helped with the correspondence and basked in the limelight. Her influence on Rachel's personal life—which cannot be wholly separated from her writing career—is more difficult to measure. It was she who, two decades earlier, had encouraged Rachel to take on the two nieces when their mother died; and this eventually led to Rachel's adopting a five-year-old boy when she herself was fifty. These family responsibilities, whatever their rewards and satisfactions, kept Rachel from enjoying what Thoreau called a broad margin to her life. And it is probably an understatement to say that Maria Carson never urged Rachel to marry (Brooks 1972, p. 242).[13]

And what are the broad margins to life that Thoreau discerned and presumably knew and enjoyed, but which Carson did not? Interestingly,

---

13. This terse, but loaded, comment has settled in like an obstinate, gray cloud forming the climate around Carson's entire life. There is now a second generation of biographers, like Fox, who reproduce and burnish the gray, slightly downcast image of the "unmarried" Carson.

Thoreau, who lived nearly a century before Carson, had talents and lived a life not unlike hers. To some he seemed austere. "But his family had all the best of him, which was affectionate, kind, and loyal" (Atkinson 1937, p. xi). Whenever Thoreau wrote to his mother or to his sisters, "the thoughts were homey, the style was glowing and the concern with family affairs was anxious." When his father died, he took over the responsibilities as head of the family, deferring pursuing his own life. "He accepted it calmly and discharged his duty, for the Thoreaus were in the habit of regarding personal honor as a natural part of their lives" (Atkinson 1937, p. xi). Thoreau distinguished himself initially by his writing on nature. It was for him in some fundamental way enough reason for its own existence and for his. Again, like Carson's final worldly work of protest and reform, this naturalist, after writing on nature, wrote an insurgent essay which helped reshape the world, *On the Duty of Civil Disobedience*. Carson protested against the evils of pollution, corporate greed, and necrophilic technologies; Thoreau personally seceded from the Union to protest a government that tolerated slavery and in speaking against slavery was "transfigured into a man of action."

Where they differed chiefly was in who they chose as life companions. "Sometimes Thoreau seemed needlessly morose in his responses to human society; it was late in life before he threw down his guards and took men as good companions with human gusto" (Atkinson 1937, p. xiv). Carson chose women as her closest friends and life companions. She gave herself completely only to two, Brooks wrote, her mother and Dorothy Freeman. When Thoreau wrote that he required "broad margins to his leisure," it was by way of expressing the need for privacy and quiet from other human beings, because of a natural pull toward reflection and critical thought. When Brooks used it of Carson—not enjoying "the broad margins to her life"—he is not referring to quiet and privacy. He refers to her not marrying. Thoreau could enjoy "the broad margins" of life without marrying; Carson could not. His homosocial world was sufficient; her female-centered world was not.

This points up the problem of a woman in the hands of a male biographer. The first is one of presence, that is, men seeing women for what men would have them be and not for who women are. A recent incident is useful here in illustrating the quality of active presence which men rarely give women. George M. Taber, a senior editor for *Time*, met Corazon Aquino twice, once the day before she fired Defense Minister Ponce Enrile. "It made all the difference to get her up close at a crucial time," said Taber, who edited the *Time* cover story in which Aquino was featured as Woman of the Year. "From a distance it was her soft style that came through. But in her presence we could see complexity and strength" (Taber 1987).

Presence is not only the fact of being up close physically or of being nearby at a critical moment. It is a listening with the willingness to see complexity and strength. It emanates, as Barbara McClintock said of her method of knowing, from the desire to understand the unexpected and to let the material speak for itself. The unexpected for Carson's biographers was that "liberty was a better husband" for her and she was happy with the friendship of women. They did not let their material speak for itself. They constructed theories about the scarcity of men and surplus of women, the chain of family responsibilities and pressure from her mother. And they saw what they expected to see: spinsterly primness and loneliness. Nor was the loneliness they "saw" existential and conducive to genius, or a tragic but great condition, as Henry Thoreau's and John Muir's biographers have granted them. In Carson it was small, unattractive, and psychological.

Men did not have the access to Carson that her closest women friends did. She kept them at a distance, having primarily professional, deferential interest in them if they were writers or prominent scientists or naturalists; whereas her letters to women are warm, supportive, and dimensioned. Women were first in her life.

Rachel Carson, if she is to be known, must be sought in the places and ways she chose to express herself. At 17, in an entrance essay to Pennsylvania College for Women entitled, "Who I Am and Why I Came to PCW," she wrote: "I am intensely fond of anything pertaining to outdoors and athletics. I am seldom happier than when I am before a glowing campfire with the open sky above my head. I love all the beautiful things of nature, and the wild creatures are my friends." She then described the sports she enjoyed playing and her love for reading, especially the classics of English and American literature. She concluded this essay on herself with a glimpse of the spark which would mark her entire life. "To become a little more personal, I am an idealist. Sometimes I lose sight of my goal, then again it flashes into view, filling me with a new determination to keep the 'vision splendid' before my eyes."

The vitality, the integrity, and a precocious attentiveness to the kernel of things, which marked Rachel Carson so indelibly by 17, also marked Carson's most personal relationships. These were with women; it was women who knew her best. Shirley Briggs first met Carson at the Fish and Wildlife Service in 1945, and was a lifelong friend. She remembers her as being "at the center of the office" by her humor and her wry observations in what would otherwise have been a humorless, bureaucratic routine. They went on many birdwatching trips and nature jaunts together. One particularly memorable one was an exploration of the Everglades and the coral reefs. Briggs has written of those times with Carson, "The worlds I explored with her will always seem richer and more vivid than others, however I may hope the keenness of perception found with such a companion persists in new scenes" (Briggs 1972, p. 148). Recently, in discussing Carson's life, she said that, "If anyone lived it at the broad margins it was she."[14] Bringing us full circle back to the 17-year-old writing of her idealism, Briggs said, "Rachel looked at the broadest and most important things she could do and imagine and set out and did them. The task of writing *Silent Spring* was something no one else probably could have tackled."

The letters which Carson wrote Dorothy Freeman may be the reservoir of her deepest feelings for her most intimate friend. They will not be available for many years, at the request of Dorothy Freeman. This act does exemplify the privacy and discretion which marked Carson, a quality which many of her male biographers have denigrated into a barren quiet about her life.

In concluding some hours' conversation on Carson, Shirley Briggs said summarily, "The story of Rachel's life is the story of her work." Her work incarnated her passion for nature, her love of ideas and the English language, and her idealism. And she found love where her work was. The title of Brooks' biography, *The House of Life: Rachel Carson at Work*, captures this.

The world was her home. She wrote her first works in love with its life, and her last one to save its life. What is living at the broad margins of existence, if not this? Let us then go on to her work, *Silent Spring*, and its impact on the world.

REFERENCES

Atkinson, B. (ed.) 1937. *Walden and Other Writings of Henry David Thoreau*. New York: Modern Library.

Berry, W. 1977. *The Unsettling of America: Culture and Agriculture*. New York: Avon Books.

Bertell, R. 1986. *No Immediate Danger: Prognosis for a Radioactive World*. London: The Women's Press.

Briggs, S. 1970. Remembering Rachel Carson. *American Forests*, July, 9.

Briggs, S. 1972. A decade after *Silent Spring*. *Friends Journal*, 1 March, 148.

Brooks, P. 1972. *The House of Life: Rachel Carson at Work*. Boston, Massachusetts: Houghton Mifflin.

Carson, R. 1962. *Silent Spring*. Greenwich, Connecticut: Fawcett Publications.

Carson, R. 1965. *The Sense of Wonder*. New York: Harper and Row.

Cole, L. C. 1962. Book review of *Silent Spring*. *Scientific American*, December, 173–180.

Devall, B. and Sessions, G. 1985. *Deep Ecology*. Salt Lake City: Peregrine Smith Books.

---

14. The quotes in this section are from a conversation with Shirley Briggs, April 1987, Silver Spring, Maryland.

Dunlap, T. R. 1981. *DDT: Scientists, Citizens, and Public Policy.* Princeton, New Jersey: Princeton University Press.

Erlich, P. R. 1979. Reconsidering *Silent Spring. Bulletin of the Atomic Scientist,* October, 34.

Fox, S. 1981. *John Muir and His Legacy: The History of the American Conservation Movement.* Boston, Massachusetts: Little, Brown.

Graham, F. Jr. 1970. *Since Silent Spring.* Greenwich, Connecticut: Fawcett Publications.

Hynes, H. P. 1985. Ellen Swallow, Lois Gibbs, and Rachel Carson: catalysts of the American environmental movement. *Women's Studies International Forum,* **8**(4), 291–298.

Keller, E. F. 1983. *A Feeling for the Organism: The Life and Work of Barbara McClintock.* San Francisco: W. H. Freeman.

Lewis, J. 1985. The birth of EPA. *EPA Journal,* November, 9.

Marchant, G. 1988. Committing science to peace. *Science for the People,* January/February, 41.

Raymond, J. G. 1986. *A Passion for Friends: A Philosophy of Female Affection.* Boston, Massachusetts: Beacon Press.

Richard, N. 1982. The mother as mentor. Paper in feminist theory, University of Massachusetts, Amherst, December.

Rossiter, M. 1982. *Women Scientists in America: Struggles and Strategies to 1940.* Baltimore, Maryland: Johns Hopkins University Press.

Sterling, P. 1970. *Sea and Earth: The Life of Rachel Carson.* New York: Dell.

Strouse, J. 1980. *Alice James: A Biography.* Boston, Massachusetts: Houghton Mifflin.

Taber, G. M. 1987. *Time,* **129**, 5 Jan., 1–33.

Wright, P. 1985. The greening of Nagasaki, *Contact,* **X**(4), 30–34, University of Massachusetts.

II

SILENT SPRING REVISITED

As man proceeds toward his announced goal of the conquest of nature, he has written a depressing record of destruction, directed not only against the earth he inhabits but against the life that it shares with him (*Silent Spring* 1962, p. 83).

The edifice of *Silent Spring* is built upon a spare, but controversial foundation: a two-page parable of a town in which wildlife, flowers and vegetation, children and adults sicken and die mysteriously. Spring is silenced by chemical poisoning. The parable enraged industry and many scientists, who accused Carson of a one-sided and grossly exaggerated account of the hazards of pesticides.

Nearly three decades later Superfund, the Environmental Protection Agency's (EPA) hazardous waste clean-up program, evaluates hazardous waste sites by the same criteria which Carson used to create "A fable for tomorrow." The elements of the "hazardous ranking system," as the methodology for identifying the most dangerous hazardous waste sites is called, include the type and quantity of hazardous chemicals; evidence of stressed vegetation, contaminated groundwater, surface water, and air; and the proximity of people, drinking water wells or supplies, and unique ecosystems to the chemicals. Those sites in which hazardous chemicals endanger most people or valuable natural resources, because of the nature of the chemicals and/or the routes of exposure, are the sites given priority for federal clean-up monies and enforcement action.

The Superfund program began in 1980. Congress gave EPA a $1.6 billion fund with the mandate to rank, investigate, and clean up the 400 most serious hazardous waste sites in the United States within a period of five years. In subsequent amendment, Congress has increased the fund and the number of sites. Today Superfund, EPA's most energetic and resource-laden program, is generally considered a failure by Congress, the newsmedia, and the public. In the early, critical years of Superfund, the program and the Agency were badly infected with the anti-environmental animus of Reagan-appointed administrators, a factor which compounded the already complex nature of the program. Thus far, the average hazardous waste site takes the Agency more than five years to study and comprehend. There have been so few comprehensive clean-ups—a handful at most—that EPA cannot yet realistically calculate the cost or time to clean up a site. "Clean-up" is most often a euphemism for capping in place chemical dumps, removing chemical wastes and storing them elsewhere, or replacing wells with an alternate water supply system without renovating the contaminated groundwater. Superfund has been slow, wasteful, and lacking in substantial accomplishment.

And its mission is meager by comparison with the problem. In the process of evaluating sites for remedial action, EPA has estimated that there may be as many as one to two million hazardous sites from chemical dumping, unlined industrial impoundments, leaking underground storage and waste tanks, and underground injection wells.

Most criticisms of Superfund center on its dearth of results: so much toxic waste buried, so few sites cleaned up. But there is an equally serious flaw, located in the thinking of Superfund, for which Carson's controversial fable is instructive. Carson describes "a town . . . in the midst . . .of prosperous farms, with fields of grain and hillsides of orchards" (Carson 1962, p. 13) on which a pesticide was sprayed. The chemical drifted everywhere, into soil, groundwater, and rivers; onto people's skin; and into the foodchain. EPA's conceptual model of a hazardous waste site is an abandoned dump or pits, ponds, and lagoons in which waste chemicals have been stored, buried, or poured and then leach into the environment. But the more direct and commonplace human exposure to toxic chemicals is where use constitutes disposal into the environment. For example, lead was used to manufacture water pipes and as solder for copper water pipes and tin food cans, to enhance pigmentation in house and commercial paints and ceramic glazes, and as an additive in gasoline. Lead has leached into drinking water and food; it has fallen out from auto exhaust into soil and onto garden vegetables; it has flaked off interior and exterior house walls in paint chips; it has dissolved from dishware into beverages and food. This cycle of hazardous chemical use constituting disposal into people's environment and nature is what Carson exposed and described in *Silent Spring*. Chapter by chapter she explains how agricultural chemicals used in chemical intensive farming migrate throughout the web of life as if they had been dumped into the environment.

Thus, while EPA has focused its entire hazardous waste program on industrial waste sites and abandoned dump sites, with little to show for it, problems of environmental contamination which don't fit that model are neglected. There are two, in particular—one rural, one urban—where chemical use, not dumping or disposal, results in the kind of extensive environmental contamination and endangerment to public health which we associate with hazardous waste dumps.

Farmers contaminate their own wells and regional water supplies with agricultural chemicals, even when they use the chemicals as prescribed by the manufacturer. What *Silent Spring* warned about has been amply documented in the states of Florida, California, Hawaii, and Massachusetts. In Massachusetts, for example, of 139 private wells in the farming town of Whately sampled by State agencies in 1984, 39 had detectable levels of ethylene dibromide (EDB), a potent carcinogen used on shade tobacco by western Massachusetts farmers. Thirty-five of those 39 wells had levels of EDB above the State drinking water guideline of 0.04 parts EDB per billion parts water. In a similar study conducted by the State Pesticide Bureau with Union Carbide, manufacturer of TEMIK(R), 114 private wells in Whately were tested for aldicarb (registered trademark TEMIK), a pesticide used by potato farmers against the Colorado potato beetle after it developed resistance to other pesticides. Aldicarb was found in 34 wells, 14 of which had levels in excess of the State and EPA standard. Many farmers' wells contained between two and five different pesticide compounds.

Private wells in Whately have been replaced with a municipal drinking water supply funded by state and town funds and homeowner fees. In a study of Whately's water quality conducted for the purpose of developing a town water supply to replace contaminated private wells, consultants drilled test wells and sampled groundwater in both the upper and lower regional aquifers. They found pesticide contamination in the upper aquifer to such an extent that they concluded the aquifer was unsafe for use as a new public water supply.

Whately is an isolated case within a much larger problem. The problem—agricultural pollution—will only take shape and definition as studies are undertaken in other agricultural areas, as was done in this case. There are tremendous pressures against this, however. One pressure comes from within public agencies. There is not enough money in the Superfund budget or individual State budgets to replace or restore all groundwater and sole source aquifers contaminated by agricultural chemicals, as was done in Whately. Without resources to solve this problem, public agencies are likely to ignore it in the hope that, unobserved, it will go away.

Another pressure is opposition from pesticide manufacturers. The Monsanto Company filed suit in a Massachusetts court to halt a January 1, 1988 state ban on Alachlor, a herbicide which Monsanto manufactures. Alachlor, a widely used herbicide and a suspected carcinogen, has been applied by Massachusetts farmers to inhibit weed growth in cornfields. The State survey of pesticide contamination in farmers' wells, which verified EDB and TEMIK contamination, also found Alachlor residues in a small number of wells. Monsanto claimed the State data are faulty and the ban is unfair.[1]

A third deterrent to action is the trendy philosophy of living with risk promulgated by some risk communication professionals. It usually devolves into a "do-nothing" philosophy which lets public agencies off the hook and allows the pesticide industries to get on with their business. "Safety is the acceptance of risk, not the absence of risk" advised Dr. Sorrell Schwartz, who downplayed the cause for concern over EDB in Whately wells since there are so many other risks in life (Bond 1984a).[2]

Finally, farmers habituated to chemical farming feel they know no other alternative except to use chemicals. The "other road" which Carson called for, one which would develop ecological alternatives to chemical pesticides and use chemicals as a last resort, has barely been traveled. Research on alternative methods to protect agriculture and forests from infestation—such as using natural predators, rotating crops, and determining what population density of insect is harmful so as to minimize the use of chemicals—grew out of the ecological reforms in agriculture and a federal research budget which were spurred by *Silent*

---

1. See Dumanoski 1987a. Monsanto won its appeal before a state administrative law judge. The terms of the agreement between the Massachusetts Department of Food and Agriculture and Monsanto were that Alachlor will be registered by the state as a restricted use herbicide, and Monsanto will conduct training sessions for users and an environmental study on the migration of Alachlor into groundwater. The State's action is more rigorous than EPA's on Alachlor. In early 1988, EPA announced that it will permit the continued use of Alachlor. After a four-year review, EPA decided that the risk of cancer from Alachlor is an "acceptable" average of one in one million Americans. (If this average is spread out over all Americans, must it not be higher for farmworkers?) Alachlor containers must bear the warning that the chemical has been determined to cause tumors in lab animals. *Valley Advocate*, 15 February 1988, p. 20.

2. Risk communication emerges from the confluence of two phenomena. One is the public participation process of Superfund, whereby people affected by a Superfund site are provided studies and information about the site and given the opportunity to provide comments on the studies and decisions about the site. The second is the use of risk analysis as a rational method by which to evaluate the hazard of a waste site and then compare all of the feasible remedial action options for their effectiveness in eliminating or minimizing hazard.

However, risk analysis is increasingly being used by industry to avoid responsibility for their hazardous products and waste and by indecisive government bureaucrats to deflect criticism from their inaction. They cite lifestyle activities—smoking, drinking, driving—and naturally occurring phenomena—radon gas in homes—as much higher in risk than their product or waste site, and thus dwarf the hazard in question. Even where public officials are sincere in presenting the risks of a hazardous waste site to people, they often talk at rather than with people and use overly technical jargon, causing antagonism and mistrust. For a lucid analysis of this latter—the failure of risk analysis professionals to understand and communicate with people, in the process of interpreting hazard—see Edwards and Santos 1987.

Spring. These more ecologically based methods require a different kind of attention to farming, one which is more observational and labor-intensive, according to Dr David Ferro, vegetable entomologist at the University of Massachusetts, Amherst (Bond 1984b). However, the current minuscule budget from the federal government for this research renders these alternatives to chemical farming a nonthreatening project conducted by a few ecologically minded entomologists with minimal resources to assist farmers. Such token support leaves the agricultural chemical industry's domain intact.

The second example of widespread environmental contamination from the routine use of chemicals is high lead levels in urban soils. A 1985 Boston City Hospital study of children suffering from blood lead poisoning calculated that the incidence of blood lead poisoning in young children may be as high as 1 in 20 children in some neighborhoods. The children studied live in the poorest neighborhoods of Boston where lead from gasoline and leaded paint from housing has contaminated house dust and the soil in which they play. Lead affects virtually every aspect of human physiology, but it is most destructive to the developing brains of children, causing mental retardation, hyperactivity, and other behavioral problems. These largely irreversible effects are compounded by malnutrition.

After a decade of effort by community public health activists and a core of local EPA and city of Boston staff, Boston received EPA monies in 1986 for a pilot project to remove lead-contaminated soil from residential properties which have been termed Emergency Lead Poisoning Areas because of the high number of lead-poisoned children.[3] This crucial

---

3. See Deland 1987. *This editorial by the Regional Administrator of EPA provides a concise summary of the serious threat to young children posed by lead contamination. It makes clear that soil removal must be one part of a concerted program to eliminate lead in drinking water and air and to de-lead the interior of houses. However, at the time of this writing, EPA's soil removal program has undergone a period of interagency disagreement that brought the program to a standstill. Over the more than two years' planning, the emphasis and resources of the program have shifted from the original legislative intent of lead abatement to an epidemiological study with more limited remedial action (see Hynes 1988).

A comprehensive bill on lead poisoning prevention in the Massachusetts State legislature was signed into law in January 1988, after an initial balking by Governor Dukakis over the cost of the law. The law provides tax credits to homeowners or tenants who remove lead paint or contaminated soil. In addition, the law provides for more screening of children for lead poisoning; loans to low-income property owners who remove lead; licensing and training of those who remove lead and inspect removal; setting safety standards for lead in soil and water; investigating less expensive methods to remove soil; directing money to inner cities and other places known to have high numbers of children poisoned; and giving lead poisoning information to all homeowners (see Tye 1988).

On November 18 1987 lawyers filed suits in state and federal courts on behalf of three

initiative is small by comparison with the Superfund program budget; it is restricted to Boston and possibly one or two other pilot areas. Yet the public health hazard to poor, primarily Black and Hispanic children, from lead compounded with malnutrition harms more children than any childhood disease. It is one of the most, if not the most, serious and widespread environmental health hazards in the country.[4]

---

lead-poisoned children. The suits seek to hold five major lead suppliers and the Lead Industries Association responsible for the poisoning of children in Massachusetts and to make them pay damages for injuries to the three children named in the suit. The suits contend that the lead industry has known since the thirties that lead poses a serious health risk to children and, through the Association, lobbied against proposed lead regulations in Massachusetts in 1934. Massachusetts did not enact legislation to combat lead poisoning until 1971 (see Dumanoski 1987b).

4. Environmentalism is often trivialized as the issue of a leisured class intent on protecting natural resources for their own personal enjoyment, for sport, for economic value, and so forth. At its worst, this is true. At its best, I think environmentalism is a "birthright" of people with wealth because they live where nature is more pristine and wild. They have the privilege of awakening to "wild and scenic" rivers, wildlife sanctuaries, and vistas unobstructed by high rises and freeways. However, they do not necessarily step beyond securing their own small, unspoiled world to challenge the larger political and economic principle that corporate profit (usually marketed as jobs, urban development, economic growth) supercedes environmental protection and people's right to a healthy environment.

In fact, environmentalism is more germane to the lives of women and the poor of this country. They are the primary victims of industrial pollution. For lack of wealth, mobility, and leisure, they are deprived of nature in the wild. A recent study by the United Church of Christ's Commission on Racial Justice found that Blacks and Hispanics are more likely to live near a toxic waste dump than a white person. Fifty percent of Hispanics and 60 percent of Blacks live in a community with at least one uncontrollable toxic waste site. Three of the five largest hazardous waste landfills are located in communities that are predominantly Black or Hispanic. The study found that in many cases siting a hazardous waste facility was linked to job opportunities and contracts with minority-owned businesses. Clearly, the economic depression and daily struggle for survival left minorities vulnerable to high-risk opportunities (see Newsnotes 1987).

In addition to being the majority of the urban adult poor, women are the caretakers of victims of pollution. Anguished by lead-poisoned children, children with birth defects and leukemia, mothers like Lois Gibbs have organized community protests to force action from public and environmental agencies. Women are treated as the sole route of exposure to contamination for fetuses, even though men may endanger or contaminate the fetus through their own gametes or through contaminating women. Women are made solely accountable for environmental and medical risks to the fetus by the medical profession. Only women suffer job discrimination for being of "childbearing" age. When global population is pitted against natural and environmental resources by governments and population experts, women in developing countries are the targets of their birth control policies. For lack of money, mobility, and leisure and because women have been socialized to make their world within the small world of the home, women have less access to nature in the wild than men.

Environmentalism is not fundamentally the privileged cause of the upper class. It is a necessary issue of women and the poor.

These two examples are undramatic and nonmacho by comparison with the warlike heroics of Superfund site descriptions, which generally depict men in moonsuits sampling corroding drums of a "witches' brew of toxic chemicals"[5] in ugly, abandoned dumps. Yet lead in urban soil and pesticides in farmers' wells bring us back to the fundamental message of *Silent Spring*, a message particularized about pesticides and herbicides but intended as a warning about the indiscriminate and arrogant use of industrial chemicals and technologies. Carson wrote:

> For the first time in the history of the world, every human being is now subjected to contact with dangerous chemicals, from the moment of conception until death. In the less than two decades of their use, the synthetic pesticides have been so thoroughly distributed throughout the animate and inanimate world that they occur virtually everywhere (Carson 1962, p. 24).

Synthetic pesticides result from the laboratory manipulation of molecules of basic chemicals like carbon, hydrogen, and chlorine into new compounds which do not occur naturally in the world. The insecticidal properties of certain synthesized compounds were discovered when they were being tested on insects for use in chemical warfare during World War II. When that war ended, the chemical industry declared war on insects and weeds and opened up a whole new market for chemical biocides. In the massive aerial spraying campaigns of the late forties and fifties, chemicals were rained on marshes, tree-lined towns, forests, and farms. The production of synthetic pesticides in the United States increased five-fold from 124,259,000 pounds in 1947 to 637,660,000 pounds in 1960 when Carson was writing *Silent Spring*.

Carson discusses two large groups of chemicals into which the majority of pesticides could be classified: the chlorinated hydrocarbons, such as DDT, chlordane, heptachlor, dieldrin, aldrin, and endrin; and organic phosphorus insecticides, two of which are malathion and parathion. All of these chemicals intended for use on crop-, tree-, and plant-destroying pests and weeds, enter humans and animals. Some

---

5. The oxymoron, "witches' brew of toxic chemicals," is an egregious reversal of history. Witches, mostly women, were alchemists, herbalists, healers and midwives of the Middle Ages. Their brews were medicinal, healing potions. For more than three centuries Christianity waged a campaign of witch trials and witch burnings to stamp out witchcraft. Witches who were healers and midwives were a major threat to the supremacy of Church clerics.

On the other hand, toxic chemicals in corroding drums are dangerous and deadly. They were mixed and dumped as cheaply as possible by corporate officers, military officials, and waste haulers. Almost exclusively, all polluters and environmental criminals are men; women don't hold positions of authority to make and carry out those decisions. Someone captured succinctly one element of the sexual politics of hazardous waste: hazardous waste exists because men never learned to clean up after themselves.

chemicals are more selective in their routes than others; but they enter humans and animals adsorbed to dust inhaled, as residue on sprayed foods, absorbed through the skin in contact with vapors, and in contaminated drinking water.

The chlorinated organics, beginning as only minute residues, can result in significant concentrations in the body due to two phenomena. One is cumulative increase in the food chain as pesticides move from one organism to another. Fields of grain are sprayed with a pesticide, leaving a small residue on the grain. The grain is fed as meal to an animal which consumes large quantities of the small pesticide residue. A higher level of pesticide becomes concentrated in the animal's tissue than was on the grain. Humans eat animal products in which the original residues are magnified. The poisons may pass from a mother to her breast-feeding child, at levels in excess of limits set by the Food and Drug Administration for food sold in interstate commerce.

The second phenomenon is persistence. Once the chlorinated organics enter the body, they are stored in organs rich in fatty substances such as the adrenals, testes, or thyroid. They are deposited in the liver, kidneys, and fat around the intestines. They accumulate and persist in the body. "Because these small amounts of pesticides are cumulatively stored and only slowly excreted, the threat of chronic poisoning and degenerative changes of the liver and other organs is very real," warns Carson (1962, p. 30). Some of these compounds undergo change into another chemically distinct compound, the latter being more toxic than the former. Heptachlor, for example, a constituent of the insecticide chlordane,[6] undergoes a chemical change to heptachlor epoxide in soil and in the tissue of plants and animals. The resultant epoxide is more toxic than heptachlor, which is four times more toxic than chlordane.

The second major group of insecticides, the organic phosphates, are closely allied to the deadly nerve gases used in World War II. They, like the nerve gases, attack the nervous system of their subject, human, animal, or insect. Specifically, they destroy enzymes which are needed for smooth functioning of the body. Repeated exposures may result in tremors, convulsions, and death. The organic phosphates are short-

---

6. More than a decade after banning chlordane in agriculture, EPA continues to allow the use of this highly toxic chemical around house foundations as a termiticide. Evidence shows that chlordane/heptachlor has penetrated into treated houses contaminating people and their possessions. This carcinogenic chemical has migrated with drainage water into nearby rivers. As with agricultural chemicals, the use of chlordane around homes constitutes disposal into and contamination of the environment. There are alternative ways to deal with termites, including safer controls and preventing infestation by sound building codes (Briggs and Epstein 1987).

lived, by comparison with the chlorinated hydrocarbons, so they do not persist and build up in human tissue. However, they still pose dangers to farmworkers exposed during or soon after application. Further, their toxicity can be increased or "potentiated" for someone exposed to different organic phosphate insecticides simultaneously (in the common salad bowl, Carson suggests) or to an organic phosphate insecticide and another compound in sequence. For example, although the liver produces enzymes which detoxify malathion, if that enzyme production is inhibited or the enzyme destroyed by another pesticide or other chemical compound, then malathion cannot be detoxified. The ever-increasing number of synthetic drugs and chemicals being marketed and consumed are being consumed in mixtures with pesticides. No one, Carson warned, can predict their effects in combination.

The significance of even minute concentrations of a chemical in a food chain is illustrated by the history of wildlife at Clear Lake, California. The lake was used as a resort by fishermen. Its waters were an ideal habitat for a small gnat, *Chaoborus astictopus*. Three times between 1949 and 1957, DDD, a close relative of DDT, was applied to the lake water in infinitesimal but increasing concentrations, initially at a strength of one part chemical for every 70 million parts water. The maximum concentration applied was one part DDD in 50 million parts water. Mysteriously, western grebes on the lake began to die. Grebes, being fish eaters, were attracted to the lake for its fish and would breed and winter there. Analysis of dead grebes' tissue subsequently revealed a concentration of 1,600 parts per million DDD. Plankton, plant-eating fish and carnivorous fish were analysed for DDD in their tissue. "The large carnivores had eaten the small carnivores, that had eaten the herbivores, that had eaten the plankton, that had absorbed the poison from the water" (Carson 1962, p. 52).

This phenomenon of increasing accumulation and storage of persistent chemical compounds has been borne out in case history after case history of harbor, lake, and river studies. Bottom sediments contain heavy metals, pesticides, PCBs, and other persistent compounds which have been discharged by industries and wastewater treatment plants located along or near those bodies of water and also carried in stormwater runoff from nearby industrial property, city streets, or farmland. Fish, lobsters, and all life which feed in these bottom sediments or eat organisms which do, and which feed from the water column above these sediments, bioaccumulate these toxic substances at 10, 100, even 1,000 times their initial concentration. Is there a harbor, major lake, or river left which is not posted to warn people of the hazard of eating fish, mollusks, and crustaceans from those waters? Who warns the wildlife which feed on them? "Can we suppose," Carson asks, "that poisons we introduce into water will not enter into these cycles of nature? . . . Here again we are reminded in nature that nothing exists alone" (Carson 1962, p. 55).

One of *Silent Spring's* most prescient concepts is the dangers pesticides pose to groundwater. Before groundwater protection was a concept, let alone a profession and public program, Rachel Carson warned: "In the entire water pollution problem, there is probably nothing more disturbing than the threat of widespread contamination of groundwater. . . . Pollution of the groundwater is pollution of water everywhere" (Carson 1962, p. 47).

Groundwater is that invisible underground sea which is recharged by rain that percolates through the pores of soil and in places moves into fractures of bedrock. Moving as slowly as a few feet a year, and as quickly as a few feet a day, it surfaces at lakes, streams, rivers, wetlands, ponds, and the ocean. In New England, water a few meters underground may be sufficient to serve an individual home; while a few large wells drilled into glacial outwash may provide drinking water for an entire community. In the entire United States, groundwater supplies nearly 50 percent of the total drinking water.

The example from which Carson drew to warn of groundwater contamination was the pollution of farm wells several miles from the Rocky Mountain Arsenal of the Army Chemicals Corps near Denver, Colorado. During the forties, chemical wastes from the manufacture of war materials by the Army were discharged to holding ponds at the Rocky Mountain Arsenal. The chemicals seeped into groundwater and in a matter of seven to eight years had migrated into farmers' wells three miles downgradient. The farmers irrigated their crops, fed their livestock, and drank from these wells. This resulted in animal and human illness and extensive crop damage. Most mysterious of all was the discovery of the herbicide 2,4-D in the well water and also in the holding basins, although it had never been manufactured at the arsenal. It was concluded that 2,4-D had been formed spontaneously in the open ponds from other compounds disposed there in the presence of air, water, and sunlight. "An extraordinary episode that may easily be only the first of many like it," she wrote (Carson 1962, p. 47).[7]

Carson's brief chapter, "Realms of the soil," displays a teeming, di-

---

7. The Army and the Shell Oil company agreed jointly to pay as much as $1 billion to clean up the Rocky Mountain Arsenal. Shell operated a pesticide plant on land leased from the Army from 1952 to 1982. Among chemical wastes at the site are the pesticides aldrin and dieldrin, two of the chlorinated organics whose toxicity, Carson wrote, exceeded that of DDT. The major public concern about the "clean-up" is that the Army and Shell will not

verse world of organic and inorganic constituents in the thin mantle that covers continents: the soil. Formed over eons from the action of water, frost, and ice wearing and cutting away at rock and from the remnants of disintegrated lichens, mosses, small insect life, flora and fauna, soil is sustenance for all living creatures and is sustained by them. The soil is enlivened by billions of microorganisms. Each acre of soil is estimated to contain about 2,000 pounds of mold, 1,000 pounds of bacteria, 200 pounds of protozoa, 100 pounds of algae, and 100 pounds of yeast. Some are the agents of decay rendering the nutrient components of plant and animal tissue available to new life. Others destroy the infectious microorganisms deposited in the soil with the dead matter and wastes of living creatures. Bacteria capture and fix nitrogen for plants and chemically transform iron, manganese, and sulfur into forms available for plants. Certain soil fungi, mycorrhiza, live in a symbiotic relationship with the roots of plants, including many food crops. These fungi may contain as much as 10 percent nitrogen in the form of protein which is digested in the plants' roots.

Earthworms by their burrowing activity aerate the soil and keep it well

remove all of the contamination, but "simply dump it into a designated area within the arsenal" (Shabecoff 1988).

The Rocky Mountain arsenal is the most infamous of thousands of military sites throughout the United States, including nuclear fuel plants and national research and testing sites for nuclear bombs, where chemical and radioactive wastes from war materials production were buried in drums or poured into open pits and trenches contaminating soil and groundwater.

Militarism—defense build-up, preparation for war, and war itself—pollutes and ravages the environment as it kills and maims people. The link between militarism and environmental degradation is most explicit today in Central America, a land of vital and fragile ecosystems which are being polluted and destroyed by chronic war. "War is Nicaragua's principal environmental problem," concluded the Nicaraguan National Park Director, who described how environmental projects and environmentalists are targeted by the *contras* (Hall 1987). Scorched earth warfare in Guatemala, a cycle of bombing villages, crop lands and forests, has caused forest fires, soil erosion, siltation of reservoirs, and clogging of natural springs. Chemical bombs contaminate soil and water. In 1986 US military assistance to El Salvador and Honduras was 18 times what the United States spent on the entire Caribbean environment. Honduras, called the aircraft carrier of Central America, is crisscrossed with US military roads, airstrips, and bases which were built without the environmental controls to which they would be subject in the United States. Wilderness is destroyed; rainforests are opened up; and peasants displaced by war move into these ecologically sensitive areas.

In war, nature is the property and the home of "the enemy," to be destroyed as the enemy is routed and killed. The lush, vegetative cover of tropical rainforests is eliminated with herbicides. An obstacle for military machinery, rainforests are slashed and ground down for military roads and aircraft. The earth is an infinitely deep landfill in which to inject, pour or bury the chemical and biological wastes of war and the bodies of raped and slain women and children.

drained, enabling plant roots to better penetrate the soil. They digest and thus help break down dead plant and animal matter, and enrich the soil with their excrement. Darwin calculated that earthworms might create an inch to an inch and a half thick layer of soil in a 10-year period.

Looking at the interdependent and vital relationships among the living and inorganic substances of the soil community, Carson asks:

> What happens to these incredibly numerous and vitally necessary inhabitants of the soil when poisonous chemicals are carried down into their world, either introduced as soil "sterilants" or borne on the rain that has picked up a lethal contamination as it filters through the leaf canopy of forest and orchard and cropland? Is it reasonable to suppose that we can apply a broad-spectrum insecticide to kill the burrowing larval stages of a crop-destroying insect, for example, without also killing the "good" insects whose function may matter? Or can we use a non-specific fungicide without also killing the fungi that inhabit the roots of many trees in a beneficial association that aids the tree in extracting nutrients from the soil? (Carson 1962, p. 59).

Carson cited studies which show that the herbicide 2,4-D causes a temporary interruption of nitrification, the process by which bacteria make atmospheric nitrogen available to plants. Chlorinated hydrocarbon pesticides, such as lindane, heptachlor, aldrin, benzene hexachloride (BHC), DDT, and DDD reduce nitrification. Many have been found to prevent nitrogen-fixing bacteria from forming the necessary root nodules on leguminous plants. Not only do the chlorinated pesticides affect the soil community quickly after application, but they also persist for years, at levels capable of killing insects and presumably soil bacteria and fungi. Consequently, apparently "safe" or "moderate" applications of a pesticide, year after year, will accumulate in a soil to extremely high levels. The interrelationship between soil and plant life inevitably results in the absorption and uptake of insecticides from contaminated soil into the tissue of plants. Carrots, sweet potatoes, and other roots and tubers have been rejected as unfit for human consumption because of pesticide residues which they absorbed into their skin from subterranean soil.

The relationship between plant and soil is a critical symbiosis of soil microbes and plant which is jeopardized by chemical agriculture. The organic agriculture specialist, Sir Albert Howard, conducted classic studies in soil fertility and its relationship to animal and plant health during the first half of the twentieth century. He argues that natural soil fertility cannot be replaced with synthetic chemicals. He contends that fertility lost by erosion or intensive farming can be repaired only by replenishing it with humus from the composting of animal and vegetable waste. One of the essential functions of humus, he maintains, is to provide certain soil fungi, mycorrhiza, for many cultivated and non-cultivated plant and tree species. Mycorrhiza form a mantle of fungus cells around feeder roots; they enter the living cells of the plant root, and send thread-like filaments into the surrounding soil.

> At the end of the partnership the root consumes the fungus and in this manner is able to absorb the carbohydrates and proteins which the fungus obtains partly from the humus in the soil. The mycorrhizal association therefore is the living bridge by which a fertile soil and the crop are directly connected and by which food materials ready for immediate use can be transferred from soil to plant (Howard 1943, pp. 24–25).

In addition to improving plant nutrition, certain mycorrhiza deter plant root infection by root pathogens. The fungus mantle serves as a mechanical barrier to the pathogen; many fungi manufacture strong antibiotics against the pathogen (Martin and Focht 1977).

In his field work Sir Albert Howard observed the effect of agricultural chemicals applied to stimulate plant growth and as insecticides and fungicides on mycorrhiza. The mycorrhiza are active in soils rich in humus, which soils he observed consistently yield crops resistant to disease and support healthy animal feed crops. They are inactive or absent in infertile soils, soils applied with chemicals which then need the assistance of insecticides and fungicides to yield uninfested, marketable crops. Howard goes so far as to call insect pests "Nature's professors of agriculture." Insects and fungi, he observes, attack unhealthy plants and thus act as censors pointing out where soil fertility and agricultural methods need improvement (Howard 1943, p. 161).

In addition to the immediate toxic effect of pesticides on beneficial organisms and insects, and soil fertility, Carson warned of the persistence of the chlorinated pesticides, like DDT and chlordane, in nature. Resisting rapid biodegradation by bacteria, these chemicals build up in soil and sediment and are available to the food chain of insects, fish, animals, and humans for years.

Recent studies are beginning to demonstrate that microbes are developing the capability to break down, and in some cases to detoxify, some of these new synthetic compounds which appeared to be relatively refractory. The breakdown of these complex molecules is being carried out by yeast mold, fungi, algae, aerobic and anaerobic bacteria in riverine sediments, in activated sewage sludge, in the rumen of animals, and in marine environments. This research has been spurred on, no doubt, by two things: the heightened public consciousness of DDT-like chemicals in the food chain; and industry's and government's dilemma of how to rid or clean wastewater, soil, and sediment of persistent chemical compounds. This quickly evolved capability of microbes is one of the most important and beneficial phenomena in nature. For the promise it offers, but also because of the rapid research effort building—in which genetic engineering is carving out space—let us take a more detailed look into the world of microbes breaking down synthetic organic compounds.

Since the early twentieth century bacteria have been used to biodegrade sewage and wastewater generated by human and, at times, industrial waste. Sewage oxidation ponds, often called lagoons, are large, shallow, lined ponds exposed to the air that hold waste sufficiently long for microbial decomposition. The activated sludge process, the core of which is an activated mass of microorganisms capable of aerobically degrading waste, consists of an aerator and clarifier. In the aerator, suspended microbes are provided air or pure oxygen to metabolize the biodegradable wastes. The microbes are separated from the wastewater in a settling tank or clarifier; and a portion of them are recycled to maintain metabolism in the aerated tank. The rest are removed as sludge and incinerated, applied to land as soil amendment, or landfilled.

Trickling filters use a biological process similar to activated sludge in that growth of microbes is encouraged to biodegrade wastewater passed through the medium. The difference lies in the fact that the microbes are attached to a fixed medium such as rocks or a synthetic medium over which the wastewater is constantly recycled. The excessive microbial growth is sloughed off the media and captured in a clarifier, after which it is handled as sludge.

Animal and human waste were biodegraded by soil microorganisms before the advent of central wastewater treatment plants. Even with the collection and centralization of waste and wastewater treatment, the role of soil microorganisms has been recognized in the concept of land application of wastewater and sludges. As decomposers, soil organisms are essential to the success of land application of organic wastes. When manure or sludges are added to the land, microorganisms continue to decompose them until the wastes are converted to gaseous carbon and nitrogen compounds, minerals, water, and microbial cells. The ability of microorganisms to decompose organic materials is enhanced by the complexity and metabolic diversity of the microbial populations in soil. Microorganisms often reach large numbers in the surface of agricultural soils. Estimates of 10^8 bacteria, 10^6 actinomycetes, 10^5 fungi, and 10^5 protozoa per gram of soil are representative values.

Compounds, such as DDT, other pesticides, plastics and industrial solvents, have been introduced into the environment only in the past 40 years. They have been formed, in the simplest cases, by substituting a chlorine atom for a hydrogen atom on an organic compound. Both what is substituted or attached, like the chlorine atom, how many atoms are substituted, and where they are attached on the new molecule, affect the new compound's toxicity and resistance to metabolizing or biodegrading microorganisms in the natural world. Many of these new compounds have seemingly resisted being metabolized by naturally occurring microbes, one reason being that the microorganisms could not produce the enzymes necessary to initiate breakdown of the new compound. In fact, strong slugs of these compounds entering a wastewater treatment plant from an industrial discharge have disrupted the colonies of bacteria in the activated sludge process. The bacteria, acclimated to a particular waste "diet," were killed by the strength and toxicity of these chemicals. For this reason, industries are required to have a permit before they can tie into a municipal wastewater treatment plant. The permit establishes pollutant levels which the industry must achieve in its discharge so as not to upset the biochemical balance to which the wastewater treatment plant bacteria are acclimated.

The recent discovery that some bacteria have evolved the ability to break down persistent chemicals offers great potential for developing biological treatment and destruction of toxic waste. One fungus, *Fusarium oxysporum*, has shown the unique ability to decompose DDT completely into its elemental components in 10–14 days, a feat observed only with this organism (Kobayashi and Rittman 1982). *Flavobacterium* is extremely effective in removing the fungicidal wood preservative, pentachlorophenol, from river, lake, and ground waters. In temperatures between 15 and 30 degrees Centigrade, pentachlorophenol concentrations ranging from 10 parts per billion to 100 parts per million were reduced to nondetectable levels within two to three days (Ghosal *et al.* 1985). Actinomycetes, a group of organisms similar to bacteria and fungi, are known to decompose a variety of complex organic compounds. The decomposition that they bring about does not thoroughly reduce the compound, as does *Fusarium oxysporum* with DDT; but the various metabolites can be mineralized to carbon dioxide and water by other organisms. Thus the actinomycetes would work in tandem with other microorganisms to achieve detoxification of unusual compounds.

Algae begin a process of pesticide breakdown by causing the chlorine atom to detach from insecticide molecules in what is thought to be a photochemical process. The algae absorb light energy and induce an electron transfer between the algae and insecticide, which causes the chlorine atom to detach from the insecticide. Phototropic organisms, such as algae, cyanobacteria, and photosynthetic bacteria, are unique in microbial degradation of environmental pollution because they obtain energy from sunlight, carbon from carbon dioxide fixation and, in some cases, nitrogen by fixing it from air. Such capabilities enable them, unlike other organisms, to thrive and decompose refractory compounds in situations which offer low concentrations of nutrients. While phototrophs do not promote complete degradation of synthetic compounds, they can transform them to metabolites which other bacteria can biodegrade (Kobayashi and Rittman 1982).

The selectivity, versatility, and diversity of naturally occurring micro-organisms suggest that even the most refractory compounds may be returned to the elemental or mineral components by a sequence of microbes, each complementing the reaction of the others. Supporting and enhancing these naturally adapted microbial environmental scavengers offers a wide open and promising field for environmental scientists and engineers, as evidenced in the expanding research on microbial degradation. Such a research partnership with microorganisms involves isolating and identifying the organisms and their interactions with other organisms; establishing their limiting reactions and their metabolic pathways; and learning the pH, amount and quality of illumination, nutrient availability, reduction–oxidation potential, and moisture content needed for them to proliferate.

However, what began in the past decade as the study of microbes' rapidly developed biodegradative capabilities and the potential to use them in hazardous waste sites and biological wastewater treatment, is now taking a seriously disturbing direction. A leap is being quickly made, away from the promising study of microbes in the environment and the potential for working with them in ways akin to biological wastewater treatment, over to genetically engineering them and releasing them into nature. One recent article speculates that "the recalcitrance of many halogenated compounds [the suite of compounds which includes all of the chlorinated pesticides] to microbial degradation presents . . . challenges to microbiologists and geneticists. . . . An understanding of the biochemical and genetic mode of microbial dissimilation of biodegradable halogenated compounds may be a logical step toward the construction of genetically improved strains that might be used in the future for enhanced removal of the more persistent compounds" (Ghosal *et al.* 1985). After a word or two about "appropriate regulations" to protect the public from genetically engineered organisms released in nature, the authors conclude that "genetically engineered organisms *are key* [emphasis mine] to solving toxic chemical pollution" (Ghosal *et al.* 1985).

This rapid shift from naturally occurring microorganisms to genetically engineered organisms carries with it at least three major risks. One is the not-understood and unpredictable risk of releasing genetically engineered organisms into the environment. The second is the deflection of resources away from purposeful and promising research on naturally occurring bacteria, which carries negligible risk, but which is not as glamorous and research-worthy as genetic engineering. The third risk is that application into nature of engineered microorganisms will be controversial; it will become embroiled in lawsuits and stalled in courts. These entanglements will delay the renovation and protection of the environment.

Finally, there is a depressing parallel between the two paths that research on biodegrading microbes is taking and the two paths which Carson saw to solve the insect problem. Carson called for solutions which understood, respected, and worked with the ecology of the insect, a path which was less traveled than the path of spraying broad-spectrum, toxic, and persistent chemical pesticides. We have a comparable choice with the direction of research into using and enhancing microbes' evolving capabilities with toxic substances. The science and engineering of figuring out how the microorganisms have so quickly evolved the capability to break down man-made toxins and how to expand upon this, is as intellectually intriguing as the techniques of genetically engineering bacteria. It is more ecologically wise and more pragmatic than the path of genetic engineering; and it continues within the tried and true tradition of biological waste treatment. Genetic engineering is novel, "state of the art," and glamorous. These attributes sell cars; they sold synthetic pesticides; unfortunately, they determine research funding priorities.

One of the best-studied compounds with respect to naturally occurring biodegradation is the polychlorinated biphenyl (PCB) molecule, a compound with chemical properties similar to chlorinated organic pesticides. PCBs were first manufactured by the Monsanto Company in the thirties. In a process similar to other chlorinated organic compounds, the 209 forms of PCBs are generated by attaching chlorine atoms to one or more of the 10 hydrogen positions of the double-ringed biphenyl molecule. PCBs were valued for their chemical stability, low volatility, and nonflammability. Mixed with oil, they served as insulating fluids in capacitors and transformers. PCBs have two distinct effects on humans and other life forms: a skin lesion known as chloracne, and a toxic effect on the liver which appears to be increased if there is simultaneous exposure to carbon tetrachloride (a solvent). They are suspected of having carcinogenic effects on humans. Laboratory studies of the reproductive effects of PCBs have shown that they decrease fertility in adult fish and decrease survivability of fish embryos and newly hatched fish.

The General Electric Company (GE), like many early industries, located manufacturing and assembly plants on rivers and waterways. Waste chemicals, washings, and spills were drained and discharged into these water systems directly or through groundwater which surfaced at influent streams and rivers. The Housatonic River, which flows south 150 miles through western Massachusetts and Connecticut to Long Island Sound, is estimated to contain about 30,000 pounds of PCBs entrained in river bottom and backwater sediments. These were discharged or spilled into the river by the GE Pittsfield, Massachusetts transformer plant over a period of 40 years until the company ceased use of this compound in the early seventies. The Pittsfield plant also had outfalls into nearby

Silver Lake, the sediments of which have served as a reservoir for about 60,000 pounds of PCBs. Like DDT, this chlorinated compound is a complex molecule, which was valued in industry for its resistance to breakdown under extreme industrial conditions. The same stability makes PCBs resistant to breakdown in the environment.

GE has numerous PCB-contaminated sites in the United States for which they are conducting research on innovative biological treatment and breakdown of PCB molecules. They report that there are specific aerobic bacteria which partially degrade PCB molecules in soil through enzymatic activity. They also observe chlorine removal from anaerobic PCB-contaminated sediments of the Hudson River in New York and Silver Lake in Massachusetts and marine sediments, where the sediments are more heavily contaminated (PCB concentration greater than 50 parts per million). Their findings point to the eventual possibility of a two-step process for marine and aquatic sediments consisting of anaerobic dechlorination as observed in aquatic sediments followed by oxidation by aerobic bacteria to complete the breakdown of PCB molecules to more elemental, safer compounds (Bedard *et al.* 1987).

The results of GE's laboratory models for evaluating the biodegradation of PCBs in soil under aerobic conditions look very promising. GE concludes that "PCB degradation on soils *in situ* is feasible, but that it will be significantly slower than in our conventional resting-cell assays." The rapid degradation achieved in the laboratory under optimal conditions of high cell concentration, optimal temperature, and aeration, will take weeks or months to achieve in the field. Repeated applications of bacteria will be necessary.[8]

Remarkable as these findings are, they do not mask or minimize the fact of present widespread pollution of rivers, harbors, and bays and its

---

8. See General Electric Company 1986, 1987, p. 3. GE's research has focused on five major areas: (1) the biochemistry and genetics of bacterial oxidation of PCBs, (2) reductive dechlorination of PCBs by anaerobic communities, (3) analysis of environmental transformations of PCBs, (4) development of laboratory models for evaluating the biodegradation of PCBs on soil, and (5) development of laboratory models for evaluating surfactant extraction of PCBs from soil. Areas 2, 3, and 4 work with naturally occurring bacteria, isolating and identifying them, their methods of PCB degradation and methods of enhancing both in the environment. Area 1 has used recombinant DNA techniques to study the genetics of bacterial oxidation. There is potential here to move from this research technique to application of genetically altered bacteria into the environment. However, the preponderance of GE's research has been toward enhancing naturally occurring bacteria, not toward application of genetically altered bacteria. This may be because it is in GE's interest to develop enhanced, efficient *in-situ* dechlorination and biodegradation technologies which are acceptable to environmental agencies who have ordered the company to remediate numerous PCB-contaminated sites throughout the country.

impacts on aquatic and bird life and ourselves. For example, even where PCB pollution is infinitesimal, the uptake and bioconcentration by fish makes even very low concentrations of this compound serious. In the Connecticut portion of the Housatonic River, where the total 15- to 40-year-old PCBs in bottom sediment were below the detection limit of 0.02 parts per million, hatchery fish accumulated PCBs in excess of the then FDA tolerance of 5 parts per million (Hynes 1983). This tolerance was recently lowered to 2 parts per million. Until they biodegrade completely, PCBs in river sediments are a continuing source of contamination both to the waters and the biological food chains of the river. High levels of PCBs and their metabolites will continue to bioconcentrate in fish and other aquatic and wetland life, even while there may be declines due to biodegradation from original levels at the time of industrial discharges to the environment.

The significance of the microbial reduction of PCBs in nature is that it offers the potential to reduce in place, not just to relocate or entomb, the problem of contaminated soil, wetlands, and aquatic sediment. This would minimize dredging sediments, which carries with it the risk of resuspending the contamination. Dredging and capping sediments in place can destroy wetlands and require the rerouting of waterways. Dredging also carries with it the complex, ancillary problem of finding a site for burying contaminated sediments. Even working with these microbes to enhance their naturally evolved capabilities, scientists and engineers must tread sagaciously, with the ecological savvy and conservatism which Carson advocated for all human intervention in nature.

> The earth's vegetation is part of a web of life in which there are intimate and essential relations between plants and the earth, between plants and other plants, between plants and animals. Sometimes we have no choice but to disturb these relationships, but we should do so thoughtfully, with full awareness that what we do may have consequences remote in time and place (Carson, 1962, p. 64).

With this *caveat*, Carson begins a powerful and prophetic chapter on herbicides, more commonly called weed killers. She tells the story of the eradication program, using chemical sprays, undertaken by "progressive" government land management agencies in the sagebrush lands in the West for the sake of establishing grasslands for cattle grazing. The program was blind to the meaning of the age-old ecosystem which had emerged there.

The low-lying and shrubby sage grows year round, through dry, searing summers and long, snowbound winters, on the lands of the high western plains and the lower slopes of the Rockies. This plant supports the lives of two animals: the sage grouse and the pronghorn antelope. It is shelter for the grouse's nests and its staple for food. In winter the antelope moves down the mountain to lower elevations and eats the protein-, fat-, and mineral-rich leaves on the evergreen sage.

What will the likely results be of destroying the indigenous vegetation which has been food for native animals and replacing it with unbroken grassland, she queries. "It is clear that the whole closely knit fabric of life [is being] ripped apart" (Carson 1962, p. 67). Wisdom suggests that the climate is too dry to support sod-forming grass and that perennial grass which grew around the sage would have provided a better supply. Sage would have provided winter food for the starving livestock. The grouse and antelope will disappear along with the sage and "the land will be poorer for the wild things that belong to it" (Carson 1962, p. 67).

A second example cited by Carson of "the shotgun approach to nature" is one witnessed by Judge William O. Douglas (1961). Yielding to the pressure of cattlemen for more grasslands, the U.S. Forest Service sprayed some 10,000 acres of sagelands. The sage was destroyed; willow trees which grew by meandering streams shriveled and died; moose who fed on the willow thickets left; beavers who fed on the willows and felled them, creating a lake out of a stream, left; the lake drained away; trout and waterfowl attracted to the lake disappeared.

Recognizing that there are situations in which it is important to eliminate brush and trees along roadsides and rights of way, Carson describes the method of "selective" spraying developed by Dr. Frank Egler of the American Museum of Natural History. The concept of spraying only select plants, such as tall woody plants, takes advantage of the inherent stability of nature. Most communities of shrubs resist the growth of trees, whereas the open space of grasslands lends itself to tree seedlings sprouting up. Selective spraying of problem trees and leaving the shrubs intact to grow in where the trees took root, uses the shrubs themselves, not chemicals, to practice vegetation control. Respraying is not needed for at least 20 years because all plants are not sprayed and killed in order to eliminate one. "The integrity of the environment is thereby preserved, the enormous value of the wildlife habitat remains intact, and the beauty of shrub and fern and wildflower has not been sacrificed" (Carson 1962, p. 74).

Biological solutions—ones which originate in nature—are some of the most spectacular successes in plant control. "Nature herself has met many of the problems that beset us and she has usually solved them in her own successful way" (Carson 1962, p. 80). The case of the prickly pear is an extraordinary example of using plant-eating insects to control a plant. In the late eighteenth century the prickly pear plant was brought to Australia. By 1925 it had spread to over 60 million acres, half of which were so densely covered as to be unusable. After researching the insect predators of the plant in its native habitat, entomologists introduced three billion eggs of an Argentine moth into Australia. After only seven years, the last dense growth of prickly pears was gone.

The chapter on herbicides concludes with a remarkably insightful discussion of the most widely used herbicides at the time of writing *Silent Spring*: 2,4-D, 2,4,5-T, and related compounds. (Agent Orange, used as a defoliant in the Vietnam War, was a 50/50 mixture of 2,4-D and 2,4,5-T. Dioxin occurs as a ˋcontaminant in the manufacture of 2,4,5-T.) Herbicides were used liberally on farms, forests, roadsides, utility rights of way, and suburban lawns. They were generally considered less toxic than pesticides, perhaps because it was thought that it did not require as toxic a compound to kill a plant as to kill an insect or animal. Even though the toxicity of 2,4-D and 2,4,5-T was largely unquestioned, Carson built the case for concern:

- People applying 2,4-D to their lawns who had become wet with spray occasionally suffered severe neuritis and paralysis.
- 2,4-D had been shown in experiment to disturb respiration in the cell and to imitate X-rays in damaging the chromosomes. Reproduction of birds may have been adversely affected after exposure to this herbicide.
- Livestock and, presumably, wildlife have died after grazing on certain weeds treated with 2,4-D. The nitrate content of certain plants increases after being sprayed with 2,4-D. Once an animal eats the high levels of nitrates, microorganisms in its digestive system convert the nitrates into highly toxic nitrites. The nitrites inhibit the transfer of oxygen in the body and the animals die of lack of oxygen.

Only a small section of *Silent Spring* focused on herbicides, with most emphasis on government plant eradication programs and roadside spraying, and briefer mention of farmers' and homeowners' use. The major part of *Silent Spring* dealt with insecticides. To Carson, however, herbicides no less than insecticides were part of a whole chemical assault on nature; they were all biocidal. It is instructive to see that, in the aftermath of *Silent Spring*, a handful of chlorinated insecticides were banned or severely restricted—DDT, aldrin, dieldrin, heptachlor, chlordane (not as a termiticide) and Mirex—but that herbicide manufacture and use escalated tremendously and outpaced insecticide use.

On the 15th anniversary of *Silent Spring*, writer Daniel Zwerdling looked over the years since the book was published. He saw a massive shift in agriculture from plowing and cultivating for weed control to no-till farming. In no-till farming, a farmer plants seeds through old crop stubble and uses herbicides like 2,4-D and Paraquat to prevent weed growth. No-till agriculture is being promoted so aggressively by the agricultural chemical industry and their trade journals, that "by the year

2000 . . . almost half the cropland in America will be managed by the no-till method" (Zwerdling 1977). In 1977 American farmers and gardeners were using two and a half times as many pesticides as in 1962; American farmers were spraying nearly 10 times as much herbicide on corn and soybeans as in the early sixties.

On the 25th anniversary of *Silent Spring*, Shirley Briggs and Samuel Epstein wrote that contamination of groundwater and surface water from pesticides "has become commonplace. Much comes from agricultural use, but increasingly we find that the most intensely contaminated areas are residential" (Briggs and Epstein 1987). They cite a National Academy of Sciences study which estimated that home lawns were averaging 10 pounds of pesticide application per acre while farms rarely exceeded two. Presumably much of the 10 pounds per acre on suburban lawns is herbicide for weed control. Slipping out from under Carson's thunder at DDT and chlorinated insecticides, the chemical herbicide industry is creating what *ABC* recently called the new "silent spring" in the suburbs.[9]

Waging chemical war on plant and insect life—and killing birds, mammals, fishes, and practically every other form of wildlife—is not just a scientific question, Carson wrote, it is a moral one. The Department of Agriculture's campaign to eliminate the Japanese beetle in the late fifties exemplifies this immoral turning "plowshares into chemical sprayguns."

The Japanese beetle, an insect common to mainland Japan, was unintentionally imported on nursery stock into the United States around 1912–16. The beetle spread throughout the Eastern states and continued moving westward. Between 1920 and 1933 some 34 species of predatory or parasitic insects were imported from the East in an effort to control the beetle population. The most widely established and effective in bringing the beetle under control is a parasitic wasp from Korea and China. The wasp attaches an egg to a beetle grub which it has paralyzed and the wasp larva feeds on the paralyzed grub and destroys it. A second natural control had been "milky spore disease," a bacterial disease specific to

---

9. Special on *Silent Spring*, ABC World News, 27 May 1987. States have promulgated Right-to-Know laws which require industries to inform and educate employees about the hazards of chemicals they handle. Increasingly, states and municipalities are considering applying the same concept to farmers and homeowners who use pesticides on their fields and lawns. The state of New York is currently holding public hearings on new state pesticide regulations which would require warning signs in establishments, apartment houses, on farmland and lawns where pesticides have been sprayed. The signs must warn of the spraying and specify the chemicals being used. See "Pesticide Rule Raises Furor in New York," Boston *Globe*, 9 November 1987, p. 12.

beetles. In an effort to enhance the effects of this natural control, many Eastern states participated in a program to apply the bacterial spore to infested lands. As a consequence they enjoyed a high degree of natural protection from the beetle.

Despite the success of the Eastern states in the thirties and forties, by the late fifties when the beetles had infested the Midwest (and "peacetime" uses of poisonous chemicals were expanding), the government reached for chemicals. "Launching an attack worthy of the most deadly enemy instead of only a moderately destructive insect," Carson (1962, p. 86) writes that they selected the most dangerous chemical insecticides and applied them by aerial spraying, thereby exposing large numbers of people, domestic animals, and wildlife to the poison intended for the beetle. For example, 27,000 acres in southeastern Michigan including numerous suburbs of Detroit were heavily spraydusted with pellets of aldrin. Aldrin is 100 to 300 times as toxic as DDT in tests on quail. In a few days an immense number of birds were dead and dying of insect poison. A local veterinarian reported that his office was full of sick cats and dogs. The local Health Department received a constant stream of complaints from people with throat and chest irritations.

In Illinois an eight-year aerial spray program using dieldrin, 50 times as toxic as DDT to laboratory quail, resulted in no sustained control of the Japanese beetle and almost unparalleled loss of rabbits, squirrels, cats, muskrats, and livestock and songbirds who ate poisoned earthworms and drank poisoned water. Carson's conclusion captures how the government masked and minimized the environmental damage in order to sustain the program:

> In spite of the enormous havoc that has been wrought in the name of eradicating the Japanese beetle, the treatment of more than 100,000 acres in Iroquois County, Illinois over an eight-year period seems to have resulted in only temporary suppression of the insect, which continues its westward movement. The full extent of the toll that has been taken by the largely ineffective program may never be known, for the results measured by the Illinois biologists are a minimum figure. If the research project had been adequately financed to permit full coverage, the destruction revealed would have been even more appalling. But in the eight years of the program, only about $6,000 was provided for the biological field studies. Meanwhile the federal government had spent $375,000 for control work and additional thousands had been provided by the state. The amount spent for research was therefore a small fraction of the outlay for the chemical program (Carson 1962, p. 92).

In the late fifties, a year after the federal government had launched a massive spraying program to control the fire ant, a woman from Alabama wrote that on her land, which had been a bird sanctuary for over 50 years, suddenly in the second week of August there were no songs of birds to be heard. *Silent Spring* warned of the specter of a world rendered moribund and silent by the eradication of any creature that may annoy or cause inconvenience. Carson uses the story of the campaign to control American elm disease and its devastating consequences for more than 90 species of birds, the robin being an exemplar, to substantiate the moral outrage she and others like the woman from Alabama felt against "the supreme value [of] a world without insects, even though it also be a sterile world ungraced by the curving wing of a bird in flight" (Carson 1962, p. 118).

Dutch elm disease entered the United States about 1930 in elm logs which were imported for the veneer industry. The disease is a fungus which enters the water-conducting vessels of a tree, and its spores are carried by flowing sap to every part of the tree. By a combination of poisonous secretions and mechanical clogging, the fungus weakens the tree. The fungus is carried from diseased tree to healthy tree by the elm bark beetle. Spores adhere to its body as it tunnels under the bark of dead trees, and are carried wherever it flies.

In the mid-fifties towns in New England and the Midwest began heavy spraying of elms with DDT in the spring, and often again in July. Robins newly arrived for spring were found dead and dying in those towns. Few nests were built; few young appeared. By the late fifties, naturalists and ornithologists were able to trace the chain of events. Poisons sprayed onto elm trees infected all insects, pollinators and predatory spiders, as well as the elm beetle. Oily DDT-filmed elm leaves were fed upon and decomposed by earthworms. DDT was found throughout the bodies of earthworms. In spring the returning robins fed on the earthworms. Less than one day's diet of DDT-contaminated earthworms can be lethal for a robin. During this period midwestern university campuses were reporting robin mortality to be as much as 90 percent. Analyses showed high concentrations of DDT in the ovaries and testes of breeding birds. DDT stored in the yolk of an egg is fed upon by the developing embryo; this explains the death of embryos and nestlings. Mortality was not the only reason for the decline in robins. One or more of a pair might die before the nesting cycle was completed. The birds might build nests but lay no eggs. Many eggs which were laid and incubated did not hatch.

After an intensive spray program of five or six years, foresters and ornithologists observed two phenomena. With any let-up in spraying, the beetles were back but insect-eating birds were gone. Second, promptness in removing diseased elm trees was more effective in protecting the remaining trees than massive DDT spraying programs. At the time Carson wrote, New York State had a most impressive record of containing and controlling the disease. It established a program of removing and burning all diseased and infected elm wood. The wood had to be burned before spring to kill adult fungus-carrying beetles hibernating under the bark. The rate of loss of elm trees due to the fungus was impressively low.

A final point Carson makes is that of preserving diversity in nature as one way of reducing the loss of trees to a particular insect or blight. A healthy ecosystem is one in which a relatively small number of many species exists. Even if one species is attacked by a blight or insect, the other species are not vulnerable and the ecosystem stays strong. If a town lined its avenues with only one species of tree, as was done with the American elm, then all of the town's trees were more likely to be destroyed by a disease-carrying beetle than if the town had planted a variety of trees. The principle of diversity in nature and the conservation of variety to sustain the strength and health of an ecosystem is one of those profound lessons of nature from which humans could take heed.

After recounting so many stories of chemical poisoning and death of wildlife, Carson ponders: "Who has made the decision that sets in motion these chains of poisonings, this ever-widening wave of death that spreads out, like ripples when a pebble is dropped into a still pond?" Who, she asks, has the *right* to destroy the beauty and ordered world of nature which still holds a meaning that is deep and imperative (Carson 1962, pp. 118–119). Not content with recounting the horrors, Carson searches for the agents. In government she saw two: the United States Department of Agriculture (USDA) and the Food and Drug Administration (FDA) who, by promoting pest eradication programs and establishing acceptable levels of chemical residues, were co-responsible with the chemical industry for the surge in chemical pesticide use.

Between 1945 and 1960 there was a five-fold increase in chemical pesticide use in the United States, a "rain of death" which Carson likened to a war on nature. One cannot wage a war without an enemy. If the enemy does not exist, it must be invented. In the case of insecticides, two military-like campaigns were undertaken in the late fifties by the Department of Agriculture, one against the gypsy moth in the northeastern states and the other against the fire ant in the South.

The fire ant, named for its fiery sting, was discovered shortly after the end of World War I. During the 40 years prior to the USDA's sudden declaration of it as a killer, the fire ant was considered a nuisance because of the large nests or mounds that it builds, a nuisance to farm machinery but not to crops or livestock. In 1957, USDA launched a publicity campaign to create an image of the fire ant as a menace to life and health and to generate support for an eradication program of the insect. The public was barraged with official releases, motion pictures, and stories portraying the fire ant as "despoiler of southern agriculture and a killer of birds, livestock, and man" (Carson 1962, p. 147). Horror stories were fabricated around the fire ant's sting. (Following that logic, Carson suggests that perhaps wasps and bees ought to be eliminated because they sting also.) The federal government then announced a pest eradication program in cooperation with afflicted states to treat 20 million acres in those states.

What was the truth of these claims? Statements made by USDA officials seeking congressional appropriations were not in accord with those contained in their own key publications. The fire ant was not even cited in the USDA's 1957 bulletin, *Insecticide Recommendations . . . for the Control of Insects Attacking Crops and Livestock*. Prominent scientists and entomologists in various Alabama research agencies and institutes stated that damage to plants by the fire ant is rare, and that they had never observed damage to livestock by the insect. In fact, they observed that the fire ant feeds on many insects which are considered harmful to human activities. After 40 years in Alabama the fire ant had not caused any human death, according to the Alabama State Health Officer, who considered medical problems arising from the bites of fire ant "incidental." A wildlife expert in Alabama, when questioned about allegations that the fire ant was a menace to game birds, stated that the contrary is more likely. In the almost 40 years that southern Alabama has had heavy populations of the fire ant, game birds have shown a steady and substantial increase.

The chemicals used in the fire ant eradication program were heptachlor and dieldrin. Millions of acres were sprayed the first year, 1958, without any consideration for the known toxicity of these two chemicals to wildlife, livestock, and humans. No effort had been made to determine an effective minimum dosage, although it was known that both poisons are many times more toxic than DDT. In some sprayed areas, all or nearly all wildlife—oppossums, armadillos, raccoons, birds, quail, wild turkeys—were killed. Farmers reported losses of livestock, poultry, and pets, poisoned by dieldrin or heptachlor. While in their publications USDA had listed the two poisons as ones not to be used on forage plants eaten by dairy cattle or animals raised for eating, their eradication program resulted in just that happening. Most likely the poisons were then transmitted by cows' milk to calves and humans.

By 1959, dissatisfaction with the program on the part of the states, locales, and people grew so that the USDA "offered the chemicals free to Texas landowners who would sign a release absolving federal, state, and local governments of responsibility for damage" (Carson 1962, p. 155). Some states found not only that the spraying was a colossal failure, but that they had higher infestations than ever before. They returned to the earlier method of destroying individual mounds. Federal appropriations for this project diminished but continued through at least 1961.

Moving from the contamination of soil, groundwater and rivers, aquatic life, and wildlife to that of human beings, Carson writes: "lulled by the soft sell and the hidden persuader, the average citizen is seldom aware of the deadly materials with which he is surrounding himself" (Carson 1962, p. 157). The litany of poisons found on shelves in supermarkets, packaged and assembled as attractively as dishwashing liquid and canned foods include: kitchen shelf paper, white or tinted, impregnated with insecticide; floor wax guaranteed to kill insects which walk on it; lindane-soaked strips to hang in closets or place in bureau drawers to kill moths; oil solutions of DDT, dieldrin, or chlordane to spray clothing, corners, closets, and walls for moths, mosquitoes, and other insects; pesticides in every manner of spray, dust, and pellet to apply to yard, garden, bushes, and trees. All are sold under brand names "that never suggest their identity or nature" (Carson 1962, p. 161) with pictorial representations of happy people creating a beautiful world, clean of ugly weeds and safe from destructive pests.

If shelves, closets, and workbenches are lined with chemical poisons, what then of the food we eat? Since the early forties—for the first time in the history of humankind—people have had pesticides and other synthetic chemicals in their body fat. In 1954 the United States Public Health Service found that every meal sampled in a study of restaurant and institutional meals contained DDT. "The fact that every meal we eat," Carson (1962, p. 163) writes, "carries its load of chlorinated hydrocarbons is the inevitable consequence of the almost universal spraying or dusting of agricultural crops with these poisons."

In one of the boldest sections of the book, Carson critiques the protection afforded people by a government which permits and encourages the application of pesticide poisons to food and its accompanying entry into fish, animals, eggs, and dairy products. By setting "permissible limits," a euphemism for slow poisoning, the Food and Drug Administration is another agent in the pollution of nature and people. Her argument unfolds accordingly.

- The Food and Drug Administration (FDA) establishes a "maximum permissible limit of contamination" called a "tolerance" for various chemicals in various food products. [For example, the tolerance for PCBs in fish was 5 parts per million; it was recently lowered to 2 parts per million.]
- The language of "tolerance" and "permissible limit" suggests that the

limits established are safe. It provides an air of security that the chemicals on food we buy are really below the tolerance.

- The FDA has jurisdiction only over foods grown and sold in interstate commerce, not for foods sold within a state. With a limited enforcement staff, only an extremely small amount of food sold ("far less than one percent") can be spot checked to ensure that levels of chemicals on it are below the "tolerances."

- In setting a tolerance level, the FDA reviews tests of the particular chemical on laboratory animals and then establishes a level allowable in foods which is much less than that required to produce symptoms in the test animal. This method can never compensate for the potential effects of certain crucial unknown chemical effects. Also, the laboratory animal lives in very artificial, controlled conditions which do not resemble the day-to-day life and chemical exposures of animals and human beings. Extrapolation from animals to human beings is always risky at best. Finally, no one is ever subjected to just one chemical at a time. Because there are thousands upon thousands of synthetic and natural chemicals used in food, clothing, industrial products, and pharmaceuticals, we can be exposed to many simultaneously in a day, eating a variety of foods, polishing our shoes; cleaning paint brushes; working in a factory; living near a hazardous waste dump; burning wood or coal in our home.

"It is meaningless, therefore," concludes Carson, "to talk about the 'safety' of any specific amount of residue. . . . In effect, then to establish tolerances is to authorize contamination of public food supplies with poisonous chemicals" (Carson 1962, p. 165).

Let us look at the tolerance established for the compound PCB in fish. The history adds another element to Carson's already sufficient case against the "safety" of FDA tolerances.

The context in which this tolerance was examined is the contamination of the Housatonic River in Massachusetts and Connecticut, a river which is used recreationally for boating and fishing. PCBs carried on suspended sediment were deposited throughout the river and its backwaters. Ingested by insects and insect larvae, which are eaten by fish, they then lodge in the tissues of fish. In order to protect people fishing the river, the State of Connecticut has posted the river warning people of the danger of eating river fish. In posting a river or harbor, a state must judge when a river is "safe" to be fished, that is, what level of PCB in fish is safe for people to eat.

In an attempt to answer that question, one researcher reconstructed the history of the FDA's "tolerance level" of 5 parts per million PCB for fish sold in interstate commerce (Hynes 1983). The 5 parts per million tolerance set by the FDA in 1973 was intended to be temporary. The temporary tolerance was based on animal and toxicological data and a total diet study which suggested that Americans were ingesting PCBs at a level which approached the Acceptable Daily Intake (ADI) of 200 micrograms per day. However, the ADI was based on a 1,000-day exposure period (not lifetime), and it was assumed that, during this 1,000-day period, PCB levels in food would decrease because PCBs were being phased out of industrial use.

In 1977 the FDA proposed reducing the temporary tolerance of 5 parts per million PCB in fish and shellfish to 2 parts per million based primarily on three considerations. First, there was new evidence that PCBs might be carcinogenic. Also there were new toxicity data which suggested a possible adverse reproductive effect; and last, several surveys had revealed widespread occurrence of PCB contamination in freshwater fish. During the 1,000-day period, PCB levels had not diminished in food according to FDA expectation. In proposing to reduce the tolerance, the FDA Commissioner felt that it would be desirable to reduce exposure to PCBs from fish to the greatest degree possible and therefore even considered a 1 part per million level (the lowest level that could be reliably determined for enforcement purposes). The commercial impact of a 2 part per million tolerance was compared with that of a 1 part per million tolerance. The FDA concluded that the increment of public health theoretically afforded by the 1 part per million tolerance was not worth the $18 million loss of food that would result from prohibiting contaminated fish in commerce to that level.

FDA is required by Section 406 of the Federal Food, Drug, and Cosmetic Act to consider the extent of unavoidability of a contaminant and, in this case, the amount of PCB contaminated fish that must be removed from commerce to reduce exposure to PCBs to an acceptable level. FDA chose the 2 part per million tolerance rather than 1 part per million, based on the calculated effect this decision would have on the food supply and the economy. The 2 part per million tolerance is not a strict reflection of a level meant to protect public health, then; economic factors—the cost of this ruling to the fishing industry—have shaped its selection.

What is the solution? No less, advocates Carson, than the elimination of tolerances on highly toxic chemicals. If it is possible to use chemicals in such a way and achieve a regulatory level of 7 parts per million DDT on foods or 1 part per million of parathion, or 0.1 part per million of dieldrin on foods grown and sold commercially, then why is it not possible to control the residue completely, she asked.[10] A zero tolerance without the ability to enforce it and without new direction in pest control, however, is useless. Carson calls for a much larger force of inspectors to ensure that public health is protected; for the use of less toxic, naturally occurring plant toxins; and for the diligent exploration of non-chemical methods, such as specific insect predators and diseases.

THE HUMAN PRICE

If *Silent Spring* were distilled to one intrinsic idea, it would be that in nature nothing exists alone. Everything is interconnected. The conservationist Aldo Leopold mapped this first law of ecology in the odyssey of an atom X locked in a limestone ledge. A bur oak root pried the rock and, after a century of cracking and dissolving, freed the atom. X was drawn into the bur oak tree and helped form a flower, which became an acorn, which fattened a deer, which fed a person, all in a single year (Leopold 1977, p. 111).

In a similar biotic drama, man-made toxins move through the pathways of nature to lodge in the tissue of living things. The end-point of pollution is what Rachel Carson calls "the human price" exacted from a lifetime exposure to chemical and physical agents that are not part of the biological experience of human beings. Unlike the diseases of the nineteenth century, such as smallpox and cholera, which were immediately evident to the infected person, the effects of eating, breathing, and drinking minute doses of a vast array of synthetic chemical compounds cycled through soil, air, groundwater, and streams into insects, food, fish, and humans are not immediately apparent. Symptoms may not reveal themselves because of the incremental and subtle nature of the effects of absorbing small amounts of pesticides and other chemicals until 20 or 30 years later.

In the "ecology of the world within our bodies . . . minute causes produce mighty effects" (Carson 1962, p. 170). A change in one molecule, even, may resound throughout the entire system and initiate

---

10. Carson was ridiculed for calling for a zero tolerance because zero is not measurable. Instruments measure above their detection limits, not below them; they measure the presence of chemicals, not their absence. I find this genre of criticism spurious. What she called for was not the measure of zero; she was insisting that, unless it were proven that residues were not harmful, there should be no pesticide or other toxic chemical contamination on food or in the environment. If industry and government cannot guarantee no residue on food for known or suspected harmful pesticides, the pesticides should not be used.

changes in tissue or organs seemingly remote from that molecule. The chlorinated insecticides are fat-soluble, so that when they enter the body they accumulate in body fat. Fats are distributed throughout the body in adipose tissue, organs, and in individual cells; thus pesticides stored throughout the body are in a position to interfere with vital and necessary functions.

Chlorinated hydrocarbons, such as DDT, carbon tetrachloride, and PCBs are known to affect the liver, the organ central to the vitality of the human body. The liver provides bile for the digestion of fats; it receives blood from the digestive tract and is deeply involved in the metabolism of all the principal foodstuffs. It keeps the blood sugar at a normal level by the storage of glycogen and its careful release as glucose. It maintains cholesterol in the blood plasma and proper levels of male and female hormones. It stores many vitamins.

The liver detoxifies the body of poisons which are the by-product of metabolism. Similarly, it works to detoxify the majority of toxic materials to which we are exposed. The incessant assault of poisons on the liver with the increased use of synthetic pesticides and organic chemicals undoubtedly damages the liver, an effect which in time will weaken the ability of the marvelous defense organ to cleanse and protect the body against the stream of poisons which pass through it. And it may potentially affect the other vital functions of this organ.

Both major types of insecticides examined in *Silent Spring*, the chlorinated hydrocarbons and organic phosphates, directly affect the nervous system. Carson cites case history after case history of insecticide poisoning where the victims suffer from effects on their central nervous systems: numbness, muscular weakness, tremors, convulsions, paralysis, depression, and a sense of mental incompetence. What of the interactive potential from exposure to more than one compound at the same time or in sequence? Methoxychlor is a pesticide considered "safe" when compared with DDT because a liver enzyme can modify it so that it is not appreciably stored. However, if the liver has been damaged by alcohol, drugs, another insecticide, or a cleaning solvent, methoxychlor is then stored up to 100 times the normal rate and then acts like DDT and can cause long-lasting damage to the central nervous system.

What of the interaction between the organic phosphates and the chlorinated hydrocarbons? The power of the organic phosphates may be potentiated if the liver has been injured by a chlorinated hydrocarbon. When liver function is damaged, the cholinesterase level drops below normal. The added depressive effect of the organic phosphate may then be enough to precipitate acute symptoms. Pairs of the organic phosphates may interact in such a way as to increase their toxicity a hundredfold. Or the organic phosphates may interact with various drugs, or with synthetic materials, food additives, or any combination of the thousands of man-made substances that now pervade our world.

Moving into the microscopic ecology of the body, Carson discusses the then current understanding of the body's energy-yielding oxidation process and the known destructive or weakening effects of certain pesticides on the oxidation process. She forcefully concludes that the realm of effects from pesticides for humans may indeed be infertility and genetic mutations.

Energy is produced in every cell of the body. Within the cell are tiny packets of enzymes called mitochondria. They are arranged to work in an orderly, step-by-step fashion to turn molecules of carbohydrate fuel into energy for the body. The energy source produced in the oxidative cycle is in the form of a molecule containing three phosphate groups called ATP (adenosine triphosphate). ATP furnishes energy in the transferring of one of its phosphate groups to other substances in need of energy. ATP then becomes ADP, a diphosphate molecule. When a free phosphate group is coupled back onto it, the potent ATP is restored.

ATP is the source of mechanical energy for muscles to expand and contract, and the source of electrical energy to nerve cells. The combining of the free phosphate group and ADP to restore ATP is essential if energy is to be continually made available. If they become uncombined or uncoupled, energy cannot be produced although oxidation is taking place. This can lead to death of tissue or the death of an organism, from embryo to adult.

Radiation is a known uncoupler, as is the herbicide 2,4-D and also the pesticide DDT. With the destruction or weakening of any one of the enzymes responsible for the cellular oxidation process, oxidation ceases. DDT, methoxychlor, and malathion are among numerous pesticides which have been found to inhibit one or more of the enzymes involved in the cycle of oxidation. Not only is no energy produced for the body by those cells, but cells are deprived of utilizable oxygen gained from oxidation. The consequences of lack of oxygen can be devastating: normal cells turn to cancer cells; malformations and other abnormalities occur in embryos; congenital deformities may develop.

It may well be that infertility is linked with the interference of biological oxidation, and the consequent depletion of ATP. Both egg and sperm must be generously supplied with ATP for successful fertilization. The ATP content of a fertilized egg must be above a critical level for the embryo to develop to completion. Pesticides have been discovered accumulated in the sex organs of a variety of birds and mammals. Affected by the loss of ATP, there could be reduced production of spermatozoa or eggs and a loss of motility in sperm. Studies of eggs of pheasants, chickens, and robins have shown that those birds exposed to DDT laid eggs with large residues of that pesticide. Carson concludes:

> Knowing that DDT and other (perhaps all) chlorinated hydrocarbons stop the energy producing cycle by inactivating a specific enzyme or uncoupling the energy-loading mechanism, it is hard to see how any egg so loaded with residues could complete the complex process of development: the infinite number of cell divisions, the elaboration of tissues and organs, the synthesis of vital substances that in the end produce a living creature (Carson 1962, p. 185).

And what of the mutagenic effects? As of 1960 there had been little attention paid to the fact that chemicals may act similarly to radiation with regard to genetic damage. Despite this, Carson assembled a series of facts on a number of pesticides to argue that they do affect vital cell processes in ways ranging from slight chromosome damage to gene mutation with the consequences of malignancy. Mosquitoes, plants, and fruit flies exposed with various pesticides have had chromosomal damage and developed horrifying mutations. The herbicide 2,4-D produced an effect like X-rays on exposed plants: chromosomes become short, thick and clumped together; cell division is seriously retarded.

Carson cogently argues that if DDT is found in the gonads and germ cells of birds and mammals, that is strong evidence that chlorinated hydrocarbons will come into contact with genetic material. And yet, "there has been no comprehensive study aimed at testing the mutagenic effects of pesticides as such" (Carson 1962, p. 191). What has been observed is a by-product of research in cell physiology and genetics. Nor, she points out, have chemical manufacturers, as yet, been required by law to test new substances for any possible genetic or mutagenic effect they might have.

The final human price taken on by Carson was the relationship between pesticides newly used since World War II and the increase in cancer. There are, in the environment, natural cancer-causing agents, such as ultra-violet radiation, radiation from certain rocks, and arsenic dissolved from soil or rocks into surface or groundwater. While the soot from coal burning has long been known as a carcinogen, the rise of industrialization has brought with it a steady and growing stream of new chemical and physical agents introduced into soil, air, water supply, clothing, food supply, pharmaceuticals, and so forth. Many of them possess powerful capacities for inducing biologic change. By the end of the nineteenth century a half-dozen sources of industrial carcinogens were known. The Office of Vital Statistics stated that in 1958 malignant growths, including those of the lymphatic and blood-forming tissues, accounted for 15 percent of the deaths that year in contrast to 4 percent in 1900. By 1960, more American school children were dying of cancer than any other disease. Large numbers of tumors were showing up in very young children, significant numbers of which were present at or before birth.

The question posed by Carson, against the backdrop of this startling increase in cancer throughout society, was whether any of the chemicals used to control nature play a direct or indirect role as causes of cancer. In 1960 there were five, possibly six pesticides known to cause cancer in animals. There were many synthetic chemicals suspected by environmental medicine physicians to cause leukemia in humans; others could be considered "an indirect cause of malignancy" because of their action on living tissues or cells. Carson carefully documents each of these categories to build a substantial case for an environmental health movement in this century comparable to the public health movement of the nineteenth century. She calls for prevention of cancer by elimination of cancer-causing chemicals from our food, our water supplies, and the atmosphere.

By 1960, DDT; two herbicides belonging to the carbamate group, IPC and CIPC; and the weed killer aminotriazole, were known to cause tumors in laboratory animals. Carson points out that what was known then about carcinogenesis was more likely the beginning of what could be known because not enough time had elapsed between exposure to insecticides and herbicides and their full effects. Many cancers caused by occupational exposure are fully evident only after 15–30 years.

Leukemia is an exception to the common long latency period. Survivors of Hiroshima began to develop leukemia within three years after the atomic bomb was dropped. Between 1950 and 1960 death from malignancies of blood and lymph increased from 11.1 to 14.1 percent in the United States. Increase of death from leukemia annually was being recorded throughout the world. Carson cites numerous case histories of people exposed to toxic chemicals, especially pesticides, documented by Dr Malcolm Hargraves in the Hematology Department at the Mayo Clinic. Hargraves saw a significant increase, particularly since World War II, in the environmental diseases, due to the use of various toxic substances. Those with blood and lymph diseases usually had a history of significant exposure to hydrocarbons such as benzene, DDT, chlordane, or lindane. Many pesticides were carried in a solvent, so that exposure to a commercial product meant exposure to a combination of chemicals.

When the FDA establishes "safe doses" of a particular chemical, they cannot predict the indirect or complex interactions which may take place in people who are exposed simultaneously, or close in time, to the regulated chemical and other chemicals. What is a "safe dose" of DDT, if DDT is mixed in a toxic solvent when sprayed, so that exposure to DDT is also exposure to another dangerous chemical? Some chemicals, while not causing cancer themselves, are thought to predispose the body to produce tumors when exposed to another chemical. They may injure or disturb the normal functioning of some part of the body, the liver, for example, in such a way that malignancy results. For example, cancers of the reproductive system appear to be related to the balance of sex hormones, which may be the result of something that affects the ability of the liver to maintain a proper level of hormones. The chlorinated hydrocarbons are all toxic to the liver in some degree and may very well be indirect agents in carcinogenesis. There may be an interaction between a physical and chemical agent, in much the same way as discussed previously. X-radiation initiates a change in cells or chromosomes which can be promoted into malignancy by exposure to a chemical such as urethane. No one can ever organize her or his life to ensure "safe doses" of the thousands of invisible chemicals we breathe, drink, and ingest. "In the kaleidoscope of shifting conditions, what dose of a carcinogen can be safe' except a zero dose?" (Carson 1962, p. 213).

This section of *Silent Spring*—on the "human price" paid in infertility, genetic damage, and cancer—was the most exacting to write. In the midst of it, Carson wrote to a friend, "What lies underneath the most important part of this chapter is a whole field of the most technical and difficult biology discoveries only recently made. How to reveal enough to give understanding of the most serious chemicals without being technical, how to simplify without error—these have been problems of monumental proportion" (Brooks 1972, p. 270). For many readers "the human price" may be the most persuasive point in her argument. For, as she once remarked, those who are not compelled by the death of songbirds must at least care about the threat to their own health. For the chemical industry, these chapters on "the human price" shut down an erstwhile era of corporate naiveté, deliberate ignorance, secrecy, and cover-up around the toxicity of chemicals.

In the subsequent 25 years, three major trends have taken shape in response to and in reaction to Carson's warning of the risks of genetic damage, cancer, and infertility with the expanded use of chemicals. First, government responded by amending the pesticide law (FIFRA) and passing the Toxic Substances Control Act (TSCA) to require that pesticides and industrial chemicals be tested for toxicity, specifically carcinogenicity; teratogenicity (causing abortion, stillbirth, growth retardation, birth defects, and long-term behavioral changes in children); and mutagenicity (causing damage to genes and chromosomes). On paper, both laws purport to solve the problem of preventing dangerous chemicals from being used commercially. At best, they keep only the worst new chemicals off the market. The US National Academy of Sciences recently estimated that some 70,000 synthetic chemicals are used and traded in the United States; 25,000 are in "common use." People may be exposed to at least 50,000 chemicals (Elkington 1985, p. 44). The majority of these 70,000 chemicals were in use when the recent toxicity protocols were promulgated. Even if the intent of the law is to have "old" chemicals tested or retested for toxicity, this has not happened. The resources—in the form of an increased EPA budget—were not provided when the laws were promulgated and the regulations went into effect. In real dollars, the EPA budget has shrunken in the past eight years under the Reagan Administration. Most chemicals to which we are exposed are untested or inadequately tested for human and environmental hazards.

Another problem with toxicity testing is the potential conflict of interest built into the testing system. Industry generates the toxicity data on its own chemicals, using in-house scientists or contract laboratories, and submits the results to EPA for review and approval. In 1983 a United States court found officials of Industrial Bio-Test Laboratories, a contract lab for industries, guilty of falsifying laboratory data. The laboratory had been under investigation for seven years. Prior to the court judgment, EPA found over 100 of its pesticide studies invalid (Elkington 1985, p. 166).

A second major trend is the rise of "the cancer establishment" and their "politics of cancer," a reaction to Carson's placing responsibility for an increase in cancer in the second half of this century squarely on industry's shoulders. The "cancer establishment" consists of the National Cancer Institute, the American Cancer Society, and lifestyle-focused academics who blame 80 percent of cancer on diet (dietary fat, not chemical additives) and smoking. They blame the victims of cancer for their lifestyle habits and take attention off environmental and occupational sources of cancer. Samuel Epstein, professor of occupational and environmental medicine at the University of Illinois, writes:

> Certainly smoking is a major but not the only cause of lung cancer. Evidence such as the following clearly incriminates the additional role of exposure to occupational carcinogens and carcinogenic community air pollutants: some 20 percent of lung cancers occur in non-smokers; there have been major recent increases in lung cancer rates in non-smokers; an increasing percentage of lung cancer is of a histological type not usually associated with smoking; high lung cancer rates are found with certain occupational exposure irrespective of smoking; and excess lung cancer rates are found in communities where certain major industries are located. Clearly, the chemical industry uses tobacco as a smoke screen to divert attention from the role of carcinogenic chemicals in inducing lung cancer (Epstein 1987).

At the same time smoking is treated as if it is a freely chosen hazard. Most people smoke because they were barraged by cigarette ads—which sexualize smoking as the pastime of hard, dominant, outdoors men and easy, sexually submissive, windblown women—and then got addicted. Cigarettes were given out free on airlines; they came packed with field rations in the war. Government subsidies to tobacco farmers exceed money spent on warnings and research. Smoking is a government-subsidized addiction for immense corporate profit, sold with images of male dominance and female submission. The same genre of analysis can be made for beef-eating.[11]

The National Cancer Institute and the American Cancer Society focus most of their resources on research and treatment rather than on cancer prevention. By talking as if the cure is around the corner and their "war on cancer" is being won, when certain cancer rates—notably breast cancer and lung cancer among women and malignant melanoma—are on the rise, they divert attention from strict regulation of industry and minimizing people's exposure to carcinogens. Recently the National Cancer Institute released the Annual Cancer Statistics Review which analyzed trends in cancer incidence, mortality, and survival rates through the 36-year period from 1950 to 1985. The study found an overall 36.5 percent rise in cancer incidence since mid-century and a 6.7 percent increase in the rate of cancer deaths. Yet the Boston *Globe* coverage of the study gave boldest coverage to dropping rates in lung cancer in an article on the 36-year study entitled, "Study finds lung cancer rates dropping." A close reading of the lung cancer statistics shows that the incidence of lung cancer has dropped among men, but not among women. When pressed for reasons to explain alarming increases in breast cancer among women, and skin cancer, the researchers speculated with explanations such as delayed childbirth, alcohol, and increased exposure to sunlight. Overall, the cancer incidence, survival, and cure rates are much bleaker for Blacks

---

11. For an analysis of how industrially based risks are minimized by "lifestyle" risk analysts, see Perrow 1984, p. 312.

Frances Moore Lappé (1971) made a compelling argument for what is now familiarly called "eating lower on the food chain." She calculates in *Diet for a Small Planet* that 16 pounds of high protein grain and soy are fed to American cattle to produce one pound of beef. The purpose of the grain and high-protein feeding is not primarily to produce animal protein but to "fatten up" the animal before slaughter. Some of the fat is trimmed and thrown away; other is marbled in the tissue. The pesticide residue in animal feed is bioconcentrated in the animal fat so that, Lappé found, chlorinated organic pesticide concentrations in meat are about 13 times more than pesticide residues found in cereals, grains, vegetables, and fruits. Lappé calls for conversion to a more plant-centered diet and an agriculture centered on feeding people in an increasingly starving world, not fattening penned up livestock for American hamburgers. The San Francisco-based Rainforest Action Network calculates that cattle in Central America raised for the American hamburger industry are eating 55 square feet of rainforest per hamburger. The cattle graze on the remains of rainforest left by loggers who export the wood of rainforests for teak and mahogany furniture, wood paneling, and so forth (Duda 1988).

and women than for white men. The sexual and racial politics of cancer are buried and unrecognizable in the heavy tome of statistics, while the National Cancer Institute depoliticizes cancer by using "lifestyle" to explain the increasing trends in cancer incidence.[12]

The third major trend is the rapid rise of the biomedical industry to treat infertility, while the environmental and occupational causes of infertility are ignored. Carson pointed to the evidence of chemical-caused infertility in wildlife and in laboratory animals, and strongly speculated about the same for humans. But unlike the other toxicity tests, there has been no legislation to require that chemicals be tested for their potential to induce infertility in women or men. Despite the regulatory vacuum, it is common knowledge that workers in certain industries have a higher incidence of infertility. One landmark study at Florida State University found a significant drop in sperm counts in male students there compared to the average American male of the early twentieth century. The same study found PCBs, a flame-retardant, and three kinds of insecticide and fungicide-like chemicals in semen (Elkington 1985, p. 49).

Like the "cancer establishment," an "infertility establishment" has sprung up—in vitro fertilization (IVF) clinics, medical practitioners, surrogacy brokers, and the American Fertility Society—who prioritize treatment, not prevention. They, also, inflate success rates by using dubious definitions of success. Success has been defined as everything from a "chemical pregnancy" (slight, temporary elevations in the level of hormones produced during pregnancy: these rarely result in a live birth) to a woman going home with a baby.[13] Their counterpart to personalizing cancer by blaming the victim is to personalize the problem in women by manufacturing a motherhood and baby craze and making women guilty for not being able to conceive a child (whether the infertility is theirs or their partner's) and desperate for the technologies. Interestingly, the fertility establishment estimates environmental and occupational causes of infertility (called "unknown causes") to be as low as 10 to 20 percent, the same percentage attributed by the "cancer establishment" to environmental and occupational sources of cancer (Saltus 1987). It is low enough to ignore the chemically and medically induced causes of infertility, to avoid social and political action, and to justify building a new

---

12. See Foreman 1988, Boffey 1988. For a personal account and an analysis of the sexual and racial politics of cancer, see Lorde 1980. For an analysis of the sexual politics of tobacco advertising, see Hynes 1987.

13. Corea and Ince 1987, pp. 133–145. Half of the 108 US IVF clinics responded to the authors' survey of success rates in IVF clinics. Half of the respondents "had never produced a so-called test-tube baby. Despite that, many claimed high success rates" when talking with the media, colleagues, and clients.

medical empire by using experimental technologies and medical chemicals on women. Most recently bills are being introduced into state and federal legislatures to have the new reproductive technologies financed by the insurance industry. Such financing will ensure that, like cancer, treatment supercedes prevention. It will expand and normalize the gender-specific nature of these technologies: risk-laden chemicals and techniques practiced on women.

CHEMICAL NEMESIS

In the final section of *Silent Spring*, Carson evaluates the "success" worldwide of chemically controlling or ridding the world of disease-carrying and crop-destroying insects. She finds chemical-induced phenomena in nature which show that the exclusive use of broad-spectrum chemicals produces damages which outweigh the benefits and that widespread spraying aggravates the environmental conditions which initially cause the problem. Insects intended to be destroyed are developing strains resistant to chemicals; and the environment's own natural controls for keeping various species in check are being weakened by the chemicals.[14]

Before 1945 only about a dozen species of insects were known to have developed resistance to the pre-DDT, inorganic insecticides. Between the end of World War II and 1960, resistance to the new organic chemical insecticides had reached a level of 137 species. In Italy, where DDT was first used to control malaria mosquitoes in 1943, the housefly began to show resistance to DDT by 1946. In 1948 a new chemical, chlordane, was introduced as a supplement to DDT and achieved control of houseflies for two years. By late summer 1950 chlordane-resistant flies appeared, and they prevailed by the end of the year. By the end of 1951 DDT, methoxychlor, chlordane, heptachlor, and benzene hexachloride were no longer effective against the housefly. In the United States, agencies used one chlorinated hydrocarbon after another as the fly became resistant. They then turned to organic phosphates with the same result of insect resistance developing. Entomologists concluded that "'housefly

---

14. There is a striking parallel between Carson's analysis of chemical-induced damage to nature's own mechanisms of control and Ivan Illich's later analysis of iatrogenic or doctor-induced illness in the increasingly drug-based and technology-based health care system. Modern medicine, he writes, produces clinical damages that outweigh its potential benefits. It enhances even as it obscures the political conditions that render society unhealthy. It mystifies and expropriates the power of individuals to heal themselves and to shape their own environment (Illich 1976).

control has escaped insecticidal techniques and once more must be based on general sanitation'" (Carson 1962, p. 236).

Among body lice, disease-carrying mosquitoes and house mosquitoes, ticks, and cockroaches, as well as insects which infest crops, by 1960 the pattern was the same. How does this resistance develop? The members of an original population of insects vary in structure, behavior, and physiology. Chemical spraying kills off the weaker members of a population, leaving the "tough" insects as survivors. It is these survivors who parent the next generation of insect. Only a few generations later, a mixed population of strong and weak insects is replaced by a population consisting of tough, resistant strains. The chemical solution produces more severe problems than it has solved. Resistance among insects to the new organic pesticides takes anywhere from a season to six years, the number of generations produced by an insect population per year being an important factor. The same principle of building resistance can be seen in human beings. However, because the rate of human population reproducing is enormously slower than insects, the capacity of the population to develop resistance to toxic synthetic chemicals could take hundreds or even thousands of years.

Modern chemical insect control ignores two critical facts about the environment it sprays in order to kill one species of insect. One is nature's own effective control of insects, through the amount of food available, the conditions of weather and climate, the presence of competing or predatory species available. The second is the explosive power of a species to reproduce once the natural resistance of the environment has been weakened by pesticides. Kill off the predatory insect, albeit inadvertently, and the prey insect surges upward.

The spider mite is one example. As DDT and other insecticides have killed off its enemies, the spider mite has become practically a worldwide pest. Having a prodigious appetite for chlorophyll, it attacks the outer cells of leaves and evergreen needles to extract the chlorophyll. There were unprecedented outbreaks of the spider mite in Yellowstone Park in 1929, in forests in Colorado in 1949, in New Mexico in 1956, and in Montana and Idaho in 1957. Each outbreak followed forest spraying with insecticides. The 1929 spraying employed lead arsenate; the others, DDT.

Three reasons have been given for the tremendous population explosion of the spider mite after insecticide spraying. It is relatively insensitive to the poisons. The predators which keep it in check, such as ladybugs, a gall midge, predacious mites, and several pirate bugs, are all extremely sensitive to pesticides and wiped out by them. Third, when sprayed, the normally densely settled community of spider mites disperses. In dispersion they find an abundance of food and space, as well as no need for protection from predators now dead. Under these conditions they have been known to increase egg production three-fold.

Carson cites a host of other pest spraying infestations worldwide, both of agricultural pests and disease-bearing insects, to illustrate the point that one insect problem is traded for a worse one as spraying upsets the population dynamics of the insect world.

In *The Pesticide Conspiracy*, Robert van den Bosch, a prominent entomologist formerly at the University of California Berkeley, reiterates Carson's warning that an agriculture dependent on chemical pesticides will nullify natural biological controls, create worse insect problems than the initial ones, and result in an upwardly spiralling use of chemicals. "The overwhelming tragedy of planet Earth is man's contempt for nature," he writes (van den Bosch 1978, p. 9). Insects are viewed as "dumb, lowly brutes" to be subdued and eliminated by the most simplistic of methods. Indeed, he warns, they are formidable animals with assets of diversity, adaptability, and prolificacy. Having appeared more than 300 million years ago, they have survived cataclysmic geological, climate, and biological changes which have rendered extinct more "advanced" animals. They are literally everywhere and comprise roughly 75 percent of all earth's described animal species.

At least a million insect species populate the planet, most of which serve as pollinators, reducers of organic material, scavengers, natural enemies of pests, and as food. While it is thought that about 10 percent of insects have a pestiferous potential, only a fraction ever attain the status of pest that is dangerous to agriculture and/or human and animal health. The physical and biological control of insects is carried out in nature by other insects, called predators and parasites. Without this ever-active balance maintained in nature by insects, it is doubtful that we could successfully carry out crucial human activities, such as agriculture.

Modern insecticides are biocides. That is, they do not distinguish between the insect destroying crops and the natural predators and parasites of that insect. When applied to a crop, the broad-spectrum insecticide will kill many species in the insect community, both pest and parasite alike. Often, the parasite and predator of the insect suffer greater losses than the insect itself because they are usually less robust than the pest species and because their food supply is depleted by insecticides. The result of spraying broad-spectrum, non-discriminating insecticides is, in van den Bosch's words:

> a virtual biotic vacuum in which the surviving or reinvading pests, free of significant natural-enemy attack, explode. Such post-spraying pest explosions . . . involve not only the resurgence of target pests but also the eruption of previously minor species, which had been fully suppressed by natural enemies. The frequent outcome is a raging multiple-pest outbreak,

more damaging than that for which the original pest-control measure was
undertaken (van den Bosch 1978, p. 24).

A second consequence is the development of resistance to the insecticide
among the insects which survive the chemical attack. Insects survive
insecticides due to the same plasticity with which they have survived
drastic changes in climate and habitat. Some carry the genetic capability
to detoxify the poison in the spray; others are physically protected by an
integument which prevents penetration of the toxic material; and others
were simply missed by the spray or are able to avoid it. With multiple
spraying, those which survive by good fortune may be killed, but those
which survive because of a natural resistance to the chemical's toxicity:

> come to dominate the population, breeding among themselves and
> producing progeny that are also survivors. It is in this way that large
> populations of insects become resistant to insecticides, and the more inten-
> sive and widespread the poisonous blanket the more rapid the selection
> for resistance in the pests (van den Bosch 1978, p. 24).

Field studies, as well as agricultural statistics from the State of California, bear out that the chemical method of insect control results in
damage to natural insect controls and ultimately causes worse infestation
and aggravated crop losses than were experienced before broad-scale,
exclusive use of synthetic chemical pesticides.

Plots treated with an insecticide for bollworm control suffered heavier
infestations of the bollworm than did untreated plots. Simultaneous
sampling of the predators showed that they were destroyed by the insecticide, thus permitting a resurgence of the pest. Plots of cotton treated
with toxaphene-DDT for Lygus bug control suffered a secondary outbreak of the beet army worm. A month after the initial application, there
were approximately 17 times the number of beet army worms in the plot
treated with toxaphene-DDT as in the untreated plot. The secondary
pest explosion was discovered to be due to its predators having been
killed by the insecticide. Studies in the resistance to methyl parathion
among the tobacco budworm show that during the period of 1967 to
1970, the percentage of that insect killed by an application of 0.5 pounds
per acre declined from 100 percent to 20 percent. Increased application,
up to as much as 3 pounds per acre, killed no more than 45 percent of
the tobacco budworm.

The State of California is one of, if not *the*, world's most intensive
pesticide users. In 1970, each of the 25 most serious pests listed by the
State Department of Food and Agriculture had cost the state economy $1
million dollars or more in that fiscal year. Seventy-two percent of them
were resistant to one or more pesticides; 96 percent are either pesticide-
created or pesticide-aggravated. By the mid-seventies, after a full 30

years of extensive application of synthetic insecticides in American agriculture, insecticide use had increased 11-fold while crop losses to insects had doubled. The outcome of embarking on the road of the chemical control of nature, concludes van den Bosch, is an increased crop loss due to pesticide-resistant insects and new pests whose predators have been diminished or eliminated; growing costs to farmers for increased use of pesticides; and a spiralling pollution of groundwater and soil.

At Cornell University, David Pimental, Professor of Entomology, reports the same pattern in his studies of corn. Crop losses from insects have increased from less than 4 percent of the crop in the forties to about 12 percent in 1974 (Zwerdling 1977). One reason is the monoculture of corn year after year. Rotation of crops would give the corn rootworm nothing to feed on after the corn was harvested. Instead the rootworm feeds on corn year after year and flourishes. To control the problem, farmers have increased their use of pesticides. In the same fields, farmers have increased the use of herbicides, 2,4-D being a favorite, to combat weeds. This is a direct result of no-till farming promoted in trade journals by herbicide manufacturers. Pimental and his colleagues found that 2,4-D increases insect and pathogen pests on corn. The insects attack corn more frequently and in larger numbers. Some insects in sprayed fields were larger and laid larger eggs than bugs in unsprayed fields. In addition the corn exposed to 2,4-D had more southern leaf blight lesions than unsprayed corn, a result, thinks Pimental, of the stress the herbicide puts on the plants.

Looking at the political conditions in which biological methods of control were being ignored for chemical ones, Carson cites the statistics on research and research money. In 1960 only 2 percent of economic entomologists (entomologists who study the relationship between insect population and crop loss to determine the optimum point of insect control) in the United States were working in the field of biological controls, while a substantial number of the remaining 98 percent were engaged in work on chemical pesticides. Major chemical companies were funding research on insecticides through graduate research programs. Biological-control studies were not so endowed; no substantial industry existed to support it or to profit from it. This was left to the state and federal agencies. Among the leading advocates of chemical control were certain outstanding entomologists whose entire research program was supported by the chemical industry. Their prestige and jobs depending on the perpetuation of chemical control methods, how could they "bite the hand that feeds them?" "Knowing their bias," wrote Carson, "how much credence can we give to their protests that insecticides are harmless?" (Carson 1962, p. 229).

Not only were most entomologists bought by the chemical industry;

but scientists were pressured to suppress findings unfavorable to chemical insecticides. Dr Robert Rudd was a zoologist at the University of California who had researched the effects of pesticides on wildlife. During the same period that Carson was writing *Silent Spring*, he was writing what would be acclaimed as a sequel to her work, *Pesticides and the Living Landscape*. His manuscript was actually completed before Carson's; but it was turned down by a prominent publisher as a "polemic" and then was held up for over a year while 18 reviewers, including an entire entomology department, debated its premises. After its publication he lost a promotion and was dismissed from the state Agricultural Experiment Station where he had worked on vertebrate pest control for five years. He wrote later, "The trouble with my own efforts is the same as with the upset following *Silent Spring*. Challenges to a basic, well-entrenched system—far more expansive and profound than most people comprehend—is simply not done" (Graham 1970, pp. 170–171).

THE OTHER ROAD

Rachel Carson surveyed the deceptively smooth, fast lane on which industry, science, and government embarked in the chemical control of nature. "At its end lies disaster," she warned. Insecticides are weapons; nature, the battlefield; insects, wildlife, fish, and farmworkers, the victims. In the final chapter of *Silent Spring* Carson calls for another road to be taken, one "'less traveled by'" which "offers our last, our only chance to reach a destination that assures the preservation of our earth." This is the path of "biological solutions which are based on an understanding of the living organisms they seek to control, and of the whole fabric of life to which these organisms belong" (Carson 1962, p. 244).

Modern agribusiness farming is one of the most disruptive activities in nature. It eliminates an abundant variety of plant and insect life, and thus many of nature's own mechanisms to resist disease and insect attack. Cultivating a single crop through vast acres creates a vulnerability to insect and weed problems. Biological control methods focus on the particular problem insect without harming other insects and without poisoning the web of life in which the insect lives.

One such method is male sterilization. Large numbers of male insects are sterilized and released to compete with "wild males." In time, so many infertile eggs are produced that the population comes under control. The screw-worm fly is a subtropical insect which can devastate warm-blooded animals. They lay eggs in an open wound; the hatching larvae feed on the flesh of the animal, killing a heavily infested animal within weeks. An infestation of screw-worms in Florida, Georgia, and Alabama, which threatened the livestock populations, was eliminated in

17 months by releasing 50 million sterilized male screw-worm flies weekly over the infested sections.

Another biological control is the development of lures or attractants which can be used to confuse male insects and distract them from the female. They can be attracted en masse and killed, a program which Carson calls "male annihilation." Males of the oriental fruit fly and the melon fly find an attractant called methyl-eugenol irresistible. On the Borin Islands south of Japan this attractant was combined with a short-lived poison and distributed throughout the island chain. Within a year, more than 99 percent of the population had been eliminated.

Bacteria, like *Bacillus thuringiensis*, are an older method of controlling insect populations. Insect pathogens are specific; they infect only a small group of insects, sometimes only a single species. Thus they do not harm the natural predators as do chemicals. Compounds containing spores of *Bacillus thuringiensis* were being used in Panama against the banana root borer as Carson was finishing *Silent Spring*. Dieldrin had been used; but the borers became resistant to it, and other insects were becoming "pests" because their natural predators had been destroyed by dieldrin. "There is reason to hope," wrote Carson, "the new microbial insecticide will eliminate . . . the borers and that it will do so without eliminating natural controls" (Carson 1962, p. 255).

Some of the most spectacular successes in biological insect control have been in introducing the control which nature uses successfully, an insect predator or parasite. Predators of the alpha aphid saved the California alfalfa industry. A wasp imported from Japan controlled an insect which attacked the eastern apple orchards. Carson cites many more examples and the fact that such successful biological control of serious pests by natural insect enemies can be found in some 40 countries over much of the world. The imaginative and creative approaches to agriculture and forest protection which rely on an understanding of the ecology of the insect are "the other road." They are measures which, to paraphrase the Dutch plant pathologist, C. J. Briejèr, guide natural processes in the desired direction as cautiously as possible, rather than using brute force.

Rachel Carson finished *Silent Spring* as she began it, calling chemical pesticides crude weapons hurled against the fabric of life. The chemical industry, in turning itself and its terrible weapons against the insects, has also "turned . . . against the earth" (Carson 1962, pp. 261–262). Chapter 3 analyses the double-edged blow of this indictment. One blow cut at the taproot of technology's myth of progress. The industry said it was ridding the world of plague and famine; she said it exacerbated the problem it purported to solve and in so doing endangered public health and polluted the world. The other blow broke ground for an ethic of the environment: a "reverence [for life] even where we have to struggle against it" (Carson 1962, p. 243).

REFERENCES

Bedard, Donna L., Wagner, Robert E., Brennan, Michael J., Haberl, Marie L., and Brown, John F., Jr. 1987. Extensive degradation of aroclors and environmentally transformed polychlorinated biphenyls by *Alcaligenes eutrophus* H850. *Applied and Environmental Microbiology*, 53(5), 1094–1102.

Boffey, P. M. 1988. Breast cancer continues gradual rise. *New York Times*, 2 February, c1.

Bond, J. 1984a. Studies: EDB overrated as cancer risk. *Greenfield Recorder*, 14 June 1984, 16.

Bond, J. 1984b. Pesticide restrictions plague area farmers. *Greenfield Recorder*, 15 June 1984, 14.

Briggs, S. and Epstein, S. S. 1987. If Rachel Carson were writing today—*Silent Spring* in retrospect. *Environmental Law Reporter*, 17(6), 2.

Brooks, P. 1972. *The House of Life: Rachel Carson at Work*. Boston, Massachusetts: Houghton Mifflin.

Carson, R. 1962. *Silent Spring*. Greenwich, Connecticut: Fawcett Publications.

Corea, G. and Ince, S. 1987. Report of a survey of IVF clinics in the USA. *Made to Order: The Myth of Reproductive and Genetic Progress*, P. Spallone and D. L. Steinberg (eds.), pp. 133–145. Oxford and New York: Pergamon Press.

Deland, M. 1987. An all-out effort needed to end lead poison danger. *Boston Globe*, 10 October, 15.

Douglas, W. O. 1961. *My Wilderness: East to Katahdin*. New York: Doubleday.

Duda, P. 1988. Worldwatch. *Valley Advocate*, 8 February 1988, 16.

Dumanoski, D. 1987a. Monsanto sues to block ban of herbicide linked to tumours. *Boston Globe*, 9 October, 20.

Dumanoski, D. 1987b. Industry sued in lead paint poisonings. *Boston Globe*, 18 November, 1.

Edwards, S. and Santos, S. L. 1987. Unraveling risk communication. Paper presented at annual meeting of American Public Health Association, New Orleans, October.

Elkington, J. 1985. *The Poisoned Womb: Human Reproduction in a Polluted World*. Harmondsworth, England and New York: Viking Press.

Epstein, S. S. 1987. Losing the war against cancer: Who's to blame and what to do about it. Paper published by Rachel Carson Council.

Foreman, J. 1988. Study finds lung cancer rates dropping. *Boston Globe*, 2 February, 1.

General Electric Company 1986/87. *Research and Development Program for the Destruction of PCBs*, Sixth Progress Report.

Ghosal, D., You, I-S., Chatterjee, D. K. and Chakrabarty, A. M. 1985. Microbial degradation of halogenated compounds. *Science*, 228(4696), 135, 141, 142.

Graham, F. Jr. 1970. *Since Silent Spring*. Boston: Houghton Mifflin.

Hall, B. 1987. Environmental action for Central America. *Science for the People*, 19(5), 27.

Howard, Sir A. 1943. *An Agricultural Testament*. London: Oxford University Press.

Hynes, H. P. 1983. PCB contamination in the Housatonic River: An overview of PCBs in sediment and fish of the Housatonic River and regulatory concerns with respect to future remedial action. Paper presented at the annual conference of the Society of Environmental Toxicology and Chemistry, Arlington, Virginia, November.

Hynes, H. P. 1989. Lead in soil: A comparative study of environmental contamination and policy in Western Europe and the United States. *International Environment Reporter*, February.

Hynes, M. M. 1987. *Smoking behavior among teenage girls*. Columbia University School of Public Health.

Illich, I. 1976. *Medical Nemesis: The Expropriation of Health*. New York: Pantheon Books.

Kobayashi, H. and Rittman, B. 1982. Microbial removal of hazardous organic compounds. *Environmental Science and Technology*, **16**(3), 172A–178A.

Lappé, F. M. 1971. *Diet for a Small Planet*. New York: Ballantine.

Leopold, A. 1977. *A Sand County Almanac*. New York: Ballantine.

Lorde, A. 1980. *The Cancer Journals*. San Francisco: Spinsters Ink.

Martin, J. P. and Focht, D. D. 1977. Biological properties of soils. *Soils for Management of Organic Wastes and Wastewaters*, 141–144. Madison, Wisconsin: Soil Science Society of America.

Newsnotes 1987. *Science for the People*, **19**(5), 2.

Perrow, C. 1984. *Normal Accidents: Living with High Risk Technologies*. New York: Basic Books.

Saltus, R. 1987. Hunt for reliable formula for in-vitro births goes on. *Boston Globe*, 16 November, 1.

Shabecoff, P. 1988. Settlement is set in vast cleanup of toxic waste. *New York Times*, 2 February, A10.

Tye, L. 1988. Dukakis balks at lead paint bill. *Boston Globe*, 15 January, 13.

van den Bosch, R. 1978. *The Pesticide Conspiracy*. New York: Doubleday.

Zwerdling, D. 1977. The pesticide treadmill. *Environmental Journal*, September, 15–18.

III

THE WORLD AROUSED

Imagine the United States were to go through a single year completely without pesticides. It is under that license that we take a hard look at that desolate year, examining . . . its devastations ("The desolate year," *Monsanto Magazine*, 1962).

The American people must understand somehow that *Silent Spring*, which they read so avidly, is not a balanced account of the place of pesticides in the world. They must know its conclusions are not endorsed by the vast majority of scientists and physicians with the background to judge. They must realize that it is a polemic, not a prophecy. (*That We May Live* [1966] Rep. Jamie L. Whitten, Chair of Subcommittee on Agriculture)

I thought she was a spinster. What's she so worried about genetics for? (Member of Federal Pest Control Review Board)

Sometime midcentury in America the new synthetic chemical pesticides gained distinction as being necessary to national food supply. On this premise the Monsanto Chemical Company published its dystopian parody of *Silent Spring*. "The desolate year" portrays a once abundant, now impoverished and infested United States overrun by insects because, one year, no one—no farmer, no cattleman, no forester, no pet owner, no housewife—used pesticides. *That We May Live* (Whitten 1966) was another projectile in the agro-chemical campaign to strafe and mortally wound *Silent Spring*. It is a folksy, patronizing to Carson, patriotic defense of "new weapons in an ancient war," written by a Congressman who was an avowed advocate for agricultural interests.

There were hundreds of attacks on *Silent Spring*. The Velsicol Chemical Corporation, sole manufacturer of chlordane and heptachlor, pressured Houghton Mifflin not to publish it. CBS was flooded with letters asking them not to air their special, "The *Silent Spring* of Rachel Carson." Most of the program sponsors withdrew support for it. Scientists were enlisted to write negative reviews of the book. Journals were forced to choose between chemical advertisements and favorable reviews of *Silent Spring*.

The original attacks on *Silent Spring* were built on twin pillars, of militarism and misogyny. Militarism is the glorification of dominance, combat, warlike relationships and policies. In this worldview security is maintained by stockpiling tools of destruction, such as bombs, missiles, and other penile weapons. A strong defense—with progressively more potent and more accurate weapons—is the best deterrent to aggression. Arms are taken up in defense of peace.

War is a world of male swagger; war legitimates male fantasies of dominance and destruction. Novels, films, war memorials, military parades, and revisionist history glorify war as an expression of virility and all manner of manly qualities. In response to a male attorney's question, on the eve of World War II, of how we are to prevent war, Virginia Woolf replied, "to fight has always been the man's habit, not the woman's. Law and practice have developed that difference. . . . Scarcely a human being in the course of history has fallen to a woman's rifle; the vast majority of birds and beasts have been killed by you, not us" (Woolf 1938, p. 8). Your question, she continued, is how to prevent war. Ours is, why fight? "Obviously there is some glory, some necessity, some satisfaction in fighting which we never felt or enjoyed" (Woolf 1938, p. 9). To prevent war, Woolf argued, women must be educated and able to earn a living. Only then, not dependent on fathers and brothers, can women possess "disinterested influence" to exert against war. Otherwise, women have only male-defined roles in support of war: providing sons for combat; replacing men in industry and retreating after the war; grieving the war dead and praying for peace; nursing the war-wounded; following soldiers in prostitution camps; being the intimate targets of male sexual aggression.

The patriarchs of agricultural politics and the chemical industry built their defense of chemical agriculture on the metaphor of war, with insects as enemies, chemicals as weapons, and themselves as heroes. When Rachel Carson exploded the myth of agricultural security through chemical aggression on nature, the chemical industry, many scientists and some politicians saw a woman who had stepped into a world where she had no place and, they alleged, no competence. Theirs was the world of rationality, technicality, public policy, and science. Her rightful and most suitable world was poetic nature writing.

Both "The desolate year" and *That We May Live* exemplify the bullish masculinism of men who see civilized life as a struggle against brutish nature. "All other professions seem to be as bloodthirsty as the profession of arms," Woolf had observed (1938, p. 96). On the battlefield of public life, women's place is nursing, healing, and soothing stressed male egos and bodies. Women write life's poetry while men handle its hard prose. Carson, opined these patriarchs, should stay with pretty books on the sea and leave the subject of intervention in nature to those qualified. "What charms and consoles in the private house distracts and exacerbates in the public office" (Woolf 1938, p. 76).[1] They despised this woman who—educated, employed, and independent of "fathers and brothers"—used her "independent opinion based upon independent income" (Woolf 1938, p. 60) against their war.

Excerpts from *Silent Spring* first appeared as a three-part series in *The New Yorker*. The Monsanto Company immediately began work on "The desolate year" and rushed the galley sheets through company hierarchy in order to publish it simultaneously with the first edition of *Silent Spring*. "The desolate year" is a hostile parody of Carson's opening chapter, "A fable for tomorrow," written in a style which mimics and banalizes Carson's writing. "Life-slowing winter lay on the land that New Year's Day, the day that Nature was left to seek her own balance," it begins. Then unfolds a drama in which bugs march across America like Sherman's army to the sea, destroying everything in their path. The first winter the Mediterranean fruit fly bored holes with "her stilleto-like appendage" into the entire Florida citrus crop, while scales and blights killed all California and Arizona groves. Throughout the northern United States, "the most numerous and ferocious of all mankind's visible natural enemies [as eggs or larvae or pupae or voracious adults] lurked quietly . . . waiting" for spring. With spring the "garrote of Nature rampant began to tighten," as early crops were plagued with cutworms, aphids, mites and "the pretty butterflies that winged over the fields." Farmers planted and cultivated; but they harvested garbage. People who processed food found the insect-ridden food so gross they could hardly handle it. The FDA could not approve such damaged food. Food was scarce; prices were spiralling upward. Insects, "creeping and flying and crawling into the open," swarmed from southern states north-

---

1. This artifice of a male public world and female private world, a ploy to keep women worldless and powerless and also to keep them available as emotional filling-stations for men, has been contrived under all kinds of pretexts. Men have considered it "bad luck" for women to enter construction sites. Gandhi allowed men into his world of history-making and used women for massage and companions on walks and then slept with them naked to prove his asceticism. Mary Daly (1984, pp. 39–41) has called this a spiritual rape of these women and "an enormous draining of these women's energies into a phallocratic cesspool." Where women have broken through the divide and moved into the public world, they have been punished and made a lesson for other women. Recently, the Defense Advisory Committee on Women in the Services found that women in the Navy and Marine Corps deployed in the Pacific region were frequently the victims of sexual harassment and abuse and appeared to be locked in dead-end jobs.

ward. "They were chewers, and pierce-suckers, spongers, siphoners and chew-lappers, and all their vast progeny were chewers—rasping, sawing, biting maggots and worms and caterpillars. Some could sting, some could poison, many could kill." The U.S. Department of Agriculture stood by, besieged but helpless, as the country's vital cotton crop was destroyed by the "worst plant-loving demon of them all," the boll weevil. Corn fields were overwhelmed by tough grasses. Eastern truckfarmers had to abandon their "deformed, wormy, rotting" vegetables. Surpluses from other years were ruined by the explosion of insects and rodents "freed from pesticidal opposition."

Under siege, but emasculated without chemical weapons, the country was helpless to fight the insect enemies. This naive woman, with her romantic notions about the balance of nature, had disarmed and endangered the entire nation. And Monsanto warned, in a slick take-off of Carson's forecast in "A fable for tomorrow":

> The terrible thing about the "desolate year" is this: Its events are not built on fantasy. *They are true.* All of them, fortunately, did not take place in a single year, because so far man has been able to prevent such a thing. But all the major events of the "desolate year" have actually occurred. They have occurred in the United States. They could repeat themselves next year in greatly magnified form simply by removing this country's chemical weapons against pests ("The desolate year," 1962, pp. 4–9).

Between publication of "The desolate year" and *That We May Live*, a review of *Silent Spring*, entitled "The myth of the 'pesticide menace'" appeared. It is particularly memorable for its mean-spirited condescension to Carson; some of its arguments appear to have influenced *That We May Live*. The author was Edwin Diamond, a senior editor of *Newsweek* and formerly that magazine's science editor. Diamond, the biographical section of the review tells us, worked with Rachel Carson in the initial stages of *Silent Spring*. However, "a disagreement over how to proceed ended the collaboration" (Diamond 1963). There is some critical misrepresentation here. Diamond was not a collaborator of Carson's; he was a research assistant hired by her publisher, the Houghton Mifflin Company. He never worked with Carson directly; his employment was terminated by Houghton Mifflin (Graham 1970, p. 78).

Diamond introduces his review by stating that "her arguments were more emotional than accurate." He is sure of this because *Silent Spring* reminds him of a book he read "bug-eyed" as a youth, in which Americans were portrayed as guinea pigs at the mercy of an "unholy trinity of government bureaucrats, avaricious businessmen, and mad scientists." The most vivid fact he recalls from that popular, alarmist book was "the danger ascribed to a certain toothpaste, which, if used in sufficient quantity, could cause a horrible death" (Diamond 1963, p. 17). This fact presumably has equal standing with the wildlife killings and the pesticide poisonings Carson cites. Why has *Silent Spring* caused such a stir in society, he asks? The reputation of Carson's other books has carried this one. Although this one has little of the beauty of her earlier books, "it nevertheless has a high expository gloss." Timing was another advantage. *Silent Spring* was published soon after the thalidomide drug tragedy. Diamond suggests that, although Carson's work is unrelated, she exploited the coincidence, when she stated in a newspaper interview that, "It is all of a piece, thalidomide and pesticides. They represent our willingness to rush ahead and use something without knowing what the results are going to be."

Diamond cites three facts to cast doubt upon the book's accuracy. The first is the expression "chemical rain of death," which describes aerial spraying with pesticides. The use of rain here is inaccurate, he says, because rain falls on all land in the United States while less than 5 percent of land is treated annually with pesticides. Clearly, he doesn't grasp that pollutants don't respect the boundaries of land in which they are used. They dissolve, adsorb, volatilize, are absorbed and move with wind, rain, ground and surface water, and in the food chain. They have been found in the remotest corners of the earth.

Diamond's second problem is Carson's statements that pesticides are dangerous and cause significant illness and death. At the time of writing his article, there were more deaths annually from bee stings and aspirin than from misuse of pesticides, he alleges. One of Carson's key points is, of course, that the harmful chronic effects of pesticides might take as long as 20 to 30 years to evaluate fully because of their subtle biological effects. Add to this that pesticide poisoning among farm workers was very much underreported then, and still is. Even when it was reported, doctors, not being trained in environmental and occupational health, rarely recognized pesticide poisoning when they treated it.

Finally, Diamond assails Carson for worrying about cats' deaths from DDT application in Java, while not mentioning the "10,000 people throughout the world who die of malnutrition or starvation every day. . . . If DDT kills some cats but saves many humans, if weed killer destroys a pocket of wildlife shelter but increases highway safety, so much the better" (Diamond 1963, p. 18). Pesticides, he holds, will save the world from famine; a return to a world without pesticides is ignorant, backward, and antihuman. Carson—"the quiet-spoken, retiring, single woman"—is a mystical bird–cat–wildflower fanatic with no concern for human beings.

Diamond accuses Carson of emotionally manipulating people's fears and insecurities, of mystifying nature, and of being naively antitechnology and nonprogressive. He projects on to Carson the "stereotyped thinking and the scattershot charges" which he himself employs in perpetuating the myth of all technology as inherently progressive and in evoking the image of Carson as a heartless, sinister spinster.

Jamie L. Whitten, a congressman from Mississippi and chair of the House Appropriations Subcommittee on Agriculture, was an acknowledged spokesman in federal politics for agricultural interests. In 1964 Whitten requested staff of his committee to "conduct an inquiry into the effects, uses, control and research of agricultural pesticides, as well as an inquiry into the accuracy of the more publicized books and articles which increase public concern over the effects of agricultural pesticides on public health" (Graham 1970, p. 165). Over 200 scientists and physicians, government and industry officials, and conservationists were interviewed. The staff reviewed numerous books, including Robert Rudd's *Pesticides and the Living Landscape* and Lewis Herber's (pen name of Murray Bookchin) *Our Synthetic Environment*, and many newspaper and magazine articles. They concluded, "in view of the opinion of representatives of Government, industry, and the scientific community" that the "alarming statements" of *Silent Spring* were by far "the most effective in influencing the public's concern over the use of pesticides" (*The Whitten Report* 1965, p. 5). So the report of this committee was limited to a review of *Silent Spring*. *The Whitten Report* was immediately reprinted by the National Agricultural Chemicals Association; and Jamie Whitten popularized it in *That We May Live*, published in 1966.

Whitten opens *That We May Live* with an elegy to the high standard of living in 1965 America: atomic submarines, missiles, satellites, jets, men in space, nuclear fission, nylon, television, teflon, and DDT. All were "unbelievably successful" and part of a piece, controlling "the air above and the elements about us." The next frontier would be the sea; for the developer of the atomic submarine had told Whitten that "in future wars the nation which controlled the bottom of the sea might well emerge the victor" (Whitten 1966, p. 2).

The thread running throughout this book is that Rachel Carson had a "magic pen," but she needed tutoring in history. She did not understand that human history has always been a struggle against nature to tilt the balance of nature for man's own well-being and comfort. DDT, aldrin, and dieldrin are "new weapons in an ancient war" against plague, pestilence, and famine. They are the most recent in a continuum of agricultural improvements: mechanization with the tractor, fertilizers, improved varieties of crops, and improved cultural practices, such as irrigation, rotating crops, planting on optimum dates, thinning or planting more thickly. The loss of chemical pesticides—the kind Carson and Whitten wrote about had been in use no more than 20 years—would be "an incalculable blow" to the farmer, to the city dweller and "to the general health of all." Production of food and fiber, Whitten predicts, citing a National Academy of Sciences report, would fall on the average more than 50 percent, close to 100 percent in some crops.[2]

What is it about Miss Carson's message that evoked such love and reverence, so that she is quoted everywhere, asks the congressman. He likes Edwin Diamond's explanation that she manipulated public distrust of scientists and that she timed *Silent Spring* so as to exploit public fear of new chemicals. The "mainspring," he decides, was her ability to evoke the past of innocent, romantic rural charm and beauty, the past when nature "did not need to be controlled to the extent it does today to meet the needs of population growth and world leadership" (Whitten 1966, p. 133). He knows because he was a farm boy himself and can remember smelling sweet green grass; hearing birdsong in spring; drinking cool, clean water from a cistern; reading before an open fire by a kerosene lamp; eating meats cured in the family smokehouse; and enjoying lots of other premodern, pristine pasttimes. Miss Carson has substituted "sentiment and nostalgia for scientific data facts" (Whitten 1966, p. 138). The charming, childish sentiment must not be allowed to blind us to the requirements of modern society, cautions the grown-up, worldly congressman. Patting Miss Carson on the head for the delightful reading she has given us in *Silent Spring*, he assures us that it is not and never was a serious book. Like a patriarchal father chiding a daughter, he suggests that her place is to entertain, not instruct; to be seen, but not heard.

> I believe all must agree that *Silent Spring*, delightful reading that it is, certainly is not and was never claimed to be a scientific document nor an objective analysis of the chemical–human life relationship. Though we give it our highest praise for its wonderful prose, for its timely warning, let us move it over from the non-science fiction section of the library to the science-fiction section, while we review the facts—in order that we may continue to enjoy the abundant life (Whitten 1966, p. 141).

Whitten's political mission on the House Appropriations Subcommittee on Agriculture was to protect the agricultural economy and the then current USDA pro-pesticide policies. President Kennedy's Science Advisory Committee had agreed with the findings of *Silent Spring* and recommended the development of biological methods and the minimization of chemical pesticides. Senator Abraham Ribicoff's subcommittee was gathering testimony to advance Carson's recommendations to re-

2. The ecologist LaMont C. Cole's comment on the dystopian picture of "The Desolate Year" also applies to the apocalyptic worldview of *That We May Live*. It is easy to become persuaded by these skillful fantasies, he writes in his review of the critics of *Silent Spring*, "that years like those just before World War II could not have possibly occurred: no chlorinated hydrocarbons, no organic phosphates, payments to farmers to reduce production and still crop surpluses!" (Cole 1962, p. 173).

duce chemical pesticide use and to reorganize the enforcement of pesticide regulation, so that it protected human health and wildlife rather than promoting pesticides use. Whitten needed to dampen the public popularity and offset the influence of *Silent Spring* on the Executive and Legislative Branches. After calling Carson's book essentially pretty but empty-headed, *The Whitten Report* and *That We May Live* attempted to rebuild the chemical industry's case for the safety and the necessity of pesticides.

The core of Whitten's findings on pesticides hazards was that, except for a few instances of suicide by using pesticides, people have been poisoned infrequently and only by accidental ingestion of high doses. Most frequently children who got hold of improperly stored pesticides were the victims. In other words, pesticide *misuse*—by children, farm workers, and others who do not follow precautions established by the manufacturer—not pesticide *use* is at issue.

The Whitten committee was advised by scientists and physicians that *Silent Spring* was "superficially scientific" because Carson made implications (about the hazards of pesticides to human health) "based on possibilities as yet unproved to be actual facts" (*The Whitten Report*, p. 6). The American Medical Association and many scientists advised the Whitten committee that no one knows the long-term effects of chemical pesticides in sublethal doses over time. There were those who opposed the use of pesticides because of this fact; on the other hand, there were those who supported their use because of the same fact. "Because no one at the present time can prove who is correct, any discussion of long-term effects of minute traces of pesticides on human beings would be fruitless," concluded the committee (*The Whitten Report*, p. 8).

Overall, *The Whitten Report* and *That We May Live* present government running a tight ship, where every chemical used in agriculture undergoes a full battery of toxicology tests to determine what level of residue is safe to allow on food. These tolerances are strictly and adequately enforced; and foods accidentally contaminated are immediately removed from the market. Where Government can improve, it has. Agricultural research programs have recently shifted their priorities to greater study of biological controls and more precise methods of pesticide application. Meanwhile, Whitten contentedly clucks, pesticide use has increased since the publication of *Silent Spring*.

FARM WORKERS AND THE SAFETY OF PESTICIDES

At the time Jamie Whitten was shoring up the safety record of pesticides, pesticide poisoning was rarely recognized by physicians when they saw it. Also, farm workers did not have the benefit of employer-paid

health insurance, so pesticide poisoning often went untreated. Even if
pesticide poisoning were treated and recognized by medical personnel,
there was no requirement that it be reported to the local or state government. Pesticide poisoning was, and still is, severely underreported.

The human health hazards of chemical-intensive agriculture are most
acute for farm workers. They are exposed to pesticides in the fields in
which they work, on the crops they cultivate and harvest, in the soil the
crops are grown in, on the drift of sprays from adjoining fields or from
their own field being sprayed. Farm workers' homes abut agricultural
fields and are at times downwind of pesticide spray. Pesticides migrate
into the irrigation water and also into the groundwater which supplies
the farm workers' wells. Farm workers are more likely to eat foods
sooner after they have been sprayed, so they probably eat more pesticides than the rest of the population. Agriculture is the only industry in
America where children comprise a significant part of the workforce.
Farm workers' occupational exposure to toxics begins at an earlier age
than for the rest of us.

Dr Marion Moses, a physician specializing in environmental and occupational medicine and an Assistant Clinical Professor at the University
of California, San Francisco, is the former director and now a consultant
to the National Farm Workers Health Group. In 1987 Dr Moses testified
before the House Agricultural Committee in their hearings on amendments to the federal pesticide law (FIFRA) and also before the Los
Angeles City Council. Her summary of the pesticide poisonings among
farm workers in California refutes the industry contention—the same
made in *The Whitten Report*—that all pesticides are safe if used properly,
that the hazards of pesticides are uniquely in misuse, and that Rachel
Carson inflated the health hazards of intensive chemical agriculture.

Farm workers in California have the highest illness and injury rate of
any workers in that state. Farm workers represent only 3.9 percent of the
workers in that state, yet they represent 9 percent of reported fatalities, 5
percent of doctors' reports, and 5 percent of compensable illness and
injuries. California is the only state that mandates physicians to report
occupationally related pesticide illness. In 1985, 1,675 such cases were
reported. Since pesticide illness is grossly underreported (as low as 1
percent in farm workers is reported, says Moses), the actual extent of
pesticide illness and poisoning is much greater. "It has been estimated
that 300,000 cases of farm worker poisoning from pesticides occur annually in the United States" (Moses 1987b, p. 3).

Federal and state regulatory agencies have failed to protect farm
workers in the two major ways advocated by Carson in testimony before
Congress in 1962 and reiterated by Moses in her 1987 testimony: more
stringent occupational protection for those who work with pesticides,
and comprehensive testing and restricting of all toxic pesticides. Unlike

other workers, agricultural workers are not covered by the Occupational Health and Safety Act, which sets exposure standards in the workplace. EPA, which is empowered to set farm worker protection standards under the federal pesticide law FIFRA, has not yet done so at this writing. For example, FIFRA should mandate that growers inform field workers about what pesticides will be sprayed in the fields, their specific hazards, what protective clothing ought to be worn, and field reentry times. In California, the state agency responsible for farm worker health and safety does not do routine field monitoring, but awaits reports of worker illness before acting.

As for the safety of pesticide residues in food sold commercially, the elaborate maze of tolerances and permissible limits of residues is more confusing than consoling. The major source of carcinogens deliberately allowed in our food supply is pesticides. The Delaney Amendment to the Food, Drug and Cosmetic Act, which forbids the use of any chemical in food that is known to cause cancer in animals or humans, does not cover pesticides in fresh foods. Nearly one billion pounds of pesticides are used on food each year in the United States. About 500 different pesticides can leave residues on food; EPA has set tolerances for only 316 of these; only 41 percent of the 316 can be detected by the current testing methods used for multiple residues. For those pesticides on which tolerances are set, most have what are called data gaps, that is, incomplete health and safety information to determine their long-term health effects.

Dr Moses cites a study of cancer among farm workers conducted by Dr Thomas Lazar, formerly of the Kern County Health Department, California. In McFarland, California, a small agricultural community in the San Joaquin Valley near Delano, Dr Lazar found an excess of cancer in children, some cancers of the type on the increase in farmers, agricultural workers, and others exposed to pesticides: non-Hodgkins' lymphoma, leukemia and testicular cancer. McFarland is surrounded by vineyards, cotton fields, almond groves, and other extensively sprayed crops. In the course of the study, Lazar found evidence of high childhood cancer rates in several other towns in the same county. Dr Lazar was forced to quit the health department in early 1987 because of harassment and pressure from the Department Director to alter his report to conclude that environmental contamination by pesticides and other toxic chemicals was not related to the cancers (Clemings 1987).

A broad-brush look at the United Farm Workers' 25-year-old struggle to win safe working conditions demonstrates the severity and persistence of pesticide hazards in agriculture. The first meeting to organize migrant farm workers into what would become the United Farm Workers movement was convened by Cesar Chavez in an abandoned theater in Fresno, California on 30 September 1962, three days after the publication of *Silent Spring*. Carson took on the agricultural chemical industry;

Chavez and the poorest workers in America would strike against agribusiness. Since its inception, the United Farm Workers have sought protection from toxic pesticides in their contracts with growers, because no occupational protection existed for them in law, and because the existing pesticide law, as enforced by the Department of Agriculture, functioned to register but not to ban extremely hazardous pesticides. In September 1965 farm workers walked out of grape orchards in Delano, California, because of unsafe pesticide exposure, unsanitary working conditions, and poverty-level wages. One result of this historic action was a ban on the use of DDT, dieldrin, and aldrin in the first contracts with grape growers. The ban on pesticide use proved to be the most controversial element of the agreement signed in 1970, after a five-year strike–boycott by the United Farm Workers of table and wine grapes. Growers held out longer on the contract clause banning the use of these three pesticides than on any other demand.[3] The ban was won by the United Farm Workers two years before EPA would rule on DDT.

In assessing the gains farm workers have made over the past few decades, Chavez recently pointed out that while there have been some economic benefits won, one aspect of farm work has worsened: the use of toxic pesticides. In 1985 the United Farm Workers called for a new boycott on fresh table grapes from California until the grape industry would agree to three conditions:

1. A ban on five pesticides used in growing grapes: Captan, Parathion, Phosdrin, Dinoseb, and Methyl Bromide.
2. A joint and well-publicized UFW/grower testing program for pesticide residues on grapes sold in stores.
3. Free and fair elections for farm workers and good-faith collective bargaining.

Grapes are the largest fruit crop in California. They receive more restricted use pesticide applications than any other fresh food crop, approximately 8 million pounds of more than 130 different pesticides. Most of the pesticides used have not been fully tested to determine whether they cause cancer, birth defects, chronic effects, sterility, or damage to genetic material. Approximately one third of them are suspect or proven carcinogens. More than half of all acute pesticide-related illness in California involves cultivating or harvesting grapes. Each of the five pesticides named in the boycott is extremely toxic; some have caused extensive worker poisoning and illness; some are known carcinogens; some leave residues on grapes.

---

3. Conversation with Roberto de la Cruz, New England Region Representative, United Farm Workers of America, AFL-CIO, 17 December 1987.

EPA's concession, which allowed grape growers to market table grapes that contained illegally high sulfite residues, is one major reason for the second condition in the recent boycott. In July 1986, the FDA ordered grocers and restaurants to stop preserving food with sulfite compounds because sulfite residues were linked to 16 deaths and 800 allergic reactions. In December 1986, EPA ordered grape growers to certify that 75 percent of their grapes contain less than 10 parts per million sulfites residue. After an intense public campaign by California grape growers, EPA relented and gave growers three options. The first was the original requirement. The second was to placard supermarkets warning consumers that the grapes were treated with sulfites. Retailers objected. The third option was to tag 40 percent of the grapes with the message, "Grapes treated with sulfites to ensure freshness and quality." The growers chose this option. Until December 31, 1987, growers could sell grapes, no matter how high the sulfite residues, if two out of five bunches were tagged.

The issue of pesticide safety, then, is not just one of misuse. Chemical-intensive agriculture is hazardous when pesticides which are too dangerous to use—no matter what precautions taken—are not banned from agriculture; when there is insufficient protection of field workers from drift and residues of spray; when pesticide tolerances on food are set without adequate data; when tolerances are not enforced; and when routine use of pesticides causes significant contamination of groundwater and the food chain of wildlife. Arguing from the same premise raised by Carson in testimony to Congress—that we ought to have a civil right to a healthful and safe environment—Dr Moses concludes her testimony:

> Neither biological controls, nor safer and more selective pesticides, nor alternatives to pesticides will be developed or used as long as agribusiness and the agricultural industry continue to refuse to accept responsibility for the actual and potential harm their products cause workers, consumers, and the environment. The burden should not be on us to prove that pesticides are harmful, but on the producers and the users to prove they are safe (Moses 1987a, p. 2).

THE WORLD CANNOT FEED ITSELF
WITHOUT PESTICIDES

Before the end of 1962, Robert White-Stevens, Assistant Director of Research and Development in the Agricultural Division of the American Cyanamid Company, had made 28 speeches in which he charged that *Silent Spring* was littered with crass mistakes. He warned that Carson, in seeking to ban all pesticides, was promoting world famine; and the victims would haunt her conscience. Before a UN conference in Rome in

1971, Norman Borlaug, a 1970 Nobel Prize winner for developing new wheat strains, declared:

> The current vicious, hysterical propaganda campaign against [pesticides], being promoted today by fear-provoking, irresponsible environmentalists, had its genesis in the best-selling, half-science, half-fiction novel *Silent Spring*. . . . If the use of pesticides in the USA were to be completely banned, crop losses would probably soar to 50 percent, and food prices would increase four-fold to five-fold (Wellford 1972, p. 264).

There were two critical flaws in the shrill outpourings (if anyone is hysterical on the pesticide issue, it is they) of Carson's detractors. First, they assume a cause-and-effect relationship between the use of pesticides and increased food supply (or its obverse, the nonuse of pesticides and a 50 to 100 percent decrease in food), which they do not prove or justify. Second, they accuse Carson of calling for a ban on the use of all pesticides, when what she advocated—the "other road"—was the development of biologically based pest control methods and a minimum use of chemical pesticides only where absolutely necessary.

At the time of White-Stevens' and Borlaug's statements, there was no established or agreed-upon method of quantifying the economic impact of minimizing the use of pesticides. Pesticide economics was a new field and only beginning to assemble the information needed for an accurate analysis of the "necessity defense" for pesticides in agricultural production. Harrison Wellford, author of a critical study on chemical agriculture and food safety, examines the fallacious and self-serving statements of critics like White-Stevens and Borlaug:

> As of 1971, the benefits and costs of pesticides even in the most narrow sense of their marginal effect on the farmer's profits . . . remain unmeasured in agriculture.
>
> On what then do USDA and the chemical companies base their claims for pesticides? One answer is that uncertainties in the methods used to evaluate pesticide benefits allow them to interpret the results as they choose. For example, one method involves comparing production figures before and after the use of pesticides from the same farms or regions over a period of years. USDA and the pesticide companies, using this method, attribute the large increases in crop yields achieved by American farmers since the early fifties to pesticides. But they do not distinguish the contribution of increased use of machinery, fertilizers, better crop strains, and other changes. Indeed, the deductive logic of the numbers game can cut both ways: at least one standard textbook on economic entomology (Metcalf and Flint) estimates that percentage crop losses to insects in 1936 and 1957 were *virtually identical*, although organic synthetic insecticides had come into widespread use in the interval (Wellford 1972, p. 273).

In other words, the great claims made by promoters of pesticides for increased crop production and food to feed the world lump together fertilizers, cultural practices, better farm machinery, and new crop strains with pesticides. Disaggregating pesticides from the other changes in agriculture, we may find, as Wellford cited, that the percentage of crop damage from insects is identical in crops grown with and without, or with minimal use of synthetic pesticides.

Wellford then proceeds to analyze how national farm policy has fostered the use of pesticides. In the fifties the government, in order to avoid food surpluses and control food prices, introduced a program of subsidy payments to farmers for nonuse of farmland. The policy limits the amount of land farmed, not the amount of food grown. The farm subsidy system, therefore, encourages farmers to use the most sophisticated mechanical and chemical technology to increase yields from the acres farmed. Some of the changes in farming which resulted from the intensive use of the land were an abandoning of crop diversity and crop rotation, which helps discourage pests, and increased application of pesticides to control the pest outbreaks which result from monoculture farming. In 1970, J. C. Headley, a professor of agricultural economics at the University of Missouri and specialist in the cost–benefit analysis of pesticides, warned that the policy of withdrawing land from farming, embodied in the Agriculture Act of 1970, "had weakened the natural ability of the biological system's capacity to control pests and overtaxed the system's capacity to dispose of chemicals safely" (Wellford 1972, p. 274).

The linchpin in the defense of the new synthetic pesticides was that they would protect agriculture from severe crop loss due to insect pests. Robert van den Bosch, a research entomologist for more than three decades and professor at the University of California, Berkeley, confirmed in field studies, his own and others, that the opposite was true. He verified, as Carson had warned, that chemical-intensive agriculture does not control insect pests, it creates them. It places an immense financial burden on farmers which he likened to a treadmill of increasing pesticide use because of rapid insect resistance. It also threatens farm workers' health, while exposing consumers to unknown risks.

Van den Bosch proposed shifting insect pest control from "the poisoning of things" to a holistic, ecologically based strategy of minimizing insect damage to crops and disease-bearing insects. Called *integrated control* or *integrated pest management* (IPM), this alternative strategy concentrates on two factors which chemical agriculture ignores: first, the agricultural ecosystem and second, the population density of the insects that could damage the crop. The first factor includes a recognition that the ecosystem contains indigenous means, including predators, to control insects and that this should be preserved. The second factor derives from a different definition of the insect problem. "Pest" refers not to a species of insect, the boll weevil, for example, but to a population large

enough to damage the crop. The focus of IPM, then, is the interaction of
the insect population with the agricultural ecosystem. IPM utilizes technical information, continuous monitoring of the pest population, assessment of the condition of the crop, control–action criteria, materials, and
methods in concert with natural mortality factors, to manage pest populations in a safe, effective, and economical way. Integrated control uses a
combination of the biological and cultural practices which Carson advocated as "the other road" in concert with a diminished use of chemicals
to minimize crop damage from insects. Integrated control achieved some
notable successes in the late sixties and early seventies. Let us look at
four of these projects—three undertaken within a decade of *Silent Spring*
and the fourth more recently—in order to see the inner workings of
integrated control.[4]

Marin County, California, has a 2,000 acre wetland, Petaluma Marsh,
which had been a major mosquito breeding ground. As a consequence
much of the marsh was aerially sprayed with the pesticide parathion five
times a year. The county entomologist responsible for mosquito control
deduced that the mosquito source was not the natural wetland waterways which are flushed daily by tides, but the "potholes" created when
the area was used as a practice bombing range by the military during
World War II. The potholes did not drain with tidal flushing, and their
stagnating water became ideal breeding sites for mosquitoes. The entomologists developed a pothole drainage system that permits daily
flushing. As a result, aircraft stopped spraying the marshes with pesticides. The mosquito problem has disappeared from nearby communities; dairy farmers reported that their herds are free of mosquito swarms
for the first time in memory.

In Washington State's Yakima, Wenatchee, and Okenagen valleys, integrated control was used to save apple orchards from an intractable
spider mite problem. The spider mite outbreak was an induced secondary outbreak because the spider mite became resistant to all of the
chemical sprays which had been used there on the codling moth and
other insects and diseases which plagued the orchards.

The Washington program is oriented to the protection of a predatory
mite which is the key natural enemy of the pest spider mite. The program investigator found that the predatory mite was resistant to a variety
of pesticides. Thus, there were some chemicals which could be used
effectively against the target pest without harming the predator mite.
The program requires continuous monitoring of the pest and predator

4. See van den Bosch 1980, pp. 129–157 for a fuller description of the first three integrated
control projects described in the following section.

populations, so that pest/predator populations are known. This information is indispensable for making decisions about selective pesticide use.

In order to sustain the predatory mite, the program also uses the apple rust mite. Formerly considering this insect a pest to be sprayed, the investigators found that it rarely causes sufficient damage to warrant spraying, but that it also serves as a source of food for the predatory mite during times of spider mite scarcity. Not only has the amount of pesticide use been lowered, but in some orchards, spider mite spraying has been eliminated. The selective and diminished use of pesticides has permitted the build-up of natural predators of other insect pests in the orchards, further reducing the need for chemical sprays. Where the program has been used faithfully, pesticide use has been reduced by 50 percent. The program is used on over 40,000 acres and has served as a prototype for apple-growing areas in the Midwest and the Northeast.

In the San Joaquin valley, Dr van den Bosch and colleagues developed an integrated control program to reduce pesticide use in cotton to the most effective minimum. In the early seventies, valley cotton growers were spending $25 million on chemicals to protect their $500 million-plus cotton crop, amounting to what researchers felt was a greatly excessive use of pesticides. Too often insects are blamed and crops are sprayed for problems which arise from agricultural practice or climate conditions. In the case of cotton, insecticides are poured onto cotton for "bug damage" when the plant injury is caused by poor irrigation, poor cultivation practices, or temperature extremes.

The program entails integrated control specialists visiting the fields frequently from mid-May until late September. They assess plant growth, note fruiting performance, measure beneficial and harmful insect populations, and record insect injury. The condition of the cotton crop is compared with the plant's optimum performance and an assessment is made of the factors that could cause any plant problems, for example, irrigation, climate, fertilizer, insects. Spraying for insects is recommended only when it is judged that they are the current cause of plant problems. Van den Bosch reports that where the program has been put into practice, insecticide use has been minimized, as much as 50 percent, and crop yields and quality were very high. Another benefit has been the disappearance of secondary pests, such as the bollworm, which have become pest problems as a result of excessive spraying for the primary pest, the lygus bug.

University of Massachusetts Cooperative Extension has been conducting Integrated Pest Management Programs in Massachusetts since 1978. The programs have developed mechanisms for accurate pest and beneficial insect estimation and spray decision-making. They use biological control agents, techniques of sustainable agriculture, and the "least is best" pesticide strategy. By 1987 the statewide program had projects under way for apples, cranberries, potatoes, sweet corn, strawberries, and turf. Their objective is to make farming viable economically and sound environmentally through providing farmers with interdisciplinary training in IPM concepts and techniques. The apple and sweet corn projects exemplify the overall success of all of the projects (Coli 1986/87).

Sweet corn is the most valuable vegetable crop in Massachusetts. The corn is attacked by numerous pests, and farmers make frequent pesticide applications in order to produce an insect-free corn. At the same time, residential neighborhoods are encroaching on farmland in western Massachusetts as financially strapped farmers sell off parcels of farmland. Therefore, an IPM program to reduce pesticide use on corn is increasingly important to public health as well as wildlife and groundwater.

In the sweet corn IPM program, sex-attractant pheromone traps are used to catch important corn pests, the European corn borer, the corn earworm and the fall armyworm. The traps are checked weekly and corn fields are scouted for pest occurrence. Spray recommendations are based on trap capture, plant growth stage, and field scouting reports. The program staff also instruct farmers in more accurate pesticide spray techniques, as a means of reducing spray and spray drift. The 1986 program worked directly with 16 growers in 23 Massachusetts towns, whose farms grow 1,000 of the approximately 8,000 acres of sweet corn in the state; the 1987 program reached a slightly larger percentage. The educational effort included instructional meetings with growers, computer-based communication, and reports offering spray recommendations left with individual growers. In the 1986 program, corn farmers used an average of 37 percent fewer pesticide treatments than farmers not using IPM, with no loss in quality in the corn. This amounted to almost three fewer sprayings per crop and a net savings of $50,000 among the participating farmers.

The sweet corn project is also researching the reduction of herbicides in cornfields through lower rates of herbicide use or use of an oat cover crop as a substitute for herbicides. The results of reduced herbicide use show that corn yields are just as high with substantially less herbicide applied to cornfields as with the standard application rate. The oat cover project was started in fall 1987, so there are no results yet for this cultural alternative to herbicide use.

The apple program is the oldest and most developed of the IPM programs. It has a comprehensive educational outreach to growers with newsletters, phone networks, meetings, orchard visits, and a manual, *Integrated Management of Apple Pests in Massachusetts and New England*. Between 1978 and 1987, pesticide use in participating orchards has been reduced by about 40 percent. Recommendations to the growers by the

University IPM staff have focused on the timing and type of pesticides used throughout the growing season. The staff relied on factors of weather, pest population, economic thresholds, and enhancing endemic biological control agents by choosing pesticides which would not harm them.

A second stage of apple IPM is being designed which is intended to move beyond pesticide management toward a more holistic orchard strategy. The program will employ methods to reduce and intercept immigrating pests at the orchard perimeter; predator releases and groundcover management practices to enhance biological mite control; and biological pesticides and pest controls. The goal with the second stage biological measures is to reduce insecticide use by up to 70 percent compared to pre-1978 levels.

Rachel Carson observed that the science of biotic control had obscure beginnings in the nineteenth century, with the effort to introduce the natural enemies of troublesome insects. However, she wrote, entomologists were dazzled by the wonders of the new synthetic pesticides introduced into agriculture in the mid-forties and turned away from biological methods. Integrated pest management (IPM) had its "sustained beginnings," according to one entomologist, in the later forties and fifties, often when insects had developed resistance to DDT or some other new synthetic pesticide. It "flowered and expanded" in the sixties and early seventies, thanks largely to a political and scientific receptivity to biological and cultural pest control alternatives generated by *Silent Spring*. It began maturing and being institutionalized in the seventies and eighties, as federal agencies, including EPA, the US Department of Agriculture, National Science Foundation, and the Cooperative State Research Service began funding projects. Institutionalization has resulted in the Consortium for Integrated Pest Management, a 17-university, interdisciplinary research project on four major crops: alfalfa, apple, cotton, and soybean. The purpose of the Consortium has been to improve integrated pest management on these crops and clearly demonstrate that it is a successful, ecological strategy to minimize insect and pathogen damage to crops, while sustaining a high and healthy yield. During this period of formal support for IPM, agriculture has suffered hard financial times—what has been described as a price–cost squeeze—with many farmers going bankrupt or operating in increasing debt. Therefore, the positive economics of IPM has been very important to demonstrate and a major objective of the Consortium.

At a 1985 symposium sponsored by the Consortium for Integrated Pest Management, the US Department of Agriculture and the Cooperative State Research Service, two speakers summarized the economic benefits for farmers using IPM as either savings from using less pesticides, or increased crop yields, and often a combination of both. In their review of six on-farm cotton IPM programs, they found that all had reduced their pesticide use; 50 percent had increased yields; and two thirds had reduced costs. Profit was realized in all six cases, ranging from $3 to $186 per acre. As for alfalfa growers, there was a 45 percent reduction in pesticide use and a $25 per acre net return in the North Central region of the country. In the South, farmers who used IPM reduced their pesticide use by 75 percent and enjoyed a net return of $28 per acre. Apple growers used an average of 0.8 pounds less insecticide and 0.35 pounds less fungicide per acre with no loss in the quality of the fruit. The IPM control strategies used in place of conventional calendar-based spraying for scab, mite and codling moth in Michigan increased apple growers' net earnings 16 percent to 40 percent. Soybeans are a major agricultural crop, grown on some 65 million acres. Therefore, although IPM programs for soybeans generally reduce costs a relatively small amount on a per-acre basis, this becomes a significant reduction in pesticides when calculated for the amount of soybeans grown (Lacewell and Masud 1985).

The current importance and the future potential of integrated pest management, if used on a large scale, is evident. On the surface this approach of studying agricultural practices, environmental factors, and the web of life within which insect pests live, as well as intervening with chemical pesticides in the most minimal way possible, meets the spirit of Rachel Carson's "other road":

> A truly extraordinary variety of alternatives to the chemical control of insects is available. Some are already in use and have achieved brilliant success. Others are in the stage of laboratory testing. Still others are little more than ideas in the minds of imaginative scientists, waiting for the opportunity to put them to the test. All have this in common: they are *biological* solutions, based on understanding of the living organisms they seek to control, and of the whole fabric of life to which these organisms belong. Specialists representing various areas of the vast field of biology are contributing—entomologists, pathologists, geneticists, physiologists, biochemists, ecologists—all pouring their knowledge and their creative inspirations into the formation of a new science of biotic controls (Carson 1962, pp. 244–245).

But we must look beneath the patina of successful projects to the philosophy, the spirit, and the future directions of this interdisciplinary scientific paradigm of insect control. Historian of science Thomas Dunlap pointed out that biological methods do not necessarily "lead to a change of heart about man and nature. . . . The use of new [biological] materials can be quite compatible with a continued emphasis on man over nature" (Dunlap 1981, p. 243).

At the same 1985 Consortium symposium, entomologist Brian Croft conducted a self-examination of the national IPM program and outlined the obstacles and challenges of the eighties and nineties for IPM. For the past 25 years in the United States, IPM "has served as the major conceptual paradigm and philosophy of pest control" (Croft 1985). For at least 20 years it has been embraced worldwide. Its strengths lie in its holistic, interdisciplinary, hierarchical (by this he means looking at the organelle and plant level equally with the ecosystem and ecosphere), and dynamic nature. In short, IPM's uniqueness, as well as its strength, is that it is a process, not a technique, product, or set of pest control tactics. The vulnerabilities or potential weaknesses of IPM include a "crisis of legitimacy" among scientists and major agricultural agencies and some loss of credibility due to a "perceived poor record of implementation"; the danger of focusing too much on the individual components of IPM and not the total system; a decline in funding, thus a decline in student enrollment and in IPM research and implementation; and last, a concern that IPM is losing ground to new biotechnologies, such as recombinant DNA, applied to agriculture. "While in the 1970's and early 1980's, IPM was a key buzz word to funding agencies countrywide; more recently it has fallen victim to a new round of competing 'hot handles' such as 'biotechnology'" (Croft 1985, p. 720). Croft concludes that, if IPM is not to lose ground in the last two decades of the century, there are three scientific arenas to occupy. One is the persistent problem of resistance to pesticides, and even to biological controls, which plants and insects develop naturally. In the dynamic world of insects and plants there is no single solution, not even a biological one, to which plants and insects cannot adapt. Second is computer technology. Since IPM is an observational and information-based process and requires a precision based on cause-and-effect relationships in the ecosystem, it can be assisted and enhanced by computer technology. Third is biotechnology and genetic engineering. These will provide IPM with "new tactical tools" including crops genetically engineered for resistance to disease, insects, or herbicides; microbes genetically engineered to be pesticides; genetically "improved" natural predators or parasites, "and other novel pest control agents." He does warn that if these new tools are embraced and used unilaterally as a single solution, and not within an integrated approach, overuse may lead to the same problems which arose with the use of synthetic chemical pesticides, namely, rapid resistance to them in plants and insects and then major pest control failures.

The future of integrated pest management, two other speakers also told the symposium, is with biotechnologies and genetic engineering applied to agriculture. They describe the recombinant DNA technologies—chiefly, transferring novel genes into plants, microbes, and insects—as progressive, necessary, and inevitable. And IPM is their natural site of application. For every 10 descriptive words used about the biotechnologies, nine are positive; one, cautious. The positive consequences—called "promising," "novel," "technically feasible," "economically beneficial," "exciting," "challenging"—are presented as actual and realizable. The negative consequence—ecological risk—is discussed as a potential one. Eloquent on the new technologies' benefits, one speaker berates the "unfounded conjecture about potential risks" (Bateman 1985). Regardless of regulatory debates, the future in recombinant DNA (rDNA) techniques, he says, appears certain. There is a compelling need for regulation of the biotechnologies. The United States must get past the impasse of public resistance to recombinant DNA technologies. The current chaos in regulation and the turf battles among federal agencies who want primacy in regulating rDNA products is stifling progress in rDNA field testing and use. A regulatory system will enable the technologies to be field tested and marketed; and the United States can begin to use them and enjoy their economic benefits. In other words, the purpose of biotechnology regulation is to give American industry a competitive edge in the new economic sector of biotechnology products (Hullar and Gilchrist 1985; Bateman 1985).

Something is critically wrong here. I would call what's wrong "bondage to unreal loyalties," to borrow from Virginia Woolf. To begin with, there is an increasing rationalistic odor about most of the symposium papers. Although IPM is an ecologically based process, the preponderance of papers present it as a technique, the results are presented as products, and much more space is given to calculation of dollars saved per acre of agriculture than to ecological meaning. One article (Lacewell and Masud 1985) entitled "Economic and environmental implications of IPM," devotes itself exclusively to savings per acre to the farmer using IPM. There is no analysis of effects or implications for the environment, which features only in the paper's title. Environmental considerations seem to be soft, intellectually and professionally; agricultural economics' analysis, hard. This may explain why the IPM scientists are so passive about the ecological questions and risks which accompany using engineered microorganisms and insects in the agricultural environment.

But why are IPM scientists falling under the spell of the "revolution" in biotechnology when (assuming their symposium project reports are accurate) IPM is enjoying great success already, with minimal risk to the environment? Is it that this is where the funding is, so this is the new frontier in agricultural research? In 1985, the US Department of Agriculture funded a national program for basic research in biotechnology for food and agriculture at a level of $28.5 million dollars. In the same year national funding for Integrated Pest Management averaged about $7 million, most of which the Reagan Administration proposed to eliminate. It was only restored to the budget in a House committee. At the same time, the pesticide chemical manufacturers report that biological control measures will not replace pesticides in the nineties. The industry spends an average of $20,000,000 to synthesize one new chemical compound; and an average of 10 new pesticides are introduced per year (Storck 1987).

Reaching back 25 years, we are reminded of Carson's inflammatory critique of certain outstanding entomologists who were on the payroll of chemical companies and were leading advocates of chemical control. Would they bite the hand that feeds them, she had asked. "Knowing their bias, how much credence can we give to their protests that insecticides are harmless?" (Carson 1962, p. 229). The politics of science, for most research scientists, is a question of where the research action is, who has money and how to get it. The real politics of science, to use Carson's lexicon, or the real loyalties, to use Virginia Woolf's, has to do with questioning the values of and the risks of what work gets funded and refusing to sell your brains for money. On this—how and why an ecologically based agricultural paradigm can be overtaken so rapidly by the latest technical "hot handle" which has complex ecological impacts[5]—the symposium papers are silent.

In April 1963, CBS brought together many elements of the world aroused by *Silent Spring* in an hour-long television documentary, compiled from interviews with government and industry officials and scientists and Rachel Carson. I recently watched "The *Silent Spring* of Rachel Carson" for some critical perspective on the emerging biotechnologies in IPM, specifically the use of genetically engineered organisms in agricultural ecosystems.

---

5. *The New York Times* fell into this same pattern in a recent overview of insect control strategies ("Smarter Ways to Fight Pests," Editorial, November 14, 1988). The editorial calls chemical pesticides a "brutal technology"; integrated pest management, a "step forward"; and introducing pest-resistant genes in crop plants, a "most promising technique." The response to this editorial was vigorous (Letters to the Editor, December 5, 1988). Directors of biotechnology and agriculture policy for the National Wildlife Federation, Enviromental Defense Fund, and Audubon Society noted that the first major use of biotechnology in argriculture is herbicide-resistant crops which will expand the herbicide market and that questions of hazard must be answered before farmers "jump on another technical bandwagon." A fourth response, from the Indonesian government, described the success of the Indonesian IPM program. Rice is the staple of 170 million Indonesian people. Increased pesticide use over 10 years has caused an increase in rice pests. In 1986 Indonesia banned 57 types of pesticides and implemented IPM. Within three crops (18 months), farmers reduced pesticide application per crop from 4.5 to 0.5. Average rice yields rose from 6.1 tons to 7.4 tons per hectare. The government saved $50 million in pesticide subsidies and decreased ecological damage.

There was the chemical pesticide evangelist, Dr White-Stevens, who said Carson's warnings about the risks of pesticides were "unsupported by scientific evidence." The Surgeon General, the Commissioner of FDA, and the Secretary of Agriculture agreed with White-Stevens that chemical pesticides were saving the world from famine and pestilence. None knew of any pesticide injuries from proper use of pesticides; all felt protected by the system of permissible residues on food. The CBS commentator pointed out that there had been no tabulation of deaths from pesticides since 1958, and there were no accurate statistics on pesticide injuries since there was no reporting system. And Rachel Carson retorted that people have heard a great deal about the safety and benefits of pesticides, but very little about their hazards, failures, and inefficiencies. Not having the whole picture, she said she set about to remedy the balance in *Silent Spring*.

Like a latter-day White-Stevens, I thought, the advocates of the recombinant DNA technologies in agriculture charge that critics of biotechnologies are full of "unfounded conjecture about potential risks." And the same imbalance exists in government and industry literature on recombinant DNA products which existed in their literature on new synthetic pesticides. According to this literature, the biotechnologies' benefits to agriculture are legion; and their risks are low, although their hazards, failures, and inefficiencies are as yet undisclosed. Pesticide proponents defended their chemical products with ideals such as feeding the world and ridding it of plague and pestilence. Biotechnology proponents cloak theirs in the same altruistic mantle: greater crop yields and food grown in heretofore unarable land. They are even more bullish on the economic engines driving the biotechnologies forward. The American biotechnology market may reach $40 billion by the year 2000, they project. However, if the United States is slowed down by a overly rigorous regulatory process or public distrust, then Europe and Japan, who have the technical sophistication and are "expected to receive special regulatory treatment from their governments," may take the lead in the market (Kingsbury 1986).

As the CBS interviewer shifted his questions from general ones about why pesticides are used to more specific questions about what was unknown—questions which had emerged from the probing and demythologizing of *Silent Spring*—something changed. Except for White-Stevens, all of the government scientists and agency heads admitted that what they did not know about chemical pesticides—their persistence in nature, the contamination of groundwater and rivers, the long-term effects on wildlife and human genes and reproduction, increasing resistance to the new chemicals in insects—was critical, critical enough to relinquish their uncritical embrace of pesticides. It was apparent, watching their reluctant, flaccid admissions about the unexamined hazards of chemical pesticides, that without *Silent Spring* and its future sisterworks, government bureaucrats would offer only weak, paper protection against the waves of new chemical products and new technologies.

As one monotonal bureaucrat after another assured the 1963 television audience that pesticide excesses were a thing of the past and improvements were being made, I thought of Rachel Carson's admonition to the United States government. The mission to protect the environment was fragmented among many agencies, compartmentalized as one of many functions each agency had, and compromised by the government's largely uncritical support of pesticides. Environmental protection, which is the protection of nature and the health of human beings, ought to be unitive, uncompromised, and fully motivated by a respect for the integrity of nature and the right of humans to a healthy environment. The responsibility to uphold the integrity of nature and ourselves in nature should belong to an agency of ecologists, wildlife biologists, toxicologists and scientists primarily trained to care for nature and human health.

This lofty admonition was the mooring from which the Environmental Protection Agency was launched in 1970. Let us look next at the institution which was created from the legacy of Carson, and was intended to embody and enforce the ideal of environmental respect she aroused.

REFERENCES

Bateman, D. F. 1985. Toward a national biological impact assessment program for biotechnology. *Integrated Pest Management on Major Agricultural Systems*, Proceedings from a symposium sponsored by the Consortium for Integrated Pest Management and USDA/CSRS, R. E. Frisbie and P. L. Adkisson (eds.), pp. 680–691, Texas: Texas A&M University.

Carson, R. 1962. *Silent Spring*. Greenwich, Connecticut: Fawcett Publications.

Clemings, R. 1987. Bungling seen in Kern cancer study. *The Fresno Bee*, 3 April, B1.

Cole, L. C. 1962. Book review of *Silent Spring*. *Scientific American*, December, 173–180.

Coli, W. M. 1986/87. IPM: A report on University of Massachusetts Integrated Pest Management (IPM) programs. Amherst: Department of Entomology, University of Massachusetts.

Croft, B. A. 1985. Integrated pest management: The agricultural–environmental rationale. *Integrated Pest Management on Major Agricultural Systems*, Proceedings from a symposium sponsored by the Consortium for Integrated Pest Management and USDA/CSRS, R. E. Frisbie and P. L. Adkisson (eds.), p. 712, Texas: Texas A&M University.

Daly, M. 1984. *Pure Lust*. Boston, Massachusetts: Beacon Press.

The desolate year. 1962. *Monsanto Magazine*, October, 4–9.

Diamond, E. 1963. The myth of the "pesticide menace." *Saturday Evening Post*, 21 September, 17–18.

Dunlap, T. R. 1981. *DDT: Scientists, Citizens, and Public Policy*. Princeton, New Jersey: Princeton University Press.

Graham, F. Jr. 1970. *Since Silent Spring*. Greenwich, Connecticut: Fawcett Publications.

Hullar, T. and Gilchrist, D. 1985. Impact of biotechnology on IPM systems. *Integrated Pest Management on Major Agricultural Systems*, Proceedings from a symposium sponsored by the Consortium for Integrated Pest Management and USDA/CSRS, R. E. Frisbie and P. L. Adkisson (eds.), pp. 673–679, Texas: Texas A&M University.

Kingsbury, D. T. 1986. Regulating biotechnology: The White House policy. *EPA Journal*, **12**(8), 5.

Lacewell, R. D. and Masud, S. M. 1985. Economic and environmental implications of IPM. *Integrated Pest Management on Major Agricultural Systems*, Proceedings from a symposium sponsored by the Consortium for Integrated Pest Management and USDA/CSRS, R. E. Frisbie and P. L. Adkisson (eds.), pp. 79–80, Texas: Texas A&M University.

Moses, M. 1987a. Statement regarding farmworker health and safety. Los Angeles City Council, 20 March.

Moses, M. 1987b. Testimony prepared for the House Agricultural Committee, Subcommittee on Department Operations and Foreign Agriculture, Hearings on FIFRA Amendments, 17 June.

Storck, W. J. 1987. Pesticide growth slows. *C & EN*, 16 November, 38–39.

van den Bosch, R. 1980. *The Pesticide Conspiracy*. New York: Anchor Books.

Wellford, H. 1972. *Sowing the Wind*. New York: Grossman.

The Whitten Report. 1965. Effects, uses, control, and research of agricultural pesticides. A report by the surveys and investigation staff, House Appropriations Subcommittee on Agriculture.

Whitten, J. L. 1966. *That We May Live*. Princeton, New Jersey: D. Van Nostrand.

Woolf, V. 1938. *Three Guineas*. New York: Harcourt, Brace.

IV

IN THE SHADOW OF
SILENT SPRING:
THE ENVIRONMENTAL
PROTECTION AGENCY

EPA today may be said without exaggeration to be the extended shadow of
Silent Spring (Jack Lewis, EPA).

EPA is now a professional agency that has no environmental soul (Thomas
Jorling, Former EPA Assistant Administrator).

In September 1960 the Natural Resources Committee of the Democratic Advisory Council submitted a report, *Resources for the People*, to
Senator John Kennedy for his use in the 1960 presidential campaign. The
report advocated that national, state, and local governments "resume
positive leadership" in protection and conservation of the country's natural resources: water, fish, and wildlife; public parks, soil, forests, minerals, and energy. The earth is a sphere of finite soil, water, air, and raw
materials which people need to sustain health and a high standard of
living. We ought not, the report cautions, to deplete or ruin irreversibly
these resources for the sake of future generations.

With this utilitarian lens, the Committee saw the earth as a warehouse
stocked with chemical and physical resources to fulfill the health, industrial, defense, recreational, and aesthetic needs of human consumers.
Politicians were charged to conserve present supplies for future use, to
manage the store as good stewards.

Will there be enough pure water for home and industrial needs? Will there
be electricity enough to light America's homes, to lighten housework, and
to serve our industries at reasonable rates? Will we have sufficient fuel to
power our engines and vehicles and to heat our homes? Will there be

attractive, uncrowded recreation sites for our families? Are we as a nation doing all we can to insure the wise utilization of our resources? (National Resources Committee 1960, p. 1).

By 1962 Rachel Carson had finished examining the same evidence, and probed and pushed its significance to points unparalleled in industrial countries. In *Silent Spring* she moved readers beyond the conservationist mentality that something is only worth respecting and saving if we can use it as an economic resource, for sport, or for personal pleasure. Nature is older than we, distinct from our uses, and not a stockpile of static, developable ingredients. The "control of nature," she wrote, "was conceived in arrogance, born of the . . . age of biology and philosophy when it was supposed that nature exists for the convenience of man" (Carson 1962, p. 261). In a society habituated to viewing nature as a bountiful supermarket of resources stocked for human purposes, Carson elevated the natural world to a position of value and respect for itself, co-equal in meaning with that of human needs. She crystallized an ethic of the environment. At the same time that she restored an understanding of nature's intrinsic worth apart from human use, she warned that to pollute nature is to pollute ourselves, because we live in and depend upon nature. Perhaps those unmoved by another species rendered extinct by pollution, she wrote, could be aroused by increased human cancer from pollution.

The period of 1962 to 1970 witnessed the awakening of a social and political environmentalism. Questions of human and planetary survival became urgent and critical. So much so that, although the Nixon Administration was wracked by the Vietnam War and preoccupied with a recession-ridden economy, Nixon took some stopgap environmental action and set up a Cabinet-level Environmental Quality Council and a citizens' advisory committee in 1969. When critics charged that these gestures were "ceremonial" but meaningless, Nixon appointed a committee in December 1969 to evaluate whether there should be a separate environmental agency (Lewis 1985, pp. 6–7). At this same time Congress sent a bill known as the National Environmental Policy Act (NEPA) to him for signature.

The National Environmental Policy Act made the integrity of the environment a central value and a primary consideration in decisions on public projects. Its purposes were, paraphrasing its own language, to encourage harmony between humans and nature, to prevent or eliminate damage to the biosphere and human well-being, and to enrich our understanding of ecological systems and natural resources. It bound federal agencies to evaluate the impacts of their proposed projects on the environment and to identify all alternatives to a proposed action which would have less harmful impact on the environment. It created a forum, unprecedented in industrialized societies, in which a "progressive" public project, such as building a dam, erecting a shopping mall, or aerial spraying for mosquito control, could be challenged and altered or stopped because of irreversible environmental harm to a wetland or wildlife. This act contained some understanding of the value of nature for its own sake, not only for its usefulness to human projects. It has been considered the cornerstone of all environmental policy and regulation (Fairfax 1978).[1]

In this era of rancorous ideological dispute, public opinion was virtually unanimous on the need for a national environmental policy. President Nixon chose to sign the NEPA bill on 1 January 1970 as the "first official act of the decade." The following month he spoke of environmental action in his January State of the Union address and announced a 37-point environmental program. On 22 April, 20 million Americans participated in Earth Day. They walked into polluted rivers with scuba gear, demonstrated at corporate polluters' stockholders' meetings, and conducted peaceful actions in front of the Department of Interior.

That same April, a commission Nixon had appointed to consider the structure of environmental regulation recommended that a new independent agency was necessary for strong, comprehensive, environmental protection. They argued that existing agencies were biased toward their own "mission," whether it be agriculture, forestry, or another. An agency should be created for the sole purposes of setting and enforcing environmental standards, conducting environmental research, and recommending to the President new policies for environmental protection. In October, Nixon consolidated responsibility for environmental protection in a new agency by executive order. The responsibilities of the new agency—air pollution, water quality, solid waste management, pesticide registration and control, and radiation standards—were pieced together from various programs in the Department of Health, Education,

---

1. Fairfax considers that "NEPA has been a disaster for the environmental movement and the quest for environmental quality." It has turned activist citizens away from challenging government to reviewing tedious, rationalistic documents. Citizen participation has been domesticated into one dimension of the bureaucratic NEPA process.

While I agree with Fairfax's description of the danger for activists to be co-opted in the NEPA review process, I do not think the fault lies in the intent of NEPA. The pitfall of any organized and institutionalized group—no matter now lofty the ideal—is to get mired in the routine of data collection, administrative technicalities, paperwork, and the nitty-gritty of institutional life. One tension of any organized group—government, nonprofit agency, environmental coalition, feminist project—is how not to get stuck in the routine and shallow, how to always be moving in the innovative and deliberative realm. See the section on Question 2 in this chapter.

and Welfare; the Department of the Interior; the Department of Agriculture; and the Atomic Energy Commission.

Rachel Carson's concept of the environment as a single, interrelated web of soil, air, water, and all attendant wild and human creatures which rely on these for life and well-being, materialized in the creation of the Environmental Protection Agency (EPA). Its sole purpose was "the protection, development, and enhancement of the total environment." EPA was charged to "view the environment as a whole" and to treat "air pollution, water pollution, and solid wastes as different forms of a single problem" (Lewis 1985, p. 9).

EPA opened in a small suite of offices at 20th and L Streets in northwest Washington, DC on December 2, 1970. Five days later the first Administrator, William Ruckelshaus, announced to the Second International Clean Air Congress that he and EPA were starting with "no obligation to promote commerce or agriculture." Rather he envisioned the mission of EPA to be the "development of an environmental ethic" (Lewis 1985, p. 9). In his nomination hearings, Ruckelshaus had been asked about the Agency's independence from industrial interests by Senator Edmund Muskie, who had introduced a bill to establish a federal environmental agency. The future Administrator said that in situations where environmental protection was in opposition with economic development, he would act for the environment.

Sprung from the ethical moorings of *Silent Spring* at a time of worldwide social and political activism, EPA has always attracted environmentalists who might otherwise disdain working for the federal government. Of the 14,000 people working in EPA in 1985, nearly 2,000 had been there since its inception. A handful of the 2,000 were interviewed about their most memorable work at EPA in a 15th anniversary issue of the *EPA Journal*. The replies fell primarily into two categories: enforcement of environmental laws against industry, and research on the effects of pollution in order to develop environmental protection standards. The enforcement actions resulted in closure of open-hearth furnaces and coke ovens which were causing massive air pollution, issuing restrictive discharge permits to the major polluters of surface waters, and initiating and testifying in the enforcement action and civil penalty process of EPA's first pesticide case. The research work included developing computer models of the Great Lakes, which resulted in EPA's identifying and limiting phosphorus levels in the Great Lakes; studies of thermal changes on lake fish to establish limits for industrial discharges affecting water temperature; and studies of the ecological impacts of wastewater discharged into the ocean, in order to enforce the adoption of advanced wastewater treatment (Popkins 1985).

What is most "memorable" for these EPA veterans is focused and tangible work: acting against pollution by aggressive enforcement of environmental laws against industry and practicing science which is nature-centered. Both the research and the environmental enforcement work demonstrate a will for ecological solutions; the people interviewed expressed deep satisfaction when their work achieved environmental protection. However, the question asked of a dozen environmental scientists and engineers, "What is your most memorable work at EPA?" casts a single, flattering spotlight upon the Agency, and a retrospective one at that. It gives only a single and a limited measure of EPA's faithfulness to its mission.

Over the past two decades the original activist passion for a world unendangered by pollution has generated a profession of environmental lawyers, scientists, engineers, analysts, and public relations people. A federal bureaucracy has grown out of EPA's original commitment to develop an ethic of the environment. One must ask if Carson's legacy of a passion for nature and for an ecological existence in nature is largely a good memory, a series of accomplishments to look back on, or if it is still a living reality in the day-to-day workings of the institution built on that legacy.

In the same 15th anniversary issue, Jack Lewis wrote that "EPA today may be said without exaggeration to be the extended shadow of Rachel Carson" (Lewis 1985, p. 6). He was intending to express a still-vital historical and ethical connection between Carson and EPA. But his choice of metaphor betrays the double-sided nature of that connection. A shadow is an imperfect and faint representation, an attenuated form. It is not its own source but a reflected image. Thomas Jorling, a former Assistant Administrator at EPA, was asked his opinion of the Agency's fidelity to its mission. "EPA is now a professional agency that has no environmental soul . . . [and] its performance will be consistent with the political ideology of the [Reagan] Administration," he replied (Cahn and Cahn 1985). In other words, EPA is not its own source but a reflected image of the Administration; it is a shadow of its former self. EPA's historical link with Carson is there; the ethical one is not.

The beginnings of EPA were charged with a lofty idealism. The mission to protect and defend people and nature from pollution was clear. The agency was not created to promote (or protect) agriculture or commerce nor to mediate between industry and environmentalists. Its purpose was to create an ethic of the environment. Does that clarity and loyalty persist today? If not, why not?

When ideals such as the integrity of nature and the right of people to live unendangered in the world are institutionalized, the complexities of institutional existence enter in. While, in theory, autonomous from in-dustrial and political interests, EPA has its own internal politics and interests. One can gauge this by the way certain laws and programs gain in prominence and resources while others decline to soporific pa-perwork exercises. Some people use the institution primarily to build their own careers and agendas, the stuff out of which is constructed another politic of the institution. The personal power politics may be immiscible with environmental idealism. The tension which results as easily erodes or edges out environmental idealism as it challenges the banality of the politics. In most cases it siphons off energy from the original purpose of the institution.

Let us pose some additional questions to EPA, questions which are analytic, rather than ones which stir up nostalgic moments. In an-swering these questions, we will assess EPA's eminence in sustaining its legacy: an ethic of the environment.

1. There was an abundance of laws and regulations written and prom-ulgated in the wake of *Silent Spring*. Do more environmental laws guarantee more abundant protection of nature and people against pollution?
   (a) Can we presume that if a program exists to enforce a law, such as the pesticide law, that the original analysis and vitality which inspired the law is *de facto* present?
   (b) The hazardous waste laws, Superfund and the Resource Conser-vation and Recovery Act (RCRA), receive more resources, political interest, and media attention than older laws, such as the toxic substances and pesticide laws. Does the trendiness and media hype over newer laws and programs cause older and equally, if not more, significant ones to be ignored and decline in impor-tance?
   (c) When laws become difficult to enforce because they challenge a fundamental, entrenched freedom and interest group, have they not been reduced to their administrative paperwork aspects, such as label and manifest violations or reporting requirements, in place of their more rigorous requirements, such as banning and restricting use of chemicals?
   (d) It has been said that the fate of most laws designed to protect the environment is that they are used as rigidly against creative op-tions as against harmful ones. In time, it becomes easier for those enforcing environmental laws to use them to prevent projects and ideas from taking effect than to permit, approve, or create solu-tions. What are the reasons and mechanisms for this?
2. As the ideal of environmental protection becomes institutionalized,

does the life of the institution, including the management infrastructure and internal politics, compete with and displace the original mission and ideals? Does institutional structure devitalize the mission so that the environment becomes, like the institution, a system for professionals to manage and regulate? Having gained what the current administrator of EPA, Lee Thomas, calls "administrative and psychological maturity," has EPA lost touch with the vitality of nature and environmental protection?

    (a) EPA was created as an independent Agency, not tied to industrial or agricultural interests. Does its apparent independence from economic and political interest groups guarantee that EPA is insulated from false loyalties, Administration politics, and conflicts of interest?

3. *Silent Spring* focused EPA on pesticides, on their carcinogenic, mutagenic, and reproductive effects on wildlife and humans, and on the interconnections of rivers, soil, and groundwater with toxics put into the environment. What other environmental problems have emerged as critical points of focus for EPA today, as pesticides did by 1970? Twenty-five years after *Silent Spring*, are there major new insights, new analysis, or fundamentally different problems that are critical to environmental protection?

The questions about the presence or erosion of vitality, the illusion or reality of environmental protection, the future directions of analysis and work, and the nature of power and loyalties in the allegedly autonomous agency form the skeletal structure of the ensuing analysis of EPA. My purpose is to examine and hold the Agency to the standard of passion and politic set by Rachel Carson in *Silent Spring*. There lie its moorings. Hopefully, the Agency can recall this and can trust the paradox, that only in holding fast to its moorings in ecology can it go forward. Otherwise, disconnected from its original integrity, it will shift with the prevailing political winds and drift into being another faceless bureaucracy with political appointees at the top, career bureaucrats in middle management, and frustrated environmentalists at the bottom. It will be more benign than the other bureaucracies—because of its mission—but it will be no less banal.

1. DO MORE LAWS MEAN MORE PROTECTION?

Today EPA is the most powerful regulatory agency in the United States government, if we define power as the scope of the Agency's authority to regulate industry and municipalities. The breadth of its regulations is both a symbol and a consequence of the ubiquity of the environment, and man-made pollution. There is not one cubic centimeter of air, one milliliter of water, one hectare of ground, one meal of food grown in soil or harvested from the sea which is not touched and contaminated by pollution. One writer has described the all-encompassing regulatory framework of EPA accordingly:

> Federal law requires the EPA Administrator to make decisions that affect everything from the cost and performance of a new Chevrolet to the way a farm community in Oklahoma disposes its sewage. Decisions that determine whether children in urban areas will breathe debilitating lead fumes and whether fish will survive in the water of rural lakes and streams (Lash *et al*. 1984, p. 15).

Throughout the seventies and eighties the Agency promulgated regulations to protect air, rivers, lakes, the ocean, and drinking water; to control the manufacture and distribution of toxic substances; to require virtually every industrial company in the United States to handle and dispose of hazardous waste safely; and to clean up every major abandoned hazardous waste site in the country.

With the Clean Air Act, EPA limits air pollution from over 150 million cars, trucks, buses, and over 20,000 factories, power plants and other major stationary sources of pollution. The Clean Water Act regulates pollution at close to 100,000 different industrial sources. The Resource Conservation and Recovery Act (RCRA) enables EPA to regulate the storage, treatment, and disposal of the 500 billion pounds a year of hazardous waste generated by industry. The new RCRA amendments require industry to minimize the quantities of hazardous waste generated in production of industrial products; they discourage, by the stringency of their technical requirements, the proliferation of hazardous waste landfills. Superfund has created a fund, from taxing industry, to study and clean up the major abandoned toxic waste dumps in the country, of which the estimate is currently greater than 10,000. EPA is responsible for evaluating all pesticides and several thousand new chemicals each year, as well as the tens of thousands of chemicals and pesticides in use when the laws were passed, for their safety. This authority also includes the power to ban a product from manufacture and distribution in the United States on the grounds that no matter what its "beneficial use," it poses too great a danger to humans and the environment.

If we partition the environment into all its elements—air, water, soil, wetlands, river, stream, ocean, wildlife, aquatic life, and human life—and match a law with each element, we appear to have a comprehensive set of federal laws protecting humans and nature against pollution. As those who use sports' analogies to explain the world would say, all the bases are covered. However, this is too simplistic a calculus by which to judge the efficacy of environmental law. The efficacy of law comes from its enforcement, and more subtly, from its intentionality. By intentionality, I mean its resolve, its purpose. This more elemental aspect of environmental law—intentionality—is one key to why initially dynamic environmental programs become static and, to paraphrase Jorling, soulless.

In order to answer whether more laws mean more protection, and the subset of related questions, let us examine the Federal Insecticide, Fungicide, and Rodenticide Act (FIFRA). This is one of the oldest laws enforced by EPA; and, being the pesticide act, it is the one most directly addressed by *Silent Spring*. Except for the Toxic Substances Control Act (TSCA), other environmental laws do not fundamentally control or challenge the generation of toxic substances. They address the waste created from making or using toxic substances. They authorize EPA to regulate how much of various waste pollutants industry can discharge into air, water or soil and to establish standards for storage, transport, and disposal of hazardous waste. FIFRA and TSCA empower EPA to judge the safety of chemicals and to prohibit or ban them from manufacture and use.

The Federal Insecticide, Fungicide, and Rodenticide Act

In his report on chemicals and food safety, Harrison Wellford observed that "it is a rule of regulatory agencies that they betray the public trust less by what they do than by what they fail to do" (Wellford 1972, p. 344). His point of reference was the 20 years which elapsed before the Pesticides Registration Division in the Department of Agriculture initiated its first action in 1967 to recall a dangerous pesticide.

The original federal pesticide law was enacted in 1947. It required that pesticides be registered by the Secretary of Agriculture before being marketed, to ensure they were effective and not acutely dangerous. Registration is basically a license for specific uses of a pesticide (e.g. a particular insecticide is registered for use on a specific food crop). The history of its enforcement demonstrates that the original pesticide law was a law to check product performance, not to protect public health.

In 1970 responsibility for administering the federal pesticide law was transferred from the Department of Agriculture to the newly created Environmental Protection Agency. In 1972 Congress passed a new federal pesticide law to which amendments were added in 1975, 1978, and 1980. The import of the new law and amendments was to refocus the law onto the safety of pesticides and to make the registration process for chemical pesticides more rigorous by requiring industry to test their chemical products for their potential to cause cancer, birth defects, and genetic mutations. EPA could also require environmental fate studies, such as the chemical's solubility and potential to migrate into groundwater, as part of the registration process. In FIFRA, EPA is given the authority to approve all new pesticides before they can be sold and used, as well as all new uses for old pesticides. EPA is, further, required by another law, the Federal Food, Drug, and Cosmetic Act, to establish tolerances ("safe" amounts of residues) for pesticides which remain in or on food or animal feed. As for the thousands of pesticides in use by the time FIFRA was enacted, they were to be reexamined and re-registered by EPA as if they were new pesticides, since none had been tested for their health and environmental effects by the new, more protective standards. By law, then, EPA is authorized to evaluate every pesticide in use or proposed to be used, by weighing its benefits to agriculture against the harm caused by residues left on food which would be eaten by animals and humans, or residues left in the environment. Those pesticides judged to cause unreasonable risk or harm to humans or wildlife are to be restricted from use or banned altogether under the authority of FIFRA.

EPA was given the formidable task of reviewing 35,000 pesticides in use when the 1972 law was passed, of establishing new tolerances for every pesticide which left residues on food, and of registering new pesticides. In 1972 Congress mandated that EPA complete re-registration of all old pesticides by 1976. By 1978, Congress eliminated the deadline from FIFRA because it was uncertain how long this task of determining the safety of pesticides in use would take. Instead EPA was required to accomplish this work "as expeditiously as possible." The 1978 amendments also sanctioned a chemical-by-chemical rather than product-by-product approach to the registration process. That is, EPA could assess the approximately 600 basic active pesticide ingredients common to the now 50,000 pesticide products, in lieu of evaluating each pesticide product. Also, a special review process was established in 1975 by EPA which would enable the Agency to conduct a rapid, detailed risk/benefit analysis of any pesticide in use, which was found to be uniquely toxic. This would enable EPA to take rapid regulatory action including canceling some or all uses, imposing use restrictions, and requiring labeling changes.

Recently, EPA's pesticide program was studied by the Government Accounting Office at the request of Congress (U.S. Government Accounting Office 1986). This study found that EPA has failed to evaluate the safety of the majority of chemical pesticides in use and those which remain as residues on food. At its current pace, EPA will not finish its review and reassessment of the safety of pesticides in use until well into the twenty-first century. Until this is completed, we will not know the full environmental and health risks of the 50,000 older pesticides which are still in use, primarily in agriculture.

As of March 31, 1986 EPA had not completed a single final reassessment on any of the 600 active pesticide ingredients. Preliminary assessments were completed on 124 of the active ingredients. This means that the data on a chemical were catalogued, data gaps identified, and requests for missing or inadequate health and environmental studies were made to pesticide firms. Some restrictions on 60 percent of the 124 chemicals were imposed.

From the beginning of the special review program in 1975 through October 1985, EPA completed 32 special reviews. As a result, five active ingredients were canceled for all uses; 26 active ingredients were restricted in use. The review process, intended to give a rapid review for chemicals found to be more toxic than originally realized, has generally taken two to six years. During the period of review, the chemical stays in use.

The registration process is further complicated by the recognition that many "inert" ingredients in pesticides—those chemicals added to affect the texture, solubility, and other physical characteristics—are themselves toxic. This was ignored when EPA established a review method which examined "active" ingredients but overlooked "inert" ingredients. EPA has since identified 100 inert ingredients with known or suspected toxicity and another 800 for which there is insufficient toxicological data. Inert ingredients comprise the majority of the pesticide; they are also in use while their hazard is undetermined.

There are two glaring failures in the pesticide program. One is a failure in enforcement or regulatory rigor: the review of, and protection from, toxic pesticides has been slow and minimal. EPA has failed less by what they do than by what they do not do. One overt reason for this failure is a lack of resources. The resources given to the pesticide program by the Reagan Administration in 1986 were 591 full-time position equivalents (this is "people" in bureaucratese) compared to 829 at the program's peak funding in 1980. Yet, problems which have arisen since 1980—pesticide contamination of groundwater, the toxicity of inert ingredients, the regulation of new, genetically engineered pesticides—have also required FIFRA program staff scientists already in short supply for the re-registration process.

But there is also a lack of felt urgency at the top. Asked if EPA "can do its job on its current tight budget," the present Administrator Lee Thomas was "confident we have enough to do the job assigned us." He "seriously doubts we could efficiently use any more" (Interview 1985). Politically, a most expedient response; ecologically, an irresponsible one.

Although EPA was created to be independent from industrial and commercial interests, it is fettered by unreal loyalties to the political ideology of the Reagan Administration.

The second failure is one of intentionality. The pesticide law and EPA's enforcement of the law offer no fundamental challenge to the mindset which became entrenched midcentury in America, that chemical pesticides are essential to agriculture. Neither the law, nor the regulatory program to enforce the law, show more than token commitment to ecological alternatives to chemical-intensive agriculture. Rather they function to register chemicals, albeit slowly, so that the chemical industry can be assured of markets, and farmers can have a steady supply of chemicals with no incentive to change to more ecological farming. And people are fed what Carson called "little tranquilizing pills" of assurances: if a registration program exists, then chemicals used on food must have undergone registration; and if chemicals are registered, they must be safe.

In an interview about the state of the pesticide program, EPA officials express much more frustration with people's distrust of synthetic chemicals than chagrin with their own pace of pesticide registration. The alternatives to exclusive farming with chemicals—integrated pest control, biological controls, and organic farming—are treated as minor tributaries to the mainstream of chemical agriculture. At the same time, the pesticide program administrators talk with strange zest about the newest alternative, biotechnology, which "may soon *revolutionize* American agriculture." (Why was IPM never so subsidized with Agency enthusiasm?) Only as an afterthought are the potential risks of bioengineering technologies in agriculture, which may be large and even "global in scale" (Moore 1984).

The failure of EPA to do more—to review and remove toxic pesticides from use more rapidly and to promote ecological solutions in agriculture—is a failure rooted in the pro-chemical pesticide bias of the pesticide law itself, a bias which has seeped into and infected EPA's enforcement program. There is no intention in the law to minimize the use of chemical pesticides and to maximize the use of ecological agriculture. Rather the law provides a safe venue for chemicals to come onto or stay on the market in a liability-conscious era.

Let us examine the intentionality of the pesticide law from two perspectives. The first is the consequence of EPA's first attempt to restrict a pesticide, DDT. The second is an analysis of the provisions of the Federal Insecticide, Fungicide, and Rodenticide Act. Both will expose the structural failures of what ought to have been a critical, ecological program. In this way, we will answer the question of whether more laws mean more protection.

DDT, the chemical dichlorodiphenyltrichloroethane, was first synthesized by a German chemist in 1874. Its ability to kill insects was discovered in 1939 by the Swiss chemist Paul Müller, who was awarded the
Nobel Prize in medicine and physiology in 1949 for this. In one of its first
field uses, DDT was dusted on people in Naples, Italy, to kill body lice in
1943–44. Subsequently it was extolled for preventing an epidemic of
typhus. The drama of this alleged success was the springboard for its use
after the war.

The typhus epidemic, writes historian of science Thomas Dunlap,
had been broken by the time DDT became available. It was the first
epidemic of its kind to be arrested by public health measures. There were
two reasons for this unique success. First, a case-reporting system was
devised which enabled public health officers to find and treat the majority of people exposed to the lice and thus break the chain of infection.
Second, a new dusting technique, using the botanical pesticide
pyrethrin, was employed which was more efficient and effective than
former methods. DDT, however, received full credit (Dunlap 1981, p. 62).
"It came home in 1945 on a wave of publicity and high hopes. It was the
atomic bomb of insecticides, the killer of killers, the harbinger of a new
age in insect control" (Dunlap 1981, p. 3).

With the postwar recycling of surplus warplanes, chemicals, spray
equipment and techniques into "peacetime" uses and the chemical
companies' quest for new markets, DDT was aerially sprayed on American crops, wetlands, towns, and forests routinely. By 1954 the Public
Health Service found that every meal sampled in a study of restaurant
and institutional meals contained DDT (Carson 1962, p. 161). Carson
would later write, "DDT is now so universally used that in most minds
the product takes on the harmless aspect of the familiar" (Carson 1962,
p. 29). Her task was to take the familiar and to enable people to see it
differently. What people saw before *Silent Spring* was mosquitos and
other "pests" killed when sprayed with DDT. What Carson showed
them was its ecological crudeness:

- DDT killed pests and beneficial insects alike.
- Pesticide-resistant strains of insects were developing.
- Increased dosages of pesticides and new pesticides were being used in
  what became a chemical war on nature.
- DDT was entering soil, groundwater, streams, and wetlands and
  bioaccumulating in animal and human tissue through the food chain.
- There were documented imminent hazards to wildlife from DDT.
- There was a threat of degenerative changes in human beings from the
  "small" amounts of pesticides stored cumulatively in the body.

Silent Spring focused national attention on DDT. Four governmental committees which studied DDT in depth between 1963 and 1969 recommended that it be phased out from use. The Presidential Science Advisory Committee declared that the national goal should be the elimination of persistent toxic pesticides. The federal Mrak Commission recommended to the Secretary of Health, Education, and Welfare that all uses of DDT not essential to public health be eliminated by 1971. The United Farm Workers struck and boycotted grape growers in their campaign to have DDT banned in the vineyards.

The Environmental Defense Fund (EDF), founded in 1967 to educate the public through legal action and to build a body of environmental case law, obtained the first temporary injunction against DDT's use. Seizing the opportunity of a hearing to decide if, according to the water pollution laws of Wisconsin, DDT were a pollutant, EDF established the best-documented case yet for the toxicity of DDT. Next, EDF petitioned the Secretaries of Agriculture and Health, Education, and Welfare (then still responsible for enforcing FIFRA) to suspend registration of DDT, start cancellation proceedings, and immediately lower the tolerance of DDT in human foods to zero. This began a process of hearings which culminated in EPA's final ban of DDT in 1972.

Wellford's summary of industry's and science's offensive against the movement to ban DDT conveys the radical threat inherent in the move to restrict one of tens of thousands of chemicals:

> The DDT fight had unleashed a virulent form of the pesticide "McCarthyism" first directed at Rachel Carson. Dr. Max Sobelman of the Montrose Chemical Corporation of California charges DDT critics with being anticapitalistic; Louis McLean of Velsicol Chemical Corporation suggests that they are "preoccupied with the subject of sexual potency." Dr. Wayland Hayes, Professor of Biochemistry, Vanderbilt University, suggests they are aiding the machinations of foreign agents; Dr. White-Stevens charges that they may be responsible for the death of millions from malaria; and *Barron's* has accused them of plotting world famine—despite the fact that banning DDT in the United States will have no legal effect on overseas shipments and that DDT critics make an exception for use of DDT to control epidemics (Wellford 1972, p. 333).

The entire, unprecedented process of placing DDT on trial and banning it was a victory on two grounds, as a symbol and as an ecological measure, although this latter has been imperfect at best. The symbolism operated at several levels. The "father of modern pesticides" was defeated, so might the sons be. Environmental risks could be judged to be more significant than economic gain from a pesticide. For environmental groups, the ban on DDT was a test of EPA's will. EPA acted on its mandate to embody an ethic of the environment, and this empowered environmentalism. However, as an ecological and public health measure, EPA's final ruling was mixed.

- DDT was "cancelled" rather than "suspended," a decision which allowed for DDT to continue to be sold while administrative and legal proceedings took place to determine the cancellation.
- Cancellation applied only to products manufactured after the effective date of ban. DDT stockpiled in warehouses and on storeshelves before the effective date of the ban stayed in circulation.
- Initially DDT was cancelled for only certain of its some 300 registered uses. Manufacturers were required merely to change labels on containers, not to remove containers of DDT from stores. This afforded no guarantee that the cancelled uses would be enforced.
- The final ban did not prohibit manufacture and sale of DDT to other countries. Banning in the United States would stimulate an international traffic in DDT. Global ecosystems would become contaminated. DDT-contaminated food would be imported back into the United States.
- The ban on DDT could be preempted by EPA approving emergency uses of DDT.

Preempted it was. In *The Pesticide Conspiracy*, entomologist Robert van den Bosch traces the weakening of EPA's authority and enforcement of FIFRA after an initial victory, to the assault on the Agency by chemical, agricultural, and commercial forestry interests in the wake of EPA's ban on DDT. Advocates of DDT took advantage of the provision in the decision that permits use of DDT in the event of a public health crisis or impending economic disaster. One example, he cites, is the emergency use of DDT against the tussock moth in 1974.

There was an extensive outbreak of the Douglas fir tussock moth in the Pacific Northwest in the early seventies. Its larvae feed on the needles of the Douglas firs, sometimes stripping and killing the trees. The problem is age-old, and aggravated by "high grade" logging; but most trees withstand attack and grow with renewed vigor. The US Forest Service, the Department of Agriculture, and Southern congressionals joined together to force EPA to allow use of DDT. Congressman Poage (Democrat–Texas), chair of the House Agricultural Committee, announced that if EPA failed to approve a Forest Service request for the use of DDT against the tussock moth, the committee would immediately seek House action on a bill to strip EPA of its authority to regulate use of the compound. EPA conceded. The Forest Service saw to it that its dissenting researchers did not testify at EPA hearings on the subject. The tussock moth population had been suffering a natural collapse when the

Forest Service started its massive DDT spray program. The consequences of the spray program read like so many of the case studies cited in *Silent Spring*:

1. $3 million to spray 427,000 acres of phantom pests;
2. thousands of birds and other creatures killed;
3. 18,000 cattle and several hundred sheep rendered unmarketable by DDT contamination;
4. compensation to the Coleville Indians whose cattle were unmarketable;
5. warnings posted not to consume meat of game animals;
6. neglect of research on DDT alternatives while money was poured into this program;
7. emboldening of pest controllers for other forest uses;
8. maneuvering to increase the agricultural use of DDT (van den Bosch 1980, pp. 96–103).

In addition to exploiting loopholes such as the emergency exemption provision in the DDT decision, these pro-pesticide forces used political maneuvers to intimidate and clutter the regulatory framework of FIFRA in order to enfeeble its enforcement by EPA. They foresaw that the ban on DDT would have a domino effect and result in the banning of other pesticides. The toxicological grounds for banning DDT were only stronger for banning other chlorinated organics. The original success in banning the manufacture and distribution of a chemical is the most important one because it is a wedge that cracks open the fortress of free enterprise. Van den Bosch writes:

> Almost immediately following Russell Train's (then EPA Administrator) announcements of the aldrin-dieldrin, chlordane and heptachlor bannings, a fierce barrage of complaints, criticisms, and threats began to pour in on EPA from a multitude of directions. Secretary of Agriculture, Earl Butz, the ag mags, the rural media, certain of the urban politicians all rained grenades on the embattled agency (van den Bosch 1980, p. 99).

The result of the onslaught was concession under duress by EPA to open up the review of pesticides for registration or cancellation to a "broader" constituency than just the pro-environmental agency. A Pesticide Policy Advisory Committee was formed and later an amendment to FIFRA was passed by Congress which gave the Secretary of Agriculture an advisory role in the cancellation of pesticides. The Pesticide Policy Advisory Committee was established to "advise, consult with and make recommendations" (in fact, watchdog and police) on EPA's use and enforcement of FIFRA. Its members were to be appointed from pro-pesticide groups such as farm organizations and other pesticide user groups,

and the pesticide chemical industry, as well as from environmental pro-
tections organizations, the public, health experts, and State governmental agencies.

The amendment added to FIFRA, HR 8841, was co-authored by the
chair of the House Agricultural Committee. It provided for review and
comment on the part of the Secretary of Agriculture on any EPA proposed or final regulations, thus giving a role in pesticide regulation and
cancellation decisions to the Department whose pro-pesticide hands
they were originally in. While the Secretary of Agriculture is not given
veto power, the effect of this regulation, van den Bosch concludes, is to
cause delays in any of EPA's pesticide-regulating actions save those in-
volving grossly apparent and imminent danger to human health. More
important, the potential of political reprisal upon EPA for a controversial
decision was writ large with the passage of this amendment. That potential, no doubt, had the effect of undermining EPA's confidence in its own
autonomy with regards to the most controversial decisions about human
health and the environment.

If there were a symbolic power in EPA's banning DDT, it was short-
lived. In 1977 Daniel Zwerdling, an environmental journalist, wrote,
"Rachel Carson would surely weep if she were alive today" (Zwerdling
1977, p. 15). Pesticide use had increased two and one-half times in the 15
years since 1962. With DDT and a handful of other chlorinated hydrocarbons restricted from use, farmers sprayed the insecticide toxaphene, a
strongly suspected carcinogen, in greater quantity than all of the banned
and restricted chemicals used together. The USDA was predicting that
farmers would spray eight times as much herbicide on corn, and nine
times as much herbicide on soybeans, by 1978 as in 1964. Pesticide
demand was expected to increase with the latest trend in agribusiness:
"no-till farming." Applying 50 percent more pesticides per acre than they
already used, farmers would rely on chemicals rather than tractors to
control weeds, insects, and disease. The USDA estimated that by the
year 2000, almost half of the cropland in America would be managed by
the no-till method (Zwerdling 1977, p. 15).

"Rachel Carson, where are you?" asked *The Amicus Journal* 20 years
after *Silent Spring*. In those 20 years, evidence had accumulated that
many pesticides cause cancer and birth defects. Agricultural chemicals
had been found in groundwater in all agricultural states. Health studies
confirmed that virtually all U.S. Americans had a host of carcinogenic
chemicals stored in their fat tissue. Farmers were losing the same percentage and, in some cases, double the crops to insects as were lost
before synthetic pesticide use. Only a handful of chemicals had been
banned by the government, and almost none in the true sense of ban:
eliminating from use altogether. Usually when a chemical is "banned"

by EPA, some uses are regulated; some applications restricted; others are allowed. Although DDT had been "banned" in 1972, nearly 50 million pounds were being produced in the United States each year and exported to foreign nations ("Rachel Carson, where are you?" 1983).

In 1986 *Newsweek* reported that although the persistent compounds like DDT were replaced with nonpersistent pesticides, some of the new pesticides are more mobile, more soluble, and more toxic. Seventeen pesticides have been found in the groundwater of 23 states. At least 447 species of insects and mites are resistant to some pesticide, compared with seven resistant ones before World War II. Twenty of the 447 are immune to all pesticides in use ("*Silent Spring* revisited" 1986).

Banning certain persistent pesticides is essentially insignificant if there is no change in pesticide policy or use, concluded Zwerdling: "Focusing on individual pesticides . . . is essentially a waste of time. . . . The problem is not one or ten or even fifty pesticides. The problem is the entire pesticide industry itself" (Zwerdling 1977, p. 16).

While a handful of synthetic chemicals have been banned, chemical farming, dependent on the use of herbicides and pesticides, has increased, with "no-till" farming opening a vast new market for herbicides. Zwerdling traces a spiralling dependency on herbicide use, once the habit is established, much as Carson did with insecticides. As farmers eliminate the more easy-to-kill weeds with an herbicide, more difficult-to-control weeds are becoming prevalent. He points to a terrible irony. Just as American commercial farming is rushing toward increased dependency on chemicals—herbicides in this case—research supported by EPA, USDA, and the National Science Foundation in integrated pest management (IPM) and organic farming has yielded such promising results.

Why then is a more biologically oriented science and economy of farming not flourishing? Zwerdling blames the collective social, political, and economic forces of the farmers, the petrochemical industry, and major agribusiness corporations. Chemicals give a control over nature, however short-lived and a-ecological. They are profitable, since their total ecological and human health costs are not calculated into their cost or the cost of farming with them. He would agree with van den Bosch that the immense political power of the agricultural–industrial complex has intimidated and disemboldened the EPA in enforcing FIFRA in such a way as to discourage pesticide use.

After an early challenge to insect eradiction by chemical warfare and a compromise victory with DDT and a few other persistent pesticides, the pesticide program has drifted into being the quietest and least notable EPA program. It collates immense piles of paperwork in establishing files on chemicals; but it does not challenge or redirect agriculture to more ecological alternatives. Why this is so is as much the fault of the law as the enforcement of it by a disemboldened agency. As law, FIFRA has no ecological vision nor "intentionality."

"Like any forty-year-old who pretends to be eighteen, FIFRA is fundamentally dishonest," Natural Resources Defense Council Senior Attorney Janet Hathaway told the Entomological Society of America on the 40th anniversary of FIFRA. "It is not what it purports to be. FIFRA is not primarily a statute which protects human health and the environment" (Hathaway 1987b). It is preoccupied with how to get chemical pesticides registered with as little social and economic costs to the manufacturer as possible, and to buffer the chemical industry against any recall of hazardous chemicals. FIFRA's cornerstone is the belief that chemical pesticides are necessary for abundant agriculture. The predisposition toward chemicals and pesticides and the softness toward the chemical manufacturing industry is manifest in numerous provisions of the law:

Approval of Registration, Section 3(c)(5) Summary: The law will not deny registering a chemical because one or more which achieves the same results already exists on the market. Lack of essentiality will not be a criterion for denying registration of any pesticide.

The law could have been intended to curb the proliferation of poisons which duplicate each other, by conditioning registration on the need for the pesticide. Instead it normalizes and protects duplicative pesticides. Access to the market through the registration process is the primary purpose of the statute registration procedures, not protection of human health and the environment, by minimization of duplicative pesticides.

Registration Under Special Circumstances, Section 3(c)(7)(c) Summary: The law allows conditional use of a pesticide by an industry "for a period reasonably sufficient for the generation and submission of required data." The data are health and environmental data necessary to evaluate the safety of the chemical pesticide.

Without knowing its toxicity, the Administrator can allow conditional use of a new pesticide in order to test its toxicity. This provision allows EPA to test chemicals on people and nature. The net effect of this prejudice in the law for the chemical industry is to make a mockery of EPA's mission, "the development of an environmental ethic."

Registration of Pesticides, Section 3(c) Summary: The law places no deadline on the Agency to re-register all pesticides being used at the time the law was enacted in 1972. It merely requires that re-registration shall be accomplished "in the most expeditious manner possible."

Without a deadline, and without a provision to make the enormous review process finance itself, EPA has languished in this most important responsibility. According to *The Amicus Journal*, "about 80 percent of all pesticides sold today in the United States have not been examined sufficiently for their ability to cause cancer" ("Rachel Carson, where are you?" 1983). The lack of deadline has enabled industry to sell, and farmers to use, untested pesticides for many years longer than they should have been able to.

Public Participation, Section 3(c)(2) Summary: The Administrator shall make available to the public the data "he or she deems relevant to his decision" in registering a pesticide.

The law does not allow for public participation in the registration of pesticides, through permitting people to review and comment on data submitted in support of a pesticide prior to EPA approval. Rather the public is notified of the Administrator's decision on a pesticide and only then provided with scientific information he or she deems relevant. This is the most closed environmental decision-making in government.

Currently, there is no "citizen suit" provision under FIFRA, while citizen suits are permissible under 12 other federal environmental statutes. Citizens cannot go to court to force the government to enforce the pesticide law or to correct governmental violations of the law. Citizen suits have proven to be an essential enhancement of EPA's limited and overburdened enforcement authority (Natural Resources Defense Council 1987).

Cancellation of Registered Pesticide, Section 6(e)(1) Summary: The Administrator may permit the sale and use of remaining stock of cancelled pesticides.

Again, out of consideration for the costs of cancellation to industry, this provision allows the Administrator to soften the impact on industry of cancelling their chemical products and to permit the sale of dangerous pesticides. If the pesticides are so hazardous that EPA has cancelled some or all of their uses, how can EPA then permit industry to continue using them on food until their pesticide supplies are used up?

Indemnities, Section 15 Summary: If EPA finds that a pesticide is too hazardous, and suspends or cancels its registration, EPA must pay the pesticide maker the retail value of all remaining stocks of pesticide. EPA must store and dispose of pesticide stocks, using Agency funds, or pay the pesticide owner his or her disposal costs.

No other law compensates companies for hazardous products. When the auto industry is made to recall defective cars, there is no governmental assistance. This provision subverts any incentive for pesticide manufacturers to make safer products, and may even encourage them to build up stocks of pesticides for which they are likely to be indemnified. Recently CBS reported that EPA paid the manufacturer of EDB, Douglas Chemical Company, $655,000 to recall its product. EPA held the chemical in storage since 1983 until it corroded its containers and started leaking. EPA then hired Douglas Chemical for almost $800,000 to drain off the leachate, repackage the chemical, and store it in railroad cars.[2] EPA recently estimated the cost of removing seven, widely-used high-risk pesticides. Removing only these seven from the market would cost $400 million dollars. These funds would be taken from the Office of Pesticide Program annual budget. "If the skimpy pesticide budget is handed over to pesticide companies that make bad products instead of being spent to improve the regulation of pesticides," writes Janet Hathaway, "Americans will continue to consume pesticides in their food and water" (Hathaway, 1987a). In the same statute there is no provision to indemnify farmers who use alternative and more ecological methods such as organic farming or IPM for loss in yields they might suffer. Indemnifying chemical companies for manufacturing toxic products, but not indemnifying farmers for risking their livelihood in changing to ecological agriculture, shows what side the law is on.

Exporting Pesticides, Section 17(a) and (b) Summary: Pesticides which are restricted, suspended, or cancelled in the United States may still be manufactured for sale in other countries. The United States must notify other countries of the enforcement action, and may recommend other pesticides in lieu of the original one.

This sweetens the blow of enforcing FIFRA by enabling industry to manufacture and use chemical pesticides elsewhere in the world which are banned in the United States. The net effect of banning in the United States is to create an international traffic in pollution. The Administrator must notify other governments of the cancellation or suspension of a pesticide and the reasons, but he can also recommend another pesticide that could be used in place of it. This puts other countries on the pesticide treadmill also and creates a global circle of poison.

Integrated Pest Management, Section 20(a) Summary: EPA shall undertake research into integrated pest management in co-ordination with the Secretary of Agriculture. It shall not duplicate research being undertaken by any other federal agency.

The minimalist treatment of integrated pest management in this act is glaring. It is given a one-sentence statement of support and two other references in a 31-Section Act. It is neither listed nor defined in Section 2

---

2. CBS Evening News With Dan Rather, October 5, 1987.

of the Act, *Definitions*, which includes definitions of Defoliant, Active and Inert Ingredients, Plant Dessicant, Plant Regulator, and Pesticide. While the law supports registration of duplicative chemical pesticides, Section 20 insists that IPM research not be duplicated throughout the government. The statute allows EPA to recommend alternative pesticides to foreign governments to replace those which are banned; however, the reference favors other chemicals, not IPM, in lieu of banned chemicals.

Cost–Benefit Analysis, Section 3 and Section 6(b)(2) Summary and Comment: In the registration of a pesticide and the decision to suspend or cancel a pesticide, EPA weighs the pesticide's benefits to the agricultural economy against the pesticide's risks when used "in accordance with widespread and commonly recognized practice." The potential harm evaluated in cost–benefit analysis is pesticide residue on crops which are eaten by domestic animals, wildlife, and humans. However, the real-world hazards of these toxic chemicals are much more complex. They are manufactured in urban, residential areas; transported through cities; applied by farm workers, many of whom are children. They do not selectively reside on the plants and insects for which they were intended, especially when they are aerially sprayed. The entire risk of the pesticide includes the risks of malfunction of manufacturing and safety equipment in the manufacturing process, and exposure of workers and people in the vicinity of the plant (e.g. Bhopal, India); the risk of accident and spill in storage and transport (e.g. the recent pesticide spill into the Rhine); risks only recently realized to entire aquifers in agricultural states; risk of upsetting the ecology of insects and creating greater insect problems than existed initially; and risks when used or manufactured in countries where there are minimal safety regulations, or training, or inadequate warning labels in appropriate language. By so limiting the scope of a pesticide's human health and environmental risk to residue left on crops, chemical pesticides are protected by the very regulations designed to protect people and the environment. As for the benefit part of the calculation, EPA assumes that if the pesticide is used, it saves crops and it contributes to the agricultural economy. This assumption does not take into account the losses to the agricultural economy caused by pesticides which accelerate insect immunity and generate an increase in the number of agricultural pests. When we discount the fact that pesticides cause worse pest infestations, the only benefit which remains in the cost–benefit analysis is the profit in manufacture and sale. And even if the market is shaky, profit is guaranteed by EPA's indemnification of pesticide manufacturers for cancelled products. EPA's simple arithmetic of subtracting the risks to health and nature of pesticide use from their alleged benefits to agriculture has always favored their use. The benefit to the agricultural economy of pesticides is assumed not proven;

and the multiplicity and complexity of pesticides' harm is covered up, excluded or disregarded.

FIFRA supports the use of chemicals as pesticides by what it ignores, omits, and tokenizes, and by how it regulates and exempts. The statute lacks an ethic of nature and any tone of high-minded idealism. It fails to implement the fundamental critique of *Silent Spring*, that chemical control is a war on nature, waged in ignorance of ecology. Rather it places a mantle of protection around the use of chemical pesticides by supporting the following assumptions:

1. If a pesticide is used, it must be registered as safe to use because EPA's literature on the law states that FIFRA requires the registration of all pesticides.
2. Labeling about toxicity adequately protects people who use them.
3. If a pesticide is "used as intended," it is reasonably safe.
4. Chemical pesticides are an effective and necessary means of pest control.
5. To remove toxic pesticides from use is a great economic risk to agriculture and jeopardizes food supply.
6. Chemicals can be supplemented but not significantly replaced with biological methods.

Assumptions 4 and 5 were the cornerstones of Carson's critics, such as Norman Borlaug and Robert White-Stevens. The law seems to be on their side.[3]

Conclusion

Do more environmental laws guarantee more abundant protection of nature and people against pollution? I chose the pesticide law; any or all of the other environmental laws could be examined to think through this question. Pesticides were an original focus of *Silent Spring* and of subsequent environmental activism. Suspending or cancelling toxic substances is more rigorous and more threatening politically than issuing permits to restrict air and water pollution or charging an industry for their apportioned cost of a Superfund site. The pesticide program is an older program. EPA has had the benefit of time to take some significant environmental actions, or not. For all of these reasons, the statute with its enforcement program is a bellwether of environmental law and environmental law enforcement.

---

3. Amendments to FIFRA in Fall 1988 have created a strict schedule of reregistration of "old" pesticides. The cost of reregistration and cancellation will be more substantially borne by industry.

The answer to the question whether more environmental laws guarantee more environmental protection is no. Environmental laws, *de minimis*, give the appearance of protection and sometimes the language of protection, but not necessarily the reality of it. For the reality of environmental protection, we need laws which have an ecological intentionality. FIFRA was written primarily to register chemicals and their uses, and to close some glaring loopholes which Carson and others identified in the sixties. It is a law which affirms the necessity of chemicals for agriculture. The law could have been written with the goal of decreasing the use of and dependency on chemicals to control insects, by a "pesticide minimization" objective. It could have intended to promote an ecological and sustainable agriculture with aggressive support for IPM, biological controls, and organic farming. It would have sparingly registered pesticides only where ecological methods proved ineffective or as part of IPM. It would contain no loophole to manufacture or sell on another continent what is banned in the United States, because it would intend to protect people and global ecology, not the chemical market. It would be a law intent on "risk elimination, reduction, and minimization," not risk management. This is what I mean by intentionality.

2. DOES INSTITUTIONALIZATION DISPLACE IDEALS?

In a treatise on the social construction of reality, Peter Berger and Thomas Luckmann describe institutions as arising to express, maintain, and transmit a social order. Institutional structure, history, and language function to maintain the institution. Institutions, they write, originate in the routinizing of actions in order to free energy for decisions and activities which are unique and complex. "The background of habitualized activity opens up a foreground for deliberation and innovation" (Berger and Luckmann 1967, p. 53). Institutions have a history which "has the character of objectivity." It confronts those who had no part in the original shaping of the institution as a "given reality . . . unalterable and self-evident" (Berger and Luckmann 1967, p. 59). But, no matter how massive and how objective sounding, that history is human produced and constructed. Institutions develop a "canopy of legitimations" to explain and justify their existence. Language is a principal instrument of conveying the meaning and logic of institutional action. In the process of being transmitted, institutional meanings tend to get simplified "so that the given collection of institutional formulae," called "sedimented meanings," can be readily "learned and memorized by successive generations" (Berger and Luckmann 1967, p. 70). Knowledge in the institution becomes co-extensive with that which is knowable and provides the framework within which new knowledge is received. Any radical deviance from the institutional order appears as a deviance from reality (Berger and Luckmann 1967, p. 66). As institutional order and life ensue, a reification of reality within and related to the institution sets in. "Reification is apprehension of human phenomena as if they were things, that is non-human or possibly supra-human terms" (Berger and Luckmann 1967, pp. 88–89).[4] It involves a forgetting of our own "authorship" of the institution and the world. This reification extends to the self so that people's identity within an institution is primarily defined by their position, assigned role, and the loyalty expected of them.

On the one hand, the routine of institutions, its "background," is intended to free up a foreground for "deliberation and innovation." In other words, organizations create efficient systems to liberate creativity. On the other hand, the language, the knowledge, and the internal life and order of the institution function to justify and sustain its political worldview. They make the institution appear different from, larger than, and more important than the individuals who comprise it, and almost unalterable. They muffle initiative. The two—being freed up for creative work and being locked into the sediment of roles, chains of command, and institutional process—are at odds. As I see it, the latter must yield to the former if an institution is to stay vital.

Increasingly at EPA, the innovative and deliberative have been buried under the weight of the administrative and the politically expedient. People retreat to the background, routine tasks—these are familiar, safe, and sufficient for the continued life of the institution—and rarely get to the foreground, innovative issues.[5] To be innovative, people need a high

---

4. This reification extends to nature when environmental protection is defined only by its benefits to humans and costs to the economy, and talked about primarily as data points on computer spreadsheets.

5. In one sense, the routine background work of institutions, business, politics, homes—in short, life—is done by women. Men conserve their time, their energy, their "talent" for the upper-level decisions and strategies, the supposed innovative foreground. Women's work is homogeneous and supportive; it dissipates quickly and must be repeated (housework, cooking, typing, filing, answering phone, bringing coffee, listening, note-taking, emotional filling-station, assisting, researching for, etc.). Looking more critically, however, at what men in the foreground of their institutions do, we see that for the most part their work, while it is authoritative about strategy, management, and the big picture, is not innovative and deliberative. It is usually politically and personally expedient. Most men at upper levels in government, with a cadre of women doing "background" work, are bureaucrats who insist on rigid adherence to rules, forms, and routines. They appear to be in the realm of freed-up foreground because of salary, status in the hierarchy, office space, etc.; but in fact they spend their time organizing, monitoring, and ruling the background. Because the foreground is false in its appearance of originality and creativity, Mary Daly has called it an

degree of individuality and a will for the innovative which propels them through the institutional drag of paperwork and routine. These qualities are not fostered nor championed by institutions; EPA is no exception. While innovative and deliberative thinking is essential for the on-going rethinking and reformulating of the deeper purpose of the institution, it is not necessary to sustain and transmit the day-to-day institutional life.

EPA is governed by the same male sports' philosophy which governs all male-dominated institutions: everyone should be a "team player" and "play by the rules."[6] When an institution which "plays by the rules" is under pressure because of budget cuts and an Administration which is averse to their mission, as EPA has been under the Reagan Administration, those managing it consolidate their resources around the politically safe, more routine work and keep a low profile. They will "not rock the boat"; they will not "make waves." So EPA Administrator Lee Thomas can say, with impunity, that the current budget under Reagan is sufficient and that it is all EPA can handle efficiently, anyway. Conscience is supplanted with duty; duty is defined by job description, what is good for one's career, and loyalty to the organization.

The majority of EPA administrators and managers spend most of their time on issues that have to do with the institutional life and image of the Agency, such as: balancing credibility with industry, which wants less regulation, and with environmentalists who want better regulations and better enforcement of them (the "embattled middle" as the balancing act is affectionately called); the murky terrain of federal–state and EPA–Congress relations; intra-agency turf and budget battles; reorganization; "chains of command"; anticipating what those above you want by way of information, strategies, and accomplishments; and so forth. All of these issues, which sound so boring and bureaucratic, can get frenzied and drama-ridden and make people feel that they are working in the thick of things. But no matter how much adrenalin flows, they are surrogates for the "deliberative and innovative."

The administrative and institutional issues have very little to do with in-depth thought about environmental problems; and they do not tap people's depths or real talent. They keep people operating in the shallow reaches of their minds. Their focus and impact is less and less on real

---

arena of false reality. She has named the real realm of creative, original being, the Deep Background (Daly 1978, pp. 2–3).
6. Gro Harlem Brundtland, the Prime Minister of Norway, and one of the women from her Cabinet, were interviewed about the Norwegian government, which has 50 percent women in top positions. Asked if they saw differences between the way women and men work in government, both women said that men are preoccupied with the "rules of the game," whereas women work to solve the problems at hand. *20/20*, 1 January 1988.

analysis and more and more on the efficiency of the routine environmental work—data collection, information sorting, data management,
reporting, program accountability—and the routine institutional life of
EPA itself. They tie up people and institutions interminably.

The foreground is more than the set of unique and urgent ecological
issues which EPA must be engaged in, although that is its material reality. It is also a depth of thinking and being, moored to an "ethic of the
environment." But like any path, the path to one's depths, if not traveled, becomes overgrown, unrecognizable, and unavailable. This kind of
depth is in distinct tension with the pressure to "play by the rules" of
whoever is the current Administration.

Deliberative thinking is untrammeled with the vocabulary of "buzz
words," acronyms and institutional jargon, which mire the thinker in a
quicksand of "fast-food" thinking. It is expressed in active voice, with
the self's "I," not the standard impersonal "it" or "we," and passive voice
of government memos and speeches. When one thinks and feels deeply,
a passion for nature and people's well-being in nature is recovered from
its muffled and professionalized state in routine technical and management reports of EPA. However, government memos written with critical
thinking and deep feeling would be routed back to the author for re-
writing into standard government style. So there is a built-in deterrent to
talking, writing, and thinking in any language other than agency language. After a steady diet of deadening institutional documents, "paralysis of analysis" and fear of politically risky and precedent-setting decisions set in.

The role of institutional language is to convey the logic of the institution and to be the institution's vehicle of public relations to the world.
The hazardous waste program literature is a case in point. EPA's promotional literature says that under the 1976 Resource Conservation and
Recovery Act (RCRA), EPA's major priority has been to develop "cradle-
to-grave" protection from hazardous waste. To do this EPA has written
regulations governing the storage, transport, treatment, and disposal of
hazardous wastes. For example, facilities permitted to dispose of hazardous waste in the ground must line under and cover the waste according to specification, and monitor groundwater around the disposal
site for 30 years or another finite period of time after the site is closed.
The reader is led to think that the wastes permitted to be landfilled can
be disposed in a way to prevent migration into groundwater and, in any
case, groundwater will be monitored to assure safety. However, all landfills leach liquids through liners (the physical rate, not the fact of leach-
ing, varies); and all liner materials degrade in time. Regulations which
require liners, covers, and groundwater monitoring for a finite period of
time do not safeguard or protect from contamination. They delay the

problem. They require an early-warning system for contamination after it happens, but they do not prevent it from happening. "Cradle-to-grave" language connotes that hazardous waste originates and then dies (detoxified or destroyed), when, in fact, it has been buried alive!

Most of the RCRA program activities are about monitoring and managing hazardous waste. They are oriented to ensure safe handling of hazardous waste by industry. This very limited concept of hazardous waste management has been routinized into industrial inspections (only a small fraction annually of all industries because of EPA budget cuts) of waste handling and storage areas, review of written safety plans, monitoring wells, and waste analysis. The inspection activities are important from an industrial safety perspective. They have discouraged industries from dumping waste into the environment except in permitted landfills (which, it may be argued, is still dumping into the environment). However, their potential is only an efficient, routine program focused on data collection, waste identification, proper paperwork, and safe packaging of waste. The RCRA program, one of EPA's two hazardous waste programs, has barely and only slowly pushed the more complex, deliberative, and innovative issues. They are: waste detoxification and destruction rather than waste monitoring and management; waste reduction and elimination; a rapid, comprehensive ban on the burial of toxic wastes; and alternatives to landfills and incinerators. The RCRA program is primarily one of routine, passive management and review tasks carried out under the canopy of legitimating institutional formulae, such as "cradle to-grave" protection. The verbs *manage, monitor,* and *review* are limp and devitalized compared to *ban, eliminate,* and *destroy.* The flatness of the activity (managing, monitoring, reviewing) saps an original meaningfulness from environmental protection.

The "reification of reality" within institutions makes people small and docile. They abdicate their own power and "authorship" in giving supra-human power to those in authority above them. They limit their work lives and hide behind mental parameters, such as:

"I have no choice; it's my job . . . I do what I'm told."
"Washington won't like it."
"It's a good idea, but it's not EPA policy."

The clean split between those who ask questions and those who decide answers is another form of reification through role. Researchers do research but don't make value judgments. Managers think about the findings and make policy and decisions. Dr Bernard Goldstein, as Assistant Administrator for Research and Development at EPA, acknowledged that EPA researchers requested funding to study the deposition of acid rain throughout the seventies, but were continually turned down by managers. Recognizing that they may have the right questions and issues, he still relegates researchers to the role of doing what they are told. "We are not policy makers," he says. "We should not, for instance, write a paper for a scientific journal having to do with, say, the levels of a pollutant in a given area, and conclude our journal article by saying, therefore that we ought to take the following management approach" (Research at EPA 1984). Goldstein overlooks the fact that managers and policy-makers at the highest levels of institutions have plastic loyalties which they mold to fit their professional situation. Managers would turn down acid rain research proposals because it is not a priority issue of an Administration which is protectionist toward the industries generating acid rain.

The reification of the self, which happens when people assume and become their institutional role, was uniquely exemplified by Anne Gorsuch. A woman with abundant surficial intelligence and ambition, Anne Gorsuch was Ronald Reagan's choice for Administrator of EPA in 1981. She willingly played the role of perfect political housewife to him. In her own words, she went to Washington "'to *do* for the President'" (Lash *et al.* 1984, p. 13). Their no-fault divorce, two years later, was amicable. He expressed regret but displaced any responsibility for the break-up. She found him blameless and loved him to the end. As happens in divorce, he was the richer; she was the poorer. He was rid of a liability to his ratings; he had the chance to recoup, replacing her with William Ruckelshaus, a popular former Administrator. She lost her job; she was scorned by the media; the country gloated over her failure.

During the late seventies, Anne Gorsuch was part of an aggressive and ideologically conservative Republican caucus in the Colorado legislature which fought environmental protection and Hispanic assistance programs, and eliminated the Colorado Commission on Women. Described as "tough," "cool," and a "sparkplug," she climbed the professional ladder as the classic "token woman." She "thought like a man," that is, within the set limitations of male-identified thought as prescribed for each situation, while at the same time she conformed to the feminine stereotype.[7] Mary Daly writes that the token woman is allowed "into pieces of patriarchal territory as a show of female presence" (Daly 1978,

---

7. Gorsuch may not have been feminine enough. Her boldness, toughness, and cool constituted her personal style as well as her professional one. This, as much as her destructive tenure in EPA, accounts for the vicious hatred of the "Ice Queen" within and without EPA. Under pressure she wouldn't crack or melt. The media scrutinized her face and composure, watching for tears, vulnerability and defeat. Her marriage to Burford, just before her resignation, was interestingly timed. Breaking up with Reagan, she married. In substituting one man for another, her actions reveal that, for all her toughness, she was a real woman who needed the strength of a man to survive.

p. 334); but she has no real power which derives from a deep-centered self or an institution built on her own political philosophy and power. The rumors and conditions around Gorsuch's administration of EPA betray the derivative nature of her power. Her proximity to James Watt, then Secretary of the Interior, fostered the impression that "she was a mere lieutenant in his army carrying out his central plan" (Lash *et al.* 1984, p. 16). Several Administration officials asserted that Gorsuch was not the real force in the Agency. Allegedly the real power was James Sanderson, her closest advisor, whose "role was in part to 'oversee' Mrs Gorsuch" (Lash *et al.* 1984, p. 17). Add to this the fact that, except for two, the White House did not allow her to choose any top appointees at EPA.

Like a zealous housewife, Gorsuch set about cleaning up and cleaning out EPA. She envisaged the Agency as a cluttered, disordered house overstuffed with excessive regulation. It had been on a 10-year spending spree; and industry had been overburdened with the bills. Her goals were to save industry and taxpayers money by an efficient sounding, but environmentally passionless, agenda. Three weeks after Gorsuch took office, she eliminated the EPA enforcement office by reorganizing lawyers, technical and support staff who enforced the environmental laws against industry into nonenforcement-sounding program offices. The message to EPA and industry was that EPA would work "in partnership" with industry, no longer in the adversial model of an environment-protecting, nonprofit agency regulating the environment-degrading, for-profit industry. She would establish the flaccid "gentleman's agreement model" between EPA and industry, so consonant with her President's personal worldview: "Industry to [Reagan] was a group of men he knew and respected, not an institution driven by the pressures of profit and competition. In his eyes, regulations were not necessary protection, but absurd restrictions on the enterprise of reasonable men" (Lash *et al.* 1984, p. xii).

Next there was a budget to be trimmed. After a battle with David Stockman's Office of Management and Budget (OMB), which wanted to cut even more than she, Gorsuch achieved a budget reduction of almost one-third of EPA's staff and research from Fiscal Year 1981 for Fiscal Year 1983. Meanwhile, reprisals against outspoken and overly zealous environmentalists, who were forced to leave EPA, left most of EPA staff demoralized. The attrition rate during Gorsuch's two-year tenure was so high that even with a drastic budget cut, few, if any, personnel had to be fired.

Gorsuch's administration was pockmarked with anti-environmental collusion for the sake of business interests. She supported her most trusted advisor, James Sanderson, despite the fact that he used his influence as her Assistant to reverse an environmental decision which he believed would be detrimental to several of his clients. Gorsuch succeeded, but only temporarily, in lifting a ban on disposal of hazardous waste liquids in landfills. Rita Lavelle, another "tokenized, cosmeticized" woman[8] was appointed head administrator of the Superfund program. From public relations in a California company, she came unqualified and unprepared for her job. It was alleged that she manipulated hazardous waste clean-up funds to help Republican candidates and hurt Democrats. Ultimately she was prosecuted and convicted of perjury and of obstructing a congressional investigation. In the end, Lavelle served as a scapegoat for the wrongdoing of the Administration. Other officials accused of wrongdoing were given the benefit of every doubt, technicality, and loophole. Lavelle apparently was the only one who could not be saved.

But neither was Gorsuch. While Reagan publicly supported her when she resigned, he did not save her from the men of his Administration with whom she was embattled, and by whom she was deserted. When Congress began an investigation of alleged wrongdoing in EPA and subpoenaed Gorsuch to appear and provide certain documents, she was advised both by the Justice Department and the White House to ignore it. Privately she argued strenuously with the White House against withholding the documents, but publicly defended the President's decision. While she was the one subject to criminal contempt proceedings and to taking the brunt of public criticism, the White House and the Justice Department not only refused to heed her advice, they would not even let her know what was going on (Lash *et al.* 1984, p. 78). Undoubtedly under pressure to do so, she resigned on March 9, 1983, professing loyalty to the President. The same day, the White House turned over the disputed documents to Congress. Gorsuch's (and Lavelle's) was the fate of the "token" woman: they were used until they were useless, then they were thrown away.

Environmentalists knew that Reagan's political agenda was to weaken the Agency's enforcement of laws and to soften the costs of environmental protection to industry. However, the Gorsuch Administration so tarnished Reagan's image that Gorsuch had to go. The assignment of top-level managers who replaced Gorsuch and her team was to patch back together a fragmented and dispirited EPA. The approach this second generation of Reagan appointees took was to treat EPA as suf-

---

8. The male contempt for Lavelle, a woman who wore a lot of make-up, and Gorsuch, called the "Ice Queen," was sexualized. Lavelle was called a whore; Gorsuch was portrayed as frigid.

fering from nonspecific institutional malaise and adolescent growing pains. They psychologized a problem which was political and erased the politics. They applied band-aids and minor surgery when radical surgery was needed.

A year after Gorsuch's resignation, Alvin L. Alm, then Deputy Administrator to the EPA, spoke to the National Conference of the American Society for Public Administration on "public sector management" as exemplified in managing EPA (Alm 1984). He cited three generic conditions in public sector management and one unique one that challenged managers at EPA.

1. Policy decision-makers (Congress) are separated from the implementation of their decisions (Executive Branch in which EPA is located). Therefore, decision-makers in Congress have unrealistic expectations of EPA.
2. Senior managers come and go with administrators. No "stable corporate memory" develops at the top.
3. In bureaucracies "there is a bias for review and reconsideration rather than a bias for action." Bureaucracies "are by nature risk-averse." They do not foster innovation.
4. The multiple environmental statutes, each of which governs a part of environmental protection, are not always consistent. The distribution and behavior of pollutants don't follow "neat prescriptions of EPA's enabling statutes." For example, the decision to use air pollution devices creates new problems: the disposal of sludge.

Alm concludes that three essential elements are necessary for EPA to function successfully. First, clear, consistent guidance from the top. Second, timely, results-oriented follow-up to ensure things are happening in the operational level. Third, technical assistance as necessary to enable the operational managers to succeed where problems arise.

The net effect of Alm's analysis and recommendations is to consolidate the fragmented Agency around bland, background aspects of issues: consistency in guidance (whether or not guidance is creative, innovative, or environmentally centered); and timely, results-oriented follow-up (his examples are data reporting from inspections and permits, which may or may not be substantive environmentally, to show Congress something is happening). It is a tranquilizing analysis and agenda which subsumes EPA as one more room in the mansion of federal bureaucracy. The managers' challenge is to keep the room neat (consistent) and clean (timely follow-up). Strategic planning replaces an examination of Agency conscience, to recall an ethic of the environment. Alm's prescriptions conjure up Thomas Jorling's image of a "professional agency with no environmental soul."

Alm's analysis is not completely far afield; it is just too shallow. He is scratching the surface when digging deep is needed. Let us return to his analysis of EPA's obstacles as a public agency and take it beyond the prescriptions he offers.

Separation of decision-makers from implementers. Congress writes laws; EPA enforces them. If the separation of powers between Congress and the Executive Branch is so obstructionist, why was Reagan able to appoint an antienvironmentalist as Administrator of EPA, cut EPA's budget so drastically, and enjoy two years of degrading the Agency, all of which required some degree of approval or tolerance from Congress. The governmental politics of recent times which have mired EPA issue first from the conflict of interest created at the heart of the Agency in the betrayal of its mission. With appointment of loyalist administrators, who were antienvironmentalists, Reagan re-created EPA into a reflection of himself. The mirror image of the Department of Agriculture's softness toward pesticides is EPA's recent softness toward industry portrayed as suffering under the economic hardship of environmental regulation. The real political issue here is not separation of lawmakers and enforcement. It is that the Executive Branch and EPA were joined at the hip. EPA is not the independent agency of environmental planners, scientists, and lawyers that it was purported to be. It is hamstrung by the Executive Branch and its anti-environmental policies.

No stable corporate memory at the top. Much more serious than how long someone is at the top is *who* is at the top. Environmentalists, not people with plastic loyalties who are tokens for the Administration, belong in EPA. At every level, EPA ought to be managed by people who have a proven record of environmental work. EPA's stability should be achieved first by a consistent philosophy of environmental protection. Only then is the issue of time in office relevant.

Bureaucracies are by nature risk-averse. EPA's enthusiasm for genetically engineered organisms in agriculture; the government's endorsement of nuclear power and the space program during and after the Challenger and Chernobyl accidents suggest differently. The same government which is reluctant to take social and political risks, such as rapid removal of toxics from the marketplace, affirmative action, and redistribution of wealth, rushes toward high-tech risk.

Inconsistency in environmental statutes. Again, the deeper issue here is inconsistent and poor enforcement of environmental statutes by EPA, not the fact that enforcing one statute creates burdens for another. For example, the majority of all pesticides sold today in the United States have not been examined sufficiently for their ability to cause cancer, birth defects, sterility, or genetic damage. This is much more serious than Alm's example of air pollution controls collecting particulates and generating ash which then need to be disposed as solid waste.

Alm ends his analysis saying that EPA "needs a vision of where we want to go and how to get there." After exclusive preoccupation with the how-to of successful, public-sector management, he touches on EPA's critical issues: movement ("moving in a well-defined direction") and vision (foresight and an ethic of the environment shaping the direction). EPA, after two years of the Gorsuch–Reagan administration, was like a ship stranded on the twin shoals of an antienvironmental, pro-industry politic and a lack of purpose among Agency environmentalists. Alm's prescriptions for EPA—clear, consistent guidance from the top; timely, results-oriented activities and targets—might dislodge EPA from the state in which it was stuck. But they offer no vision of where to go and how to propel the Agency forward. His analysis centers on the life of the institution as institution—how to get it efficient and successful—not on the problem of how to revive an original mission.

Alm is resuscitating an institution and preparing it to move again. He does not discuss what direction it ought to take, how quickly it must move, where to find power to move, how to regain an "environmental soul." These are the complex, unique, and necessary issues if EPA is ever to be a vital institution of environmental protection and not just a well-managed public-sector agency. His solutions may bring efficiency and the odor of success to the institution's background agenda (e.g. quick response to public information requests, routinizing inspections and permits, data call-ins, generating environmental statistics, etc.). But, without vision and without an environmental mission, they cannot draw EPA into the more important arena: the foreground of deliberative and deeply ecological thought and action.

Conclusion

The second question addressed to EPA is whether ideals and loyalty to those ideals can survive within a political institution. For EPA to be a vital public agency of environmental protection, I would offer the following prescriptions.

Seek a Center, not the Middle Ground. In 1970 William Ruckelshaus, EPA's first Administrator, said that he and EPA were starting with "no obligation to promote commerce or agriculture." EPA's crucial role was to develop an environmental ethic. Fifteen years later the agency has drifted from its centering on the environment to becoming a balancer between industry and environment. "We are neither pro-industry nor anti-chemical. . . . We are often in . . . 'the embattled middle'," said one manager recently, referring to industry on one side and environmentalists on the other.

Lacking its own center on the issue of toxic chemicals, EPA seeks in its stead a middle ground. In the June 1984 *EPA Journal* it presents a positive perspective on pesticides by the executive vice-president of Monsanto Chemical Company side-by-side with an article by two farmers who stopped using chemicals and operate a successful organic farm. EPA could have concluded that the organic farmers have proven the pesticides' experts wrong. Their food supplies have not decreased by the 30 percent or more predicted by pesticide experts. Instead the Agency performs a balancing act, suggesting that there are merits on both sides, and focuses on safe transport, use, and disposal of pesticides rather than on restricting and banning them. Ultimately, EPA's position is indistinguishable from that of the National Agricultural Chemicals Association' member companies whose "highest priority is . . . the safe manufacture, transportation, use, and disposal of agrichemicals" (Reding 1984).

EPA speaks about having a mission, but the agency has no ecological worldview or philosophy of the environment to undergird and fortify the mission. Having a mission is like being given a destination and a compass. A philosophy or center offers the grounding and fortitude to stay on course in the face of obstacles. An ecological worldview would clarify for EPA that its constituency is the health and well-being of humans and the environment, not industry beleaguered by the high costs of pollution control. There are plenty of agencies, politicians, associations, and lobbies who represent industry.

Re-enchant the Mission. The metaphors and conceptual language which predominate in EPA's literature reify rather than revitalize its mission. In an interview in which he was asked to assess its 15-year history and the major issues facing EPA, Lee Thomas, the current Administrator, compared environmental regulations to a "nine-dimensional chessboard." He is confident that the environment can be "monitored, analyzed, controlled and gradually upgraded." When asked what he sees to be EPA's greatest strength, he replied: "It's our administrative and psychological maturity . . . We recognize as never before the urgency of balancing our various environmental control responsibilities and pursuing them within the context of economic growth and having to compete within the global marketplace" ("Past, present, and future" 1985).

EPA is not a business project. The environment is not a chess game. Protecting the environment is not a balancing act between the costs of pollution control to industry and industry's ability to compete in the global marketplace. I miss here what the Dutch scientist, C. J. Briejèr, called for in science: "a more high-minded orientation and a deeper insight" (Carson 1962, p. 243).

Beyond the Bureaucratic Background. EPA must minimize the amount of time and energy people give to routine background work. The goal would be to minimize the number of people who would describe themselves as bureaucrats. Institutionalization is not irreversible. Within, EPA could create islands of deinstitutionalized existence which would be creative sources of energy, policy, and ideas for the Agency.

EPA will never recover a capacity for innovative and deliberative environmental work unless people appointed to direct the Agency are environmentalists who have a substantive record of environmental accomplishment. The same is true for all management. Those promoted within the Agency must be judged by evidence of their environmental record, as well as good management and personal skills. The recent progressive human resource initiatives within the Agency are aimed at professional career development and cultivating "excellence" in managers. But this is no guarantee of an environment-centered excellence. EPA's history of political appointments and criteria for managers has not demonstrated an "ethic of the environment." Lee Thomas cited EPA's greatest asset to be "administrative and psychological maturity." We can hope that some day an Administrator, when asked the same question, could cite "environmental purpose and activism."

3. WHAT ARE THE MAJOR PROBLEMS AND PRIORITIES FOR EPA TODAY?

As this century draws to an end, most environmental professionals are asking the same question, as they pronounce on the state of the environment and set agendas for the twenty-first century. Apologists for EPA say that the Agency has solved the obvious and worst problems— soot and smoke coming out of cars and industrial smoke stacks and dying rivers—with wastewater treatment plants and air pollution devices installed in the seventies and early eighties. In the mid-eighties EPA spent most of its resources on emergency actions at Superfund sites, such as removal of abandoned rusting, corroding containers of chemicals, and providing potable water for people whose drinking water had been contaminated. What remains, they say, is less visible, more exotic, and more intractable.

> Air quality is generally better now than in 1970, despite a growth in the gross national product of 50 percent and an increase of 17 percent in population. As a dramatic example, ambient lead concentrations in urban areas dropped by 79 percent from 1976 to 1985. Most of our rivers are cleaner now, or at least are holding their own . . . the challenges of the 1990s are fundamentally different from those of 1970 (Russell 1987).

The author, an Assistant Administrator at EPA from 1984 to 1987, says that one issue of the nineties is toxic substances, which are ubiquitous but also "essential to daily life." The corollary issue is realizing that "the enemy is us," and that we either limit risk in our lives by the choices we make or "learn how to live with risk." In any case, he writes, we should stop looking to the EPA regulatory system to provide the substantive environmental and health protection that we have expected. This shrinking of environmental protection to the individual's personal choices at the supermarket and hardware store depoliticizes the nature of pollution. But even with its deficiencies, this assessment does help with answering the question of where EPA ought to be going.

Toxic synthetic chemicals, over 50,000 of them, are ubiquitous. Their hazards are much less understood than their alleged benefits. (This is why Rachel Carson wrote *Silent Spring*.) But toxic substances are not a new environmental issue. They are an issue of the nineties because they have been neglected during the past two decades. This is EPA's unfinished business. While casting about for the critical issues of the end of this century, EPA must recast this one.

In February 1987, EPA released a self-study entitled *Unfinished Business: A Comparative Assessment of Environmental Problems.*[9] It originated from the suspicion that emerging or existing problems, such as acid rain and indoor radon, may be more grave and more important than those on which EPA expends its resources. This special task force of senior managers and technical experts assembled masses of data on pollutants, exposures, and the risks they posed. But ultimately they had to fill substantial data gaps with their collective judgment. "In this sense, the project represents expert opinion rather than objective and quantitative analysis" (EPA 1987, p. xiv). The group found that the priorities of the Agency—Superfund hazardous waste sites, the hazardous waste industrial inspection program, and underground storage tanks—are of lower risk to people than environmental problems which have low, if any, priority in EPA. These are toxic substances, like pesticides; global problems, such as acid rain, global warming because of carbon dioxide, and depletion of the ozone layer; discharges to estuaries, coastal waters, and oceans; and indoor air pollution. They also acknowledged that the best understanding environmental science has about the human health effects of toxic substances has to do with cancer, but even this under-

---

9. This report is more honest, more tangible, more useful, and less "institutional" than most agency documents. It is an example of "innovative and deliberative" work done in an "island of de-institutionalized existence."

standing is weak. There are no generally accepted methods for assessing non-cancer health effects, such as infertility and genetic damage, and effects on ecosystems of pollutants. The conclusions of *Unfinished Business* resonate with much of my remaining response to Question 3.

Twenty-five years after *Silent Spring*, the problem of toxic substances put into food supply, drugs, home furnishings, and everything we use, ingest, and touch, persists. As pollution becomes increasingly global and irreversible, EPA and industry get increasingly individualistic about risk, blaming most health problems on "lifestyle," such as driving, smoking, and drinking coffee. As EPA retreats from an ethic of the environment to "the embattled middle ground," there has been an erosion of the ecological base of environmental protection. Nature is only worth preserving if it benefits the human economy. Biology, the science from which Rachel Carson expected ecological and life-respecting solutions, is bringing forth its own arrogant and risk-laden technologies: "the altered harvest" (Doyle 1985) of genetically engineered crops, insects, and microorganisms and the new reproductive technologies. These issues, in brief, are EPA's new and unfinished work. Let us look at them in more depth.

EPA can no longer treat pollution as if it stays within national boundaries. The United States' responsibility for global pollution includes:

* an international traffic in toxic chemicals and toxic waste;
* exporting a model of industrialization to developing countries which exploits the resources of nature for short-term economic advantage with no consideration for the integrity or ultimate survival of nature;
* the most intensive use of nature's resources and the highest rate of waste generated per person in the world; and
* the maximum use per person of synthetic chemicals and technologies which affect global climate, atmosphere, and air quality.

The chauvinism of statements such as those by the former EPA Administrator, William Ruckelshaus, to the National Wildlife Federation, demonstrates how urgently EPA must develop a global consciousness:

> Ours is probably the only age that has ever cared about the environment as an entity [He has just erased native Americans and the nineteenth-century conservationists]. . . . In a little over two decades we have evolved from blithe indifference to irrevocable commitment, [He had recently replaced Gorsuch] and I have no doubt that by the turn of the century this country will be safer and less defiled than it is now . . .
> Elsewhere in the world things are not so good. Indeed, the real challenge of the 80s and 90s may be to *export environmental consciousness* [emphasis mine. The ideal export policy would be to ban American toxic

products and to support indigenous models of development in other countries which would sustain their own resources] ("Ruckelshaus reviews year
at EPA" 1984).

Silent Spring laid the groundwork for a nature-centered as well as a
human health-centered system of environmental protection. Carson argued that people and nature have the right to exist unendangered from
pollution and should be enabled to do so. On the whole, environmental
accomplishments in the United States have kept the air and rivers from
worsening since 1970, despite an increase of 50 percent in gross national
product and a population increase of 17 percent. And emergency re-
movals of exposed toxic waste at Superfund sites have protected some
communities from potential explosions or fires.

However, there has been an erosion of the ecological base of environmental protection. EPA has admitted that there are no generally accepted
methods for assessing the effects of pollution on the well-being of ecosystems. Increasingly, tourism and the pleasure boat industry become
the primary justifications for cleaning up harbors and bays. And contaminated groundwater is only worth restoring if it is or will be a drinking-
water source. The wetlands protection program exemplifies how nature,
apart from its economic resourcefulness and its direct effect on human
welfare, has little if any value.

Wetlands are characterized by saturated soils and plant life which are
adapted to flooding. Wetlands protect downstream land and communities from flooding; they prevent erosion along river banks and sea coasts;
they help remove and biodegrade pollutants. They are sanctuary to
scores of endangered birds, mammals, amphibians, plants, and fishes.
Some are critical groundwater recharge areas. Wetlands have been
drained and filled since the arrival of European immigrants. They are
destroyed by farmers, foresters, and commercial developers wanting wa-
terside views. Although there are federal, state, and local laws to protect
wetlands and numerous agencies responsible, wetlands are being lost at
the rate of 300,000 acres per year. Many bird, plant, and animal species
are imperiled with the destruction of their habitats. About wetland protection, environmental attorney Malcolm Baldwin concludes "at best,
existing wetland laws and programs only slow the rate of loss" (Baldwin
1987).

Finally, there is the modern counterpart of the synthetic pesticides.
Rachel Carson's work gave us the analytic tools with which to critique
and protest a world increasingly dominated by technologies and by a
philosophy of exploitation which endanger ecosystems. But it is likely
that she would look more critically at the uses of biology today than in
1960 and look in other places for an "understanding of . . . living organisms and the whole fabric of life to which they belong." The new agricul-

tural biotechnologies and the new reproductive technologies promise a lot. They are, however, experimental and risky; and they are being developed and carried out in a vacuum of woman-centered and nature-centered law and public policy. Let us, then, take the tools Carson gave us and apply them, together with our own, to the new technologies of biology.

REFERENCES

Alm, A. 1984. Managing government programs: The Environmental Protection Agency in transition. Presented to the national conference of the American Society for Public Administration, Denver, Colorado, 10 April.

Baldwin, M. F. 1987. Wetlands: Fortifying federal and regional cooperation. *Environment*, **29**(7), 18.

Berger, P. L. and Luckmann, T. 1967. *The Social Construction of Reality*. Garden City: Anchor Books.

Cahn, R. and Cahn, P. 1985. The environmental movement since 1970. *EPA Journal*, **11**(9), 35.

Carson, R. 1962. *Silent Spring*. Greenwich, Connecticut: Fawcett Publications.

Daly, M. 1978. *Gyn/Ecology: The Metaethics of Radical Feminism*. Boston, Massachusetts: Beacon Press.

Doyle, J. 1985. *Altered Harvest*. New York: Penguin.

Dunlap, T. R. 1981. *DDT: Scientists, Citizens, and Public Policy*. Princeton, New Jersey: Princeton University Press.

Environmental Protection Agency 1987. *Unfinished Business: A Comparative Assessment of Environmental Problems*.

Fairfax, S. K. 1978. A disaster in the environmental movement. *Science*, **199**, 743–747.

Hathaway, J. S. 1987a. Eating wisely gets harder all the time. *Los Angeles Times*, 8 October, part II, 1.

Hathaway, J. S. 1987b. The future of pesticide regulation. Presented to the Entomological Society of America, 1 December.

An interview with Lee Thomas. 1985. *EPA Journal*, **11**(9), 4–5.

Lash, J., Gillman, K. and Sheridan, D. 1984. *A Season of Spoils*. New York: Pantheon.

Lewis, J. 1985. The birth of EPA. *EPA Journal*, **11**(9), 6–9.

Moore, J. 1984. Pesticide regulation: An overview. *EPA Journal*, **10**(5), 2–3.

Moore, J. 1984. Insuring safety in genetic engineering. *EPA Journal*, **10**(5), 32.

Natural Resources Committee of the Democratic Advisory Council 1960. *Resources for the People*, 1.

Natural Resources Defense Council 1987. *Citizen suits under FIFRA: Enforcing the Federal Insecticide, Fungicide, and Rodenticide Act*. Washington, DC: NRDC.

Past, present, and future: an interview with Lee Thomas, 1985. *EPA Journal*, **11**(9), 4.

Popkins, R. 1985. Memorable moments at EPA. *EPA Journal*, **11**(9), 45–47.

Rachel Carson, where are you? 1983. *Amicus Journal*, Summer, 3.

Reding, N. L. 1984. Seeking a balanced perspective. *EPA Journal*, **10**(5), 28.

Research at EPA: an interview with Dr Bernard Goldstein. 1984. *EPA Journal*, **10**(4), 2–6.

Ruckelshaus reviews year at EPA. 1984. *EPA Journal*, **10**(4), 49.

Russell, M. 1987. Environmental protection for the 1990s and beyond. *Environment*, **29**(7), 12.

Silent Spring revisited. 1986. *Newsweek*, 14 July 1986, 73.

US Government Accounting Office 1986. *Pesticides: EPA's Formidable Task to Assess and Regulate their Risks*. GAO/RCED-86-125.

V

SILENT SPRING:
A FEMINIST READING

DDT . . . came home in 1945 on a wave of publicity and high hopes. It was the atomic bomb of insecticides, the killer of killers, the harbinger of a new age in insect control (Thomas R. Dunlap 1981. *DDT: Scientists, Citizens and Public Policy*).

Major technological breakthroughs have occurred in our own precisely defined area of specialization. . . . And we can only be overjoyed and exhilarated and consider ourselves extremely fortunate to be working during a time when such paramount advances have been made. How thrilling it must have been to be Chaucer writing when Gutenberg invented the printing press, or be a physicist working on the Manhattan project! (Alan De Cherney, reproductive endocrinologist and head of Yale University School of Medicine's *in vitro* fertilization team).

I get overwhelmed by a feeling of terrible guilt when I think about the history of the bomb. . . . This is what bugs me more than anything else—I don't remember having any strong feelings about [the bombings] at the time. I guess I just got caught up in the mindless hysteria (Seth Neddermeyer, physicist who developed plutonium implosion for the atomic bomb. Peter Wyden 1984. *Day One: Before Hiroshima and After*).

At their fortieth anniversary reunion in Los Alamos, New Mexico, 70 of 110 physicists who had worked on the atomic bomb signed a statement in support of nuclear disarmament. Many had changed their minds about the bomb long ago (Wyden 1984, pp. 362–366).

It is probably unprecedented in science that the brightest physicists of their day have admitted that the most notable work of their lives was a colossal mistake. Yet this collective turning point is irrelevant to those scientists who valorize their own work by comparing it to the atomic bomb project. Gauging by the "new frontier" frenzy of biotechnologists, whose time in the science sun has come with genetic engineering and the new reproductive technologies, it will be 40 years—time enough to win Nobel Prizes—before the majority regret what they have done and defect from the brotherhood of these biotechnologies. "On the 40th anniversary of the first human in vitro fertilization, what grief will we [have] witness[ed]?" asks feminist critic of the new reproductive technologies, Gena Corea (1986).[1] In the end, writes Jack Doyle of the Environmental Policy Institute, genetic engineering of plants, bacteria, and insects could produce a "house-of-cards" agricultural system. "One unforeseen mutation or errant gene could bring down the whole system" (Doyle 1986).

The atomic bomb was the mid-century touchstone of male dominance, with nature as the instrument of destruction. Rachel Carson told students of Scripps College in 1962 that "in the days before Hiroshima," she thought that there were powerful and inviolate realms of nature, like the sea and vast water cycles, which were beyond man's destructive power. "But I was wrong," she continued. "Even these things, that seemed to belong to the eternal verities, are not only threatened but have already felt the destroying hand of man" (Carson July 1962). However, the history of the atomic bomb, which holds such romance for a new generation of dominance-driven scientists, also gives us critical guideposts by which to judge the new biotechnologies. Let us use them.

The bomb was developed in secret. Once it was deployed, it became an inevitable and necessary part of defense. Nuclear weapons build-up was encased in a mythology of freedom and security through military dominance. Then "peacetime" uses of the atom were rapidly developed to make the nuclear industry respectable. Regulation and policy do not stop its continued development and use; rather they ensure it. Those responsible for national and international regulation of nuclear power ignore the substantive question of whether it is necessary or it ought to be employed. Instead they draw media attention to derivative issues, such as treating the effects of radiation exposure, international reporting and information systems in the event of an accident, evacuation plans in case of an accident, controlling who has access to nuclear arms, and keeping weapons-grade plutonium out of the "wrong" hands.

There were alternatives to dropping the bomb in Japanese cities, but those who developed it insisted on its use. They blunted the growing critique among some scientists of using the bomb, and they sheltered the

---

1. Corea draws very clear parallels between the original Manhattan Project and the Reproductive Manhattan Project: the lure of history-making science for the ambitious; the fast pace and competitiveness of the technology development; a hard, high-tech solution to a social and political problem; the effect of the atomic bomb on world consciousness; the effect of the new reproductive technologies on women's consciousness.

military and political decision-makers from that critique. The decision to use the bomb was made quickly, in secret, and in an atmosphere of crisis. In that environment the alternatives were shut out from consideration.

The bomb's technical effectiveness was better analyzed and understood than its health effects on human beings. The extensive radiation sickness suffered by Hiroshima victims had not been anticipated by American scientists. So when Japan reported the vast number of people suffering from radiation sickness, they were not believed. A second bomb was then dropped on Nagasaki. Although the bomb was developed for a specific war situation and a specific target, nuclear weapons have proliferated beyond the reasons for which they were developed. There is no earthly or atmospheric sanctuary from them. The bomb has shrunken the vastness and power of nature; nothing is inviolate from nuclear holocaust (Pacific War Research Society 1972; Wyden 1984).

These guideposts, learned from the development of the atomic bomb, will direct our analysis of the new biotechnologies. In summary, they are:

- A mythology encases the technology to make it necessary and acceptable. Once it becomes technically possible, it becomes inevitable.
- Regulation and policy are used to protect the technology, to ensure that it can profitably survive conflict, public distrust, and even failure.
- Public policy, ethical analysis, and analysis of the technologies' risks lag behind the technology development. Carson (July 1962) described this erosion of an ethical base in science, "If we know how to do something, we do it without pausing to inquire whether we should." In the absence of an ethical analysis, the proponents of the technologies generate a plethora of derivative issues which distract from the central ones and which eventually come to replace them (e.g. the legality of patents for genetically altered plants and animals; the ethics of "pregnancy reduction" or inducing a woman to abort some fetuses because she is carrying multiple ones as a result of superovulation, etc.). The derivative issues, complex in themselves, replace the fundamental questions of whether the technologies should exist at all and what the preferred alternatives to the technologies are, where a genuine need or problem exists.

Those who develop the technologies, who promote them and stand to profit most from them, are not those who suffer their risks. The analysis of the technologies is biased toward their use because the technology promoters generally lack the expertise and the incentive to analyze the risks of the technologies for human health and the environment. In their risk–benefit analysis, the technologists do not take into consideration the social, political, and spiritual price paid by those on whom the technologies are used.

• The new technology is not presented as one among many solutions to a problem, but as the dominant one. The alternatives to the technology, the "other road," are shut out.

Both biotechnology and the new reproductive technologies are called a "revolution," one in agriculture, the other in reproduction. The latter is said to offer hope for the infertile; the former, to feed the world in the twenty-first century as developing countries "explode" in population. Both are based on the premises that, first, the technologies guarantee self-sufficiency and self-determination, and second, that no matter what the social impacts from their use, people have the right to these technical turnkeys to self-determination. Both biotechnologies are driven by twin engine partnerships of scientific "initiative" and commercial interests. Both rely on the reduction of the "raw material"—plants, microbes, animals, and women—to parts of themselves: genes, eggs, and wombs. Both diminish the whole to the sum of dismembered and recombined parts.

The genetic engineering revolution in agriculture is unabashedly worldwide: every country, every farm, every international agricultural development project is envisaged. This revolution that has been carried out "in virtual silence, spawned in test tubes and directed from corporate towers, with little public involvement or oversight" is ready to happen (Matthiessen and Kohn 1985). Yet, with its readiness and gargantuan economic power, the applications in agriculture are hamstrung by regulatory confusion and court injunctions. On the other hand, the new reproductive technologies, which were supposedly developed for a small number of infertile women with blocked or absent fallopian tubes, are flourishing in hundreds of clinics throughout the world. Physicians now prescribe in vitro fertilization (IVF) for increasing numbers of women who are fertile if they are married to men with low sperm counts. Neither court injunctions nor a lack of regulatory framework are keeping them from proliferating.

Biotechnology, in agriculture and in reproduction, is referred to as a revolution, by its developers and users, in the most expectant sense of the word: "an assertedly momentous change." There are, however, two other definitions of revolution which more truthfully describe what kind of revolution is taking place: (1) "a turning or rotational motion about an axis"; and (2) "a forcible substitution of rulers or ruling cliques" (*American Heritage Dictionary* 1981).

The new reproductive technologies are the most recent technical interventions in a continuum of medical manipulation of women's fertility and childbirth experiences. These include: birth control technologies developed exclusively for women, that carry significant risk, such as the pill, the Dalkon Shield, and Depo Provera; unnecessary hysterectomies; forced sterilization of Third World women; and the routinizing of fetal monitoring, amniocentesis and cesarian section. The latest reproductive technologies, most notably the test tube baby procedure and embryo flushing and transfer, are new, in that they are more novel and insidious forms of intervention. But, like the "old" ones, they keep women caught circling the same axis of increasing biomedical manipulation of women's bodies.

The new biotechnologies in agriculture will, in some cases, ensure the continued and increased use of herbicides in agriculture: more of the old cycle of chemical-intensive agriculture. In other cases they will force farmers into high-yield technologies for which farmers, already strapped with surpluses, are not asking. But the choice facing American farmers will be either to use them, or to foreclose on farming. Vertically integrated ownership of agriculture—from seeds, patents on plants, microbes and animals, to fertilizer, herbicides and pesticides, together with the political power that such economic power wields—is shaping and forcing the biotechnology revolution in agriculture.

BIOTECHNOLOGY IN AGRICULTURE

1. Bovine Growth Hormone

There are enormous surpluses of milk, butter, cheese, and nonfat milk; so much so that, under a 1985 farm bill, the United States Department of Agriculture (USDA) is paying dairy farmers to remain out of dairying for five years. The government buyouts are intended to reduce the amount of dairy products by 8 percent, thus to relieve dairy farmers of low prices which result from surpluses and to cut government surplus storage costs. At the same time that dairy cows are being slaughtered for meat and exported because too much milk is being produced, a bovine growth hormone is about to be approved for commercial use in the United States.

Major chemical companies, like Monsanto, American Cyanamid, and DuPont, who recognize the market potential of biology-based technologies in agriculture, have retooled for the Age of Biology. One of the biotechnologies closest to fruition is use of growth hormones in cattle. Scientists have isolated the genes in a cow's cells that control the synthesis of bovine growth hormone (BGH). The BGH gene has been transplanted into microbes which manufacture commercial quantities of the hormone. The synthesized hormone is injected on a daily basis into the dairy cattle. The increased growth hormone boosts the cow's appetite in part by diverting more of the food from ordinary metabolism to milk production. Eating more fodder, cows have produced between 10 and 25 percent more milk during their peak milking period that follows calving. The U.S. Food and Drug Administration has approved experiments on cattle with BGH and the marketing of milk produced from experiments. Approval for commercial use is expected to follow by 1989.

The effect of these growth hormones on the animal is to burn her out rapidly, so that within a few years she is exhausted from the speeding up of her biological processes. Already, Holstein cows which should be able to produce milk for about 15 years are finished within four or five years because of other "enhancement" techniques. As for health effects, cows treated with BGH have more infections, particularly mastitis, an infection of the mammary glands. They become more sensitive to heat, so they suffer more from heat stress, and their fertility is reduced. These health effects have been observed only incidentally during milk production trials. They are not from comprehensive studies on the health of animals treated with growth hormones (MacKenzie 1988, p. 28).

The social impacts of this biotechnology will never be calculated in the corporate cost–benefit analysis of it. With the surplus of dairy products which BGH will create—some predict the already existing surplus will triple—dairy prices will drop. Small dairy farmers and entire dairy communities will be economically and socially devastated. Only large corporate farms, which will be able to absorb the initial losses and costs, will survive and adjust. The industry pushing the growth hormone sees the eventual bankruptcy of what may amount to half of American dairy farmers, as salutary. It will weed out the inefficient from the efficient (Andrews 1986).

The forward march of a technology—which is cruel to animals, which is not sought by dairy farmers, and which is not needed by a country with milk surpluses—demonstrates how much the forces controlling and driving the new biotechnologies have come to dominate the discourse and direction of agriculture. This is a repugnant revolution, which is forcibly substituting dairy farming as caretaking of animals with an industrialized farming that reduces animals to fast-food factories.

2. Herbicide-Resistant Crops

In the agrichemical industry, more than 25 companies are engineering crops to make them genetically resistant to specific herbicides. Chemical companies, like Monsanto, Ciba-Geigy, Stauffer Chemical, W. R. Grace, and Du Pont have teamed up with biotechnology companies and university scientists to engineer resistance and to regulate growth in plants. In

May 1988, the Monsanto Chemical Company field tested a strain of canola, a variety of rapeseed used for cooking and salad, which was genetically engineered to resist Monsanto's herbicide Roundup.

Ciba-Geigy, for example, is funding research to develop a soybean that is resistant to the herbicide atrazine, a herbicide sold by Ciba-Geigy, and which is widely used on corn. Corn contains enzymes which enable the plant to detoxify atrazine, but soybeans do not. If farmers rotate their corn crop with soybeans, the beans are damaged by residual atrazine in the soil. Scientists studied how weeds develop an immunity to the herbicide through mutation in their DNA. They have isolated and cloned the atrazine-resistant gene and are working to transfer the gene to soybeans and other crop plants.

Researchers at DuPont have developed tobacco strains resistant to two DuPont herbicides, Glean and Oust. Scientists studied chemical-induced and random mutation in bacteria that are resistant to these two herbicides. The gene responsible for resistance was then transferred to the tobacco plant. Until now, Glean has only been able to be used on cereals, since it kills most other crop plants. The market for these herbicides will dramatically increase with the development of herbicide-resistant strains of agricultural crops.

Herbicide-resistant research is being conducted by all major herbicide manufacturers, for all major crops, including corn, alfalfa, soybeans, tobacco, and cotton. Prior to biotechnology, scientists achieved herbicide-resistance by observing which varieties could tolerate a given herbicide, and then cross-breeding that variety with others. Tissue culture techniques have speeded the process of developing herbicide-resistant mutated varieties. Plant tissue is cultured and then exposed to lethal doses of herbicide. Survivors are plated out for regeneration into whole plants, then transplanted into fields, and treated with herbicide. Those variants are identified which have field resistance to herbicide.

Genetically engineered herbicide resistance in agricultural crops is a logical outgrowth of both the agrichemical industry in quest of new markets for herbicides and also the bias for chemical agriculture within existing pesticide law and law enforcement. The industry argues that it is only doing what has been observed in nature: transferring the genetic capability to resist or detoxify a herbicide to crops which do not have it. Gene transfer just speeds up the process. As one biotechnologist put it, "'Nature took her own sweet time, but with genetic engineering, you can speed up evolution'" (Ellington 1988).

What is being proposed here is more of the same chemical-based agriculture. It is now being extended with the assistance of new biology techniques. Nothing changes in this revolution, except the scale of the problem. The shift in agriculture from traditional methods of weed control—cultivation and crop rotation—to herbicides was hastened with the advent of "no-till" method of weed control (planting seeds through the stubble of old crops and relying on chemicals to control insects and weeds). It will be further hastened with herbicide-resistant crops. This marriage of biology with chemistry will augment herbicide sales for industry. Farmers will increase herbicide use without fear of losing their major cash crop now engineered for herbicide resistance. Farm workers will be exposed to more herbicides. Soil and groundwater contamination will increase. As insecticides resulted in increased insect resistance and created an insecticide treadmill, so with herbicides. While herbicides may control weeds on a short-term basis, in the long term they may worsen the problem they were intended to control.

During the 25 years that atrazine has been used, over 30 types of weeds have developed resistance to the herbicide. Dr Ross Feldberg, a Tufts University biochemist, warns that herbicide resistance may be transferred by engineered plants to surrounding weeds. The combination of genetically engineered crop strains, together with increased application of herbicides which those crop strains can tolerate, may set up the conditions that lead to gene transfer between plant species" (Matthiessen and Kohn 1985). This could accelerate herbicide resistance in weeds and cause an upwardly spiralling use of herbicides. Dr David Pimental of Cornell has studied corn exposed to the herbicide 2,4-D. He concludes that the herbicide has increased insect and pathogen pests on corn; the sprayed plots of corn were attacked by larger numbers of insects, and insects which were bigger and laid more eggs. He found that herbicides also stress and weaken the plant's resistance to disease; corn exposed to 2,4-D had significantly more southern leaf blight lesions than unsprayed corn (Zwerdling 1977).

This revolution in agriculture merely deepens the grooves of the senescent circle trod by agribusiness around the axis of a chemical-based agriculture. There are no line items in their cost–benefit calculus of herbicide-resistant crops to account for the costs of an increasingly herbicide-based agriculture on human health, soil, and groundwater, and on weed resistance.

3. Genetically Engineered Microorganisms

The widespread spraying with synthetic chemicals, which *Silent Spring* protested, can seem crude today by comparison with genetic engineering of plants, animals, and microbes for use in agriculture. The biotechnology industry anticipates inserting viral, yeast, or bacterial genes into plants to make the plants resistant to pathogens and organisms; and inserting genes into or excising genes from bacteria which are cultured and released into agricultural fields for a variety of agricultural purposes: "The genetic engineer can take a gene from any organism and add that gene to the chromosome of another organism. The recipient cell does not have to be related to the donor. Scientists are adding bacterial genes to plants, plant genes to bacteria, animal genes to plants, etc." (Brill 1986).

Genes, inserted into plants or microorganisms, might speed up a plant's uptake of fertilizer or its rate of nitrogen fixation. Genetically altered bacteria might slow ice formation on a plant's vegetative surface. Or they might act as a fungicide, herbicide, or insecticide to protect plants from pathogens, weeds, or insects. Here is a partial list of genetically engineered organisms and their potential uses in agriculture which EPA published in October 1986:[2]

Engineered marine algae. Protoplast fusion and other recombinant DNA techniques are being used in marine algae to increase their production of beta-carotene, agar, and other algal by-products.

Fungus strains altered by ultraviolet irradiation. Four strains of the fungus *Sclerotinia sclerotiorum,* which are genetically mutated with ultraviolet radiation, are being tested for their efficacy as herbicides against Canada thistle and spotted knapweed.

Cell fusion product for fungus control. A genetically altered strain of the fungus *Trichoderma harzanium* was produced by fusing cells of two closely related strains of the fungus. The new strain is being studied for its ability to control fungi responsible for damping off and plant rot diseases. The hybrid fungus will be applied to pea and cucumber seeds.

Baculoviruses as pesticides. Researchers are attempting to enhance the pesticidal ability of baculoviruses by genetically manipulating the organization and expression of viral chromosomes.

Killed bacteria as pesticide. The delta-endotoxin gene from the bacterial pesticide *Bacillus thuringiensis* (Bt) is cloned and inserted into a species of *Pseudomonas* which is cultured to produce large amounts of the protein that acts as a pesticide. The bacteria are then killed, their cell walls fixed, and the resulting toxin used as an insecticide. Monsanto is working on a similar product using live *Pseudomonas fluorescens* with the Bt gene.

---

2. "Some possible uses for biotechnology," 1986. In March 1988 EPA approved field tests of a bacterium which has been genetically engineered to increase nitrogen fixation. The bacterium *Rhizobium meliloti* grows naturally on alfalfa roots. BioTechnica Inc. of Cambridge, Massachusetts has reinserted the genes responsible for nitrogen use back into the organism, giving it two copies of the genes.

The most publicized case of a bacterium genetically engineered for use in agriculture is the "ice-minus" bacterium. A University of California, Berkeley scientist, Steven Lindow, discovered that there are two kinds of bacteria that populate the vegetative surface of most plants, *Pseudomonas syringae* and *Pseudomonas fluorescens*, which facilitate the ice-forming process that causes frost damage to crops and fruit trees. Frost damage occurs as moisture on the plant's surface begins to freeze. Expanding ice crystals puncture and dehydrate the plant's cells. Ice forms on plants only around certain kinds of impurities which serve as a nucleus for ice crystal formation. It is thought that these two bacteria contain molecules on their cell membranes which react with the water molecules. The bacteria serve as the nucleus of ice formation when ambient temperature is at or below freezing, 32 degrees Fahrenheit. Lindow found that in more than 100 different agricultural crops these two bacteria were the center of frost formation. He found that plants that had the bacteria removed from their leaves could survive without frost damage to temperatures of 23 degrees Fahrenheit. He experimented with killing and inhibiting the bacteria, using antibiotics and chemical compounds applied as plant nutrients which disrupted the arrangement of molecules on the bacteria. With two colleagues at Berkeley, Lindow found that he could remove a gene in both bacteria which governed the arrangement of molecules on the bacteria's membrane that supported ice nucleation. Testing bacteria from which the ice-nucleating gene had been removed on laboratory plants, he found that the plants survived temperatures as low as 23 degrees Fahrenheit.

The next step was to test the genetically altered bacteria's performance in the field. Lindow was funded by Advanced Genetic Sciences, a firm interested in the agricultural applications of "ice-minus" bacteria, as well as in the development of other genetically altered strains for artificial snow-making. Since his work was in part funded by The National Institutes of Health (NIH), he was required to obtain approval for the field test from the Recombinant DNA Advisory Committee of the National Institutes of Health. The approval was granted. However, the test was halted by a court injunction won by a coalition of environmentalists.

The environmental plaintiffs argued that the environmental impacts of the open-air test had not been comprehensively evaluated. NIH's Recombinant DNA Advisory Committee, which approved the field test, was dominated by molecular biologists and had no ecologists, botanists, plant pathologists, or population geneticists. They were not qualified, therefore, to make the evaluation of possible environmental impacts, an assessment which is required by the National Environmental Policy Act. Clearly, the expertise to tinker with nature, to alter bacteria genetically and achieve a specific effect was there. But the scientific depth and expertise to understand the potential impacts of releasing genetically altered organisms on the larger ecosystem was not.

The specific risks, which the environmentalists raised in their suit against the field study of the "ice-minus" bacteria, demonstrate the critical lag which exists between the laboratory know-how and an ecological and ethical analysis of the new biotechnologies. The environmentalists suggested that frost-preventing bacteria could be swept up into the upper atmosphere, where ice-nucleating bacteria have been found, and ultimately affect local and global climate. A senior scientist with the Humane Society testified that the proposed action could have adverse impacts on animal life, since frost kills or arrests certain microorganisms which cause disease in animals. Eugene Odum, a nationally recognized ecologist, wrote in an affidavit that the project of introducing microorganisms into the environment is especially hazardous because of their high reproductive potential and their interrelationships with other organisms in the environment, which are not well understood. He pointed out that higher plants, like trees and crops, are slow to develop immunity to new microorganisms (Doyle 1985, p. 238).

Genetic engineering of microbes can increase the mutational frequency of organisms far beyond their natural rate of mutation in the environment. What happens when microorganisms with a gene implanted or excised are introduced into the environment? Cornell's Dr Martin Alexander says that no one can predict their survival ability. Although the likelihood may be low that they will persist, "the probability of persistence for an unknown organism . . . is not zero" (Doyle 1985, p. 240). Genetically modified microbes and plants will be used in agricultural ecosystems, systems which ecologists consider simplified. Agricultural environments consist of crop and animal monocultures, environments which are less diverse and in which one small genetic change could have more significant consequences than in more natural, diverse ecosystems. Ecologist Frances Sharples warns that it may be difficult to keep genes inserted into bacteria isolated in those bacterial strains. Bacteria can transmit certain genetic material by means of plasmids from one species to another and from one genus to another (Doyle 1985, p. 243).

Only since 1983 have government and science begun to consider what would happen with the release of genetically engineered organisms in the environment. In February 1985 the Cornell University Ecosystems Research Center concluded that the methods for predicting the survival and proliferation of bioengineered microorganisms in nature are crude and the effects are unpredictable. Only since June 1985 have ecologists and molecular biologists begun a formal scientific dialogue on the subject. In 1986, EPA's Scientific Advisory Board echoed the same concerns as the Cornell Ecosystems Research Center. Eighty to 90 percent of soil microbes have never been cultured in the laboratory and are unnamed. It is possible to measure if microbes have "died back"; but it is not possible to tell when microbes have died back completely (Doyle 1986). The consensus among ecologists is that no one can predict the outcome of introducing a new species into the environment.[3]

At this juncture in the recent history of recombinant DNA and using genetically engineered organisms in agriculture, there is a profound sense of *déjà vu*. Has anything changed, I pondered, as I reread Rachel Carson's chapter, "The obligation to endure." Writing of the intensive use of synthetic organic chemicals in agriculture and forestry, she cautioned:

> The rapidity of change and the speed with which new situations are created follow the impetus and heedless pace of man rather than the deliberate pace of nature . . . The chemicals to which life is asked to make its adjustment are no longer merely the calcium and silica and copper and all the rest of minerals washed out of the rocks and carried in rivers to the sea; they are the synthetic creations of man's inventive mind, brewed in his laboratories, and having no counterpart in nature (Carson 1962, p. 17).

What has changed from the era of spraying broad-spectrum pesticides to the era of introducing specific, genetically mutated organisms into nature are the metaphors. Chemical companies openly declared a war on nature with synthetic pesticides. The biotechnologists present their technologies as assisting nature. "Farming, in the future, will be based more on biology than chemistry. Biotechnology means going 'back to nature,'" said one bio-entrepreneur (Brill 1986). And it means improving on nature. "'You will be able to find more variability than you can in nature,'" said another, referring to plant genetic engineering which could some day generate genetic varieties not naturally present in cultivated plants (Doyle 1985, p. 197). The entire plant world will become one open-ended gene pool in which, for example, genes from a tree species resistant to a fungus can be spliced into a wheat strain which is susceptible to that fungus.

In other words, as plants and animals are going extinct at an increasing rate, biotechnology is selling itself on its ability to create genetic diversity in agriculture. It is being offered as a technical band-aid for a

---

3. In 1987 Advanced Genetic Sciences (AGS) did win a court challenge to field test ice-minus bacteria. In April 1987 scientists sprayed a strawberry field in northern California. It was the first *authorized* outdoor release of genetically engineered bacteria in the United States. The EPA had fined AGS for injecting the bacteria into trees growing on a laboratory roof in 1985.

tragedy in nature, that "species are disappearing at rates never before witnessed on this planet" (World Commission on Environment and Development 1987, p. 148) in tropical forests, temperate forests, mangrove forests, coral reefs, savannahs, grasslands, and arid zones. But, even with concocting their own genetic varieties, biotechnologists will still need a continual source of genetic diversity from plants and animals in the wild, which happen to be richest in the tropics, subtropics, and regions such as the Mediterranean basin. So biotechnology companies, major corporations, and national governments of industrial countries are all trying to "collect, save, and in some cases, own, the genes of the Old World" (Doyle 1985, p. 198). A new form of First World dominance of the Third World is emerging, this time for gene wealth. Nature in the wild has come to interest biotechnology, as a source of genes and germ plasm, which become all the more valuable a raw material for the genetic technologies' industry as wild flora and fauna become scarce and endangered. The more genetic material the biotechnology industry can collect, save, and own today, and the more ingenious their preservation and storage methods, the more dispensable wild nature becomes tomorrow.

Preserving genetic diversity in a species-endangered world is one part of the mythology which encases biotechnology development. The other element of the mythology is that this "green-gene revolution" will solve the growing world population's food needs. This is, again, a technical band-aid offered for the profound human tragedy of hunger and malnutrition. People dying from hunger when surplus food stands in silos elsewhere is not a failure of agricultural technology. This tragedy is caused by militarism which uses hunger as a weapon and siphons off countries' economic resources for guns, tanks, and planes that should be used for sustainable agriculture. It is caused by economic and agricultural development which depletes and erodes soils rather than replenishing and sustaining their fertility. It is caused by structures of poverty which drive people in developing countries to live in and wear out fragile ecosystems. It is caused by agricultural policies in the West which use food surpluses as cheap aid to developing countries and, thus, undercut their indigenous agricultural economies.

Writing on global food production and global hunger, the World Commission on Environment and Development of the United Nations concludes that the problem of hunger is now primarily social and political, not technical: "The agricultural resources and the technology needed to feed growing populations are available. . . . Agriculture does not lack resources; it lacks policies to ensure that food is produced where it is needed and in a manner that sustains the rural poor" (World Commission on Environment and Development 1987, p. 118).

This same analysis was presented by Robert W. Kates, Director of

Brown University's World Hunger Program, to the American Association of the Advancement of Science 1988 annual conference in Boston. The end of hunger is in sight, he said. World food production first matched global food needs in the sixties and continues to increase. Hunger and famine are failures of human institutions: "Today the basic dietary needs of the world's 5 billion people can be met with only 80 percent of the world's food production. . . . but the failure of human values and institutions has skewed worldwide food allocations, creating waste in the face of starvation (Murphy 1988).

Since the causes of hunger are primarily social and political, so ought the solutions to ending hunger and famine be social and political ones, for which safe and predictable agricultural technologies serve as appropriate tools. But who will ensure that only safe and predictable agricultural technologies and technology products are approved for use?

It will not be the federal government, which has not allowed, and will not allow, the regulation of chemicals or biotechnologies to stifle their economic potential for industry. David Kingsbury of the National Science Foundation developed a policy framework on regulating biotechnology for the White House. Biotechnology will affect the United States economy substantially, he says, to as much as $40 billion by the year 2000. Although the United States is currently the leader in this field, he warns that Japan and many European countries will probably get special government financial assistance and special regulatory treatment. They may surpass the United States if "an irrational or burdensome regulatory climate . . . fatally impede(s) the eventual introduction of products now under development and lead(s) to future disinterest in this area (Kingsbury 1986).[4] In Kingsbury's view the major goal of regulating agencies is to educate the public out of "irrational" fears about the risks of the biotechnologies.

---

4. This image of United States biotechnology strapped by regulation while Japan and Europe are specially protected contradicts Yale sociologist Charles Perrow's findings. He writes that the current laissez-faire attitude toward DNA research among American biotechnology researchers distinguishes them from European and Japanese counterparts. In Britain, for example, gene-splicing technology is constrained by a stricter set of standards and containment levels than in the United States. Japan has implemented a strict set of policies patterned after the original NIH guidelines, which have since been softened in the United States. "The [American] economic projection, the great interest of private, for-profit firms and the popularity of such U.S. firms as Genetech [sic] in our stock market may have something to do with this international difference" (Perrow 1984, p. 301).

David Kingsbury is currently under investigation for his ties to a British biotechnology company, according to *Science* and *New Scientist*. In 1986 Kingsbury reelected himself to the board of directors at IGB, Inc., a medical diagnostics research company and part of Porton International plc (Anderson & Connor 1987, p. 24; Crawford 1987, p. 742).

The biotechnology industry is also forcing its view of the purpose of regulation on those federal agencies which were established to protect human health and the environment against the hazards and risks of technologies. Winston Brill, Vice President of Research and Development of the biotechnology firm Agracetus, writes that "The release of genetically engineered organisms into the environment . . . brings EPA into the picture. The task of EPA and also of the US Department of Agriculture is to regulate released organisms without inhibiting the advance of biotechnology as a whole" (Brill 1986). And EPA, which expects to have the primary role in regulating all of biotechnology in the development of pesticides, backs down from the bullish biotechnology industry and speaks in synchronicity with Kingsbury, who speaks for the White House. When EPA's Assistant Administrator for Pesticides and Toxic Substances was asked what was the greatest risk in the emerging field of biotechnology, he said that it was people who distrust the technologies and the regulatory agencies: "The greatest risk we face right now is failure to develop public confidence in the process that leads from the laboratory to the marketplace" ("Developing confidence in biotechnology" 1986).

The real risk EPA faces in the emerging field of biotechnology is that it will end up enforcing laws whose primary intent is to protect the economic benefits of the American biotechnology industry. EPA's role will be merely risk management and risk communication: analyzing the biotechnologies' risks to human health and the environment in such a limited way that, like agricultural chemicals, the technologies become acceptable and can go forward; and convincing people that risks of releasing mutated organisms into nature can be managed and that they have to be lived with.

Risk/benefit analysis is a limited, rationalistic tool which cannot comprehend values which are deep, long-lived, far-reaching, cultural, philosophical, or existential, and essentially unquantitative. How do we measure what is lost when agriculture—the culture of life and living land—becomes agribusiness, with farmers as business clients of major chemical and biotechnology companies? An American farmer and philosopher, Wendell Berry, expresses some of the nonquantifiable losses in the transition from agriculture to chemical and biotechnical food production. He says that agriculture is not, and cannot be, an industry. Agriculture has to do with life and life processes; industry uses inert materials and mechanistic processes. A factory has a limited life; tools and buildings wear out and depreciate over time. Topsoil, if well cultivated, will not wear out; some agricultural soils have been farmed for 4,000–5,000 years or more. The best farms have been those which are people's homes as well as their workplaces. Unlike a factory worker, a farmer is at home when at work. Finally, industry takes raw materials, uses and exhausts them, and pollutes. Agribusiness uses methods of the factory, not replenishing organic soil fertility; polluting soil and groundwater; treating animals, plants, and soil as minable raw materials to be used, manufactured into new products, and exhausted. Farming is a "replenishing economy" which takes, makes, and returns fertility to the soil, not just a physical organic fertility but also care and respect (Berry 1987, pp. 123–124).

How do we measure in cost–benefit terms the effect that the new biotechnologies will have on developing countries? The technology know-how is in the industrial developed countries. Those uses which will be commercialized first will be ones in their own self-interest, like the bovine growth hormone and herbicide-resistant crops. These technologies, then, will exacerbate the problem of food surpluses in the global market and depress further the agricultural economy of the Third World. There are those who say that the biotechnologies in the right hands—the hands which need them, the Third World nations—could pull those countries above famine and malnutrition into the era of scientific agriculture. The biotechnologies could be used for developing drought-resistant crops, more productive food plants, and livestock that grow more quickly. However, these new plant and animal life forms will have patents held by First World commercial companies who will require Third World farmers to pay royalties for extended periods of time. The royalties will become another form of economic bondage. This analysis of the technologies in the right hands presumes also that the technologies are progressive, beneficent, and will work. If, as one agriculture analyst has written, "one unforeseen mutation or errant gene could bring down the whole system," is it conscionable to risk agricultural catastrophe in developing countries where food supply is still precarious?[5]

5. Tanzania has embarked on a new national agricultural policy which now emphasizes improving the peasants' agriculture through crop rotation, composting, and village-based agriculture, over the high-tech practices of the Green Revolution. Originally, President Nyerere sought to modernize the country's agriculture by imitating the American and Canadian model: mechanization, chemical fertilizers, chemical pesticides, and herbicides. Compost-making was no longer taught in agricultural schools, because it was discredited as old-fashioned. Farmers found themselves dependent on an unreliable supply of chemicals. Returning to indigenous methods of organic agriculture gives them a self-reliance which they had lost (Doyle 1985, pp. 275–276).

There may be another reason for the return to indigenous farming in Tanzania. Women do most of the agricultural field work, yet the government allotted the new hybrid maize seeds, fertilizer and pesticides to men. The Tanzanian women neglected the new crop because the profits from Green Revolution agriculture would go to the men. Women—who work an average of 3,069 hours per year to men's 1,929—continued with indigenous agriculture. This fact, that women boycotted Green Revolution agriculture, may be the crux of why the high tech revolution in agriculture failed in Tanzania, and the country returned to indigenous agriculture (Dankelman and Davidson 1988, pp. 3, 18).

How do we measure the risk to the ecosystem, whether it be in the First World or Third World or both, of this new revolution, when many ecosystem accidents cannot be calculated in advance? With recombinant DNA technologies, there will be linkages, writes Perrow, between parts of ecosystems thought to be independent, which will create new relationships and sequences of activity in nature. These will not be expected, understood, or easily traced, once it is apparent that they have taken place. "Knowledge of the behavior of the human-made material in its new ecological niche is extremely limited by its novelty" (Perrow 1984, p. 296).

To make this analysis of the risk of the unexpected more tangible, let us look at an example. Two New Zealand plant scientists, K. L. Giles and H. C. M. Whitehead, used a cell fusion technique to combine the genetic material of a fungus, *Rhizopogon* sp., which lives symbiotically on the roots of the pine tree, *Pinus radiata*, with a nitrogen-fixing bacteria, *Azotobacter vinelandii*. They hoped to create a modified strain of fungus with the ability to fix nitrogen. In the laboratory, Giles and Whitehead applied the new fungus to pine-tree seedlings. Some of the test seedlings exposed to the modified fungus died. Analysis of their roots showed that the new hybrid fungus had penetrated the cells of the root cortex. The root cells appeared dead and empty of cytoplasm. There was no intercellular growth on the pine seedlings roots by wild strains and control strains of fungus. While the scientists did not know whether the genetically modified fungus killed the root cells or just entered the cells when they had died, they feared that the new organism might be pathogenic, and destroyed the remaining plants and organisms (Doyle 1985, pp. 243–244).[6]

Even with the novel risks posed by these biotechnologies, this biotechnology revolution is not new. It recalls an earlier one, in which the unexpected risks of chemical pesticides became reason to write *Silent Spring*. Rachel Carson chronicled the movement of pesticide: from point of application to soil, then washed by rain to streams and into groundwater, carried on wind beyond agricultural fields, and ultimately transported through plants, herbivores, and carnivores, from insects and worms to birds, from animals and fish to humans, bio-magnifying at each step in the food chain. It was possible to render a species extinct without killing a single individual, she wrote of birds laying infertile

---

6. Doyle writes that when this incident was used in a House Subcommittee to refute the biotechnology contention that the whole (modified fungus) cannot be more dangerous than the sum of its parts (a beneficial fungus and a beneficial bacterium, in this case), the study was denigrated as bad science. NIH and the American Society for Microbiology contended that the study was poorly designed and lacked good statistical controls.

eggs or eggs whose shells were too thin to withstand the adult bird's weight during incubation. It did not occur to the agrichemical industry that persistent synthetic pesticides would have such pathways and relationships in nature. They disputed and denied the significance of these links when they were chronicled. They trivialized Carson's research and they sexualized their contempt for a woman who would challenge their masculinist worldview: that nature exists for their use and convenience and should be taken by force.

The force, then, was an armament of synthetic chemical pesticides, broadcast like a "chemical rain of death." Now it is the reduction of nature to a pool of genetic units which can be spliced and recombined—bacterial gene to plant, plant gene to bacteria, animal gene to plant, and so on—with the arrogant claim of improving on nature. Now it is the reduction of women to egg hatcheries and wombs for hire in order to manufacture life better than women can birth.

THE NEW REPRODUCTIVE
TECHNOLOGIES

Two researchers have developed a chart entitled, "Alternative Reproductive Methods," which lays out, matrix fashion, all of the permutations and combinations which are loosely called the new reproductive technologies (NRTs). The chart has three columns: Sources of Gametes (husband, wife, donor, or surrogate); Site of Fertilization (wife, laboratory, or surrogate); and Site of Pregnancy (wife or surrogate). To date, the researchers count 16 possibilities in the mix and match of gametes and the optional sites of fertilization and pregnancy. These include husband or donor sperm used in artificial insemination or in vitro fertilization; wife or donor eggs harvested and used in in vitro fertilization; embryo transfer from a wife to another woman or the reverse; and surrogate motherhood.[7] Surrogate motherhood has the widest array of options, eight in all. The husband or the donor provides the sperm; the wife or the surrogate provides the egg; the wife is the "site of fertilization" and the embryo is flushed, transferred into and carried by surrogate; the laboratory is the site of in vitro fertilization and the embryo is transferred into the surrogate woman; or the surrogate is artificially inseminated and is the "site of pregnancy." The researchers note an option they entitle "planned procreation for placement": a donor sperm is used to insemi-

---

7. The surrogate mother is not the substitute parent, as the language implies. She is the real mother. The language of surrogacy is a duplicitous construction which enables men driven to procreate—the reproductive technologists, and the surrogate industry entrepreneurs—to exploit women as reproductive vehicles (see Raymond 1988b).

nate a surrogate who produces a baby "for placement" (Ethics Committee of the American Fertility Society 1986). The chart is very helpful. It enables the researchers to display graphically the expansionist nature of the technologies, lest anyone think they are beneficent technologies developed only for a small number of infertile women. Eight of the 16 options include a second woman, the surrogate. For every child "alternately reproduced," there will be two women's lives consumed by reproductive technologies. Everyone and every reproductive activity in the chart is represented by letters: H–husband, W–wife, S–surrogate or third-party substitute, and L–laboratory. Done for compactness' sake, this technique is more honest than pictures of healthy in vitro babies, smiling mothers, and stories about happy surrogates who love breeding. For this revolution is fundamentally thingifying: women (W and S) are interchangeable with the laboratory test tube (L) as the "site of fertilization." Women are egg hatcheries (sources of gametes) and wombs for rent (sites of pregnancy).

Embedded within this chart is the underside of this "reproductive revolution." While war is traditionally portrayed as men against men in combat, this revolution is men against women. Women's bodies are the battlegrounds of this revolution in which men use a form of chemical warfare to induce superovulation, capture eggs with invasive instruments, and then claim women's fallopian tubes and uteri as their bases of operation. Women are generally not permitted in combat; but women are expected to labor, shed blood, and suffer in childbirth. This social expectation compels women to want the technologies; and it permits technologists to practice experimental and high-risk procedures on women.

The new reproductive technologies have deceived women. The myths which encase these technologies, making them acceptable and almost inevitable, are that they offer hope for the infertile; that they improve upon nature and expand women's reproductive choices; and that motherhood is essential for a woman's fulfillment.

Myth 1. Hope for the Infertile

In 1985, journalist Gena Corea and medical writer Susan Ince conducted a survey of the success rates of 54 of 108 IVF clinics registered with the American Fertility Society. They found that clinics had different definitions of success and different methods of dropping women clients from their statistics in order to enhance their "success rate." Half of the 54 clinics—in business for one month to three years, with a total of 600 women from whom they had collected over $2.5 million in fees—never sent a woman home with a baby. Most clinics calculated their success rate by the "percentage of pregnancies per laparoscopy." This allowed clinics with some pregnancies but no births to claim success rates as high as 25 percent. Clinics' definitions of "pregnancy" and "laparoscopy" differed. But the overall intent of the statistic-keeping was to maximize the countable pregnancies and minimize the countable laparoscopies, so as to have the highest "success" rate (pregnancies per laparoscopy) possible.

A laparoscopy is an operation in which a woman's eggs, which are usually chemically induced to ripen, are removed with a series of instruments which are inserted into her abdomen to hold the ovary, pierce the egg follicles, and suck out the eggs. Corea and Ince found that some clinics counted laparoscopies only when eggs were recovered; others only when recovered eggs were successfully fertilized in vitro; still others only when fertilized eggs develop to embryos. Therefore, a lower number of laparoscopies are counted than are performed. As for pregnancies, a larger number of successful pregnancies are reported than children born. Some clinics counted pregnancies as those implanted embryos which were confirmed by ultrasound and fetal heart tone. Others counted something called a chemical pregnancy as a successful pregnancy, when one or two elevated human chorionic gonadotrophin levels were detected. Embryos which were transferred from test tube to womb and were aborted or miscarried were often included as a successful pregnancy, as were tubal pregnancies. Many clinics admitted to using only a subset of their patients from whom they have had the best results to report pregnancy rates. Some used their current success rate, rather than a less flattering overall success rate. The survey revealed the calculated cover-up of low results by the IVF industry (Corea and Ince 1985).

France is one of the western countries that has invested substantially in IVF research and IVF centers. By 1987, of the fewer than 5,000 IVF babies born worldwide, 1,500 had been born in France. France has nearly as many IVF centers as the United States. Sociologist Françoise Laborie reports the same inflation of success rates in France as Corea and Ince found in the United States. Success rates are calculated as "pregnancies by embryo transfer." Pregnancy includes "biochemical pregnancy" which lasts only a few days; "clinical pregnancy" which may be ectopic or terminate by abortion; "ongoing pregnancy," 15 to 20 percent of which end up in spontaneous abortion; and finally, "completed pregnancy." Transfer refers to embryo transfer, which is the last of several IVF stages: hormonal stimulation of the ovaries, laparoscopy to harvest eggs, and in vitro fertilization of the eggs to obtain an embryo. Many women never reach the stage of embryo transfer and, thus, never appear in the statistics as failed IVF attempts. Laborie reports that when success is defined as live births per hormonal stimulation, two highly regarded IVF centers have success rates of 5.9 and 1.0 percent, respectively! (Laborie 1987).

The American and French studies demonstrate the extent to which the new reproductive technology clinics deceive women by disguising a technology which fails for most women with the false gilding of "hope for the infertile." Is there any other medical procedure or commodity which carries the risks of so much medical intervention as these do, which fails so many as these do, which is so costly as these are for women, and which carries so much potential for exploitation as these do for women, and purports to offer hope? I think not.

Myth 2. Expanding Women's Options

To help the reader grasp the rich array of biotechnical options which the new reproductive technologies offer NRT practitioners, I looked up "in vitro fertilization" in the index of a critically acclaimed book on the new reproductive technologies, published in 1985. In vitro fertilization is the process by which the first test tube baby, Louise Brown, was conceived in 1977. An egg or oocyte is taken from a woman and fertilized with sperm in a Petri dish; the resulting embryo is transferred into the woman's womb. Under "in vitro fertilization," I found 25 entries. They include: egg donation in, egg maturation in, embryo freezing in, embryo screening in, eugenics in, genetic engineering, hormones in, nonreproductive uses of, sex predetermination with, sperm capacitation in, and superovulation in (Corea 1985, p. 368). Lots of options, but for whom, women or the technologists?

Recently, a French researcher wrote that new and more drugs and mixtures of drugs and hormones are being tested on women in IVF and that standard IVF procedures are being prescribed for an increasing number of women. *Buserline*, a drug manufactured by Hoescht Laboratories and licensed for treatment of testicular tumors, is now being used on European women in IVF. *Buserline* suppresses the natural production of hormones needed to induce ovulation. Other drugs are then used to induce the ovulation exogenously once it has been blocked. However, *Buserline* begins by inducing the opposite effect. Before the drug blocks the hormonal cycle it causes a flare-up of hormonal activity. This strong overstimulation can cause the production of cysts on the ovaries. Animal toxicological data show that the drug, at different dosages, has opposite effects, and that animal fetuses exposed to this drug in utero suffered retarded development. However, Hoescht has concluded the drug is not teratogenic (Laborie 1987).

Clearly, new drugs are being developed and used on women in the interests of reproductive technologists to obtain more eggs, more in vitro fertilizations, more embryo transfers, but not necessarily more completed pregnancies. The new reproductive technologies show no evidence of expanding women's choices. Women are given only one fundamental option, while technologists devise all kinds of new ways to play with egg, sperm, and embryo. Women still have only one choice: to submit themselves to a cadre of medical people who are inured to the profoundly unethical nature of using whatever is the latest in reproductive drugs and surgery on women as experimental subjects.

The other expansion in IVF is the numbers of women for whom IVF is being prescribed. A human menopausal gonadotrophin, hMG, which has been used in IVF to stimulate the production of eggs in one cycle, is now being prescribed for all kinds of menstrual irregularities, for women who have had successive abortions, for women whose husbands have defective sperm and for women whose infertility cannot be explained. IVF was first developed for infertility due to blocked or diseased fallopian tubes. Throughout the world, it is now being used on women in response to *male infertility* and other, unexplained sources of infertility. A French survey of 53 IVF centers reveals that only 60 percent of IVF treatments relate to tubal diseases; 16 percent are for male disorders and 24 percent for unexplained infertility. This trend will only increase in the competition for more "clients" and with the trend of increasing male infertility (Laborie 1987).

Women's options, as the media and medical promotional literature would suggest, are not expanding. What is expanding is the number of women for which the technologies are prescribed, and the biotechnologists' portfolio of technical and chemical procedures to stimulate ovulation, to capture eggs, to fertilize eggs, to implant embryos. The technical and career options of the NRT practitioners are expanding. The amount of research and number of papers and symposia are expanding. The number of indications for which IVF is prescribed is expanding. The number and types of reproductive businesses are expanding. The choices of women, the freedom of women from medical manipulation, and the ability to refuse these procedures are diminishing as IVF expands as a general pattern of procreation.

Myth 3. Fulfillment through Motherhood

Recently *Parade* magazine featured a photo of "test-tube baby families" in Britain with a short article entitled, "Yesterday's miracle." The photo shows three men standing in the background; the foreground is a semicircle of women sitting with babies and young children who fill up the space between the women. Most of the women clutch babies; a young girl is holding a baby, so is a young woman who could be a teenager, but might be a young mother. The men appear in the picture primarily in relationship to themselves, distinct from the women and children, and at the pinnacle of the group. Viewing the picture, one's eye begins with them, is led down and around the semicircle of women and children and returns back to finish on them. They are the first and final point of interest. An anomalous woman is outside the cluster of women and children. She stands at the group's outer edge between two men. Being a woman, she is not, as the men appear, sufficient in herself. Without children, like all of the other women, she appears out of place. She is the only person in the picture not smiling at the camera.

The story accompanying the photo tells us that all of these people are members of test-tube baby families in Britain. "The children owe their existence—and the adults owe their parenthood—to the scientific techniques pioneered by Drs Patrick Steptoe and Robert Edwards." Their first successful test-tube baby was Louise Brown in 1978. The article finishes in saying that women giving birth by in vitro procedures is so common now that it is no longer newsworthy, "except by the new mothers with defective fallopian tubes" who desperately want babies ("Yesterday's miracle" 1988).

It is difficult to tell whether the men in the picture are IVF doctors who made it all possible or test-tube baby fathers. Either way, they stand on their own. It is apparent that the women who cluster with the children are test-tube mothers. The picture mimics the myth: that women are full and complete with babies. Without babies, their lives are off-focus and uncentered, like the woman standing among the men. Without motherhood, they are not real women.

"The rise of the new technologies is happening at a time when women in the west are being reminded by the media that if they reach thirty without having borne children, they are living half-lives," writes medical ethicist Janice Raymond (1988b). At the same time, reproductive technologies like sterilization, Depo-Provera, and sex-predetermination to eliminate girl children, are being pushed on Third World women, because they are defined as the "population problem." Raymond traces the strategies used by the media, the state, and institutions to pressure women into conforming to the ideology of motherhood as the natural and most fulfilling state for women. Motherhood most often places women in a position of subordination to men: the father of the child and the doctor who increasingly controls biological motherhood. At the same time it compensates for much of the oppression women experience inside and outside of the home, for not being valuable outside of motherhood. Motherhood also keeps women in abusive and dead-end situations with men for the sake of the children. Men have a great stake in women being mothers. Media fabricate the softsell of single women's increasing loneliness, and the working woman's goal of how to do it all. The State uses a hard sell, making it more difficult to have access to birth control, abortion information, and federal funding for abortion. The church creates obstacles, by manufacturing internalized guilt in women for using birth control and by influencing governments from implementing voluntary family planning services. The Left, in opposing family planning, fails to distinguish between family planning imposed on developing countries and birth control availability for women who want it.

Above all, the myth of women's fulfillment through motherhood covers up two divergent realities. First, women are socially pressured into relationships with men, into marriage, and into motherhood. It is radical, nonconformist, and at times difficult to choose against this and live with the consequences. Second, women's fulfillment through biological motherhood is necessary for men's professional fulfillment. Edwards and Steptoe are "immortalized" in Britain: women's biology has become the professional destiny of the reproductive biologists. Alan De Cherney, head of Yale School of Medicine's in vitro team, compares himself to a physicist working on the Manhattan Project. His professional fulfillment will be achieved in collaborating with his team on the prospect of unlocking the secrets of women's reproductive biology. Women's bodies are his future. If women refused to be clinical experiments, these men would have no professional future. The biotechnologists are heavily invested in the ideology that unless a woman has a child, she is less than herself.

> Above all, it is clear that women are the best subjects for experimentation. As opposed to mice or monkeys, women are intelligent and talk. They are conscious of how and when their ovulation occurs; they can observe and describe to the doctors the effects of different medications; they don't have to be purchased, fed, or kept in a clean cage; they come to the hospital all by themselves, on the right day, at the right time, and . . . they pay for that privilege (sometimes exorbitantly) (Laborie 1987).

Regulation and Policy

The original court injunction which environmentalists obtained against the "ice-minus" bacteria field study was based on the fact that the Recombinant DNA Advisory Committee of the National Institutes of Health did not have the expertise to evaluate the risks to the environment of releasing mutated bacteria. The NIH committee consisted of biochemists; there were no terrestrial ecologists, plant pathologists, or botanists. Consequently, the committee was ignorant and nonchalant about the ecological risks of this field study and favorably disposed toward recombinant DNA field trials. This is precisely the situation under which the new reproductive technologies are being practiced world-wide.

The new reproductive technology profession is self-regulating, in those countries where national ethics committees are comprised primarily of reproductive technologists who are invested in the technologies. Their concerns are generally issues of licensing, patenting, defining which aspects of the technologies are experimental, and getting professional consensus so the experimental work can go forward. In other countries, governments have set up committees to define the issues and recommend policy. In these cases, issues and policy are framed by patriarchal government concerns: paternity; the "cheapening" of life inherent in the commercialization of eggs, sperm, and embryos; research on embryos; and restricting technologies to married, heterosexual couples. What is lacking in the policy of every government and professional ethics committee is the central issue of how the new reproductive technologies affect women's dignity and bodily integrity: in short, how these technologies can and do exploit women.

A recent international report on the new reproductive technology developments and policy discloses the male state-centered and male profession-centered nature of regulation (Spallone and Steinberg 1987). In Australia, for example, various governments and councils ban cloning, fertilization of human eggs with non-human gametes, mixing of sperm in AID (artificial insemination by donor), sale of gametes and embryos, commercial surrogacy, and research on human embryos. IVF is restricted to married couples. At the same time, there is major on-going research *on women* to improve ovulation stimulation methods, egg capture, and embryo transfer. Government and medical professional concerns center on respect for paternity; respect for human embryonic life; and the cheapening effect of commerce in reproduction. Meanwhile experimental technologies and drugs are being used on women to improve the doctors' success rates, with no acknowledgement that it is cheapening and unethical to experiment on women.

France has as many as 150 IVF clinics. In almost all of them, research on egg freezing and hormonal stimulation—which requires using women's bodies as the site of experimentation with fertility drugs—is being done. The primary ethical issues which have preoccupied national ethics committees are commercial surrogate motherhood, utilization of fetal tissue, and experimentation on embryos. Again, we witness more respect for fetal life than for women's bodily integrity.

In the United States there are at least 200 IVF clinics. Commercial surrogacy agencies are flourishing, initially with no regulation, now with minimal state regulation. Gamete intrafallopian transfer (GIFT), a variation of IVF in which extracted ova and sperm are being injected into a woman's fallopian tube for fertilization there, is being touted as more "successful" than IVF. Drs Randolf Seed and Richard Seed, founders of the firm Fertility and Genetics Research, plan to open 20 to 30 for-profit embryo transfer clinics throughout the United States. No federal legislation exists to regulate the technologies; at most, a Congressional decision was made not to use public funds for reproductive research. In early 1988, 10 presidential candidates were asked whether they would support a law banning surrogate motherhood. Eight out of 10 had no policy or no comment on the issue. In the same survey, 7 out of 10 had no policy on releasing genetically engineered microorganisms into the environment; 6 out of 10 had no policy on supporting viable alternatives to laboratory experimentation on animals. However, 9 out of 10 had a position on virtually every other issue which ranged from domestic issues like AIDS, nuclear power, and Star Wars to international issues on *Contra* aid and the Middle East. Apparently, every other social and political issue, including microorganisms and lab animals, has captured more of their attention and holds more value than one concerning the traffic in women's bodies (Presidential candidates' quiz 1988).

While there has been a vacuum of government interest in the US reproductive revolution until recently, when some "surrogate mothers" have decided to keep their biological children, the biomedical profession has decided to advise itself on the ethics of what it is doing. In September 1986 the Ethics Committee of the American Fertility Society published its report on the ethical considerations of the new reproductive technologies. The 11-member committee consisted of 10 men and 1 woman. Seven of the 11 were practitioners of the technologies. The chair of the committee, Dr Howard Jones, who heads the foremost IVF clinic in the United States, may have more invested professionally in IVF than any other person in the States.

On the surface, the report appears to stand on three legs: concern for the potential harms and long-term social impacts of the new reproductive technologies; the autonomy of persons making reproductive decisions; and the autonomy of IVF researchers and clinicians. This is cosmetic. In fact, it has only one sturdy leg and two atrophied ones.

The report is an ode to the autonomy of IVF researchers and technologists. Where a technology is unproven, has a low probability of success, or is risk-laden (often all three conditions are present), it is declared a "clinical experiment" and then approved for practice. (Clinical experiment means that researchers and practitioners who are heavily invested in the autonomy of IVF research review their colleagues' work.) For example, cryopreservation of eggs carries significant potential for genetic damage in the freezing/thawing process. Therefore it is approved as a clinical experiment. The committee expresses reservations about the risk of cryo-injury to embryos which could cause birth defects, since it appears that only 50 to 60 percent may be viable after thawing. Therefore, cryopreservation of embryos is approved as a clinical experiment.

Uterine lavage for preembryo transfer carries numerous risks to the donor woman from whom the embryo is flushed, and to the receiving woman into whom it is transferred. These are risks of intrauterine infection, ectopic pregnancy, and multiple pregnancies. The committee finds, however, that trying this technology out on women "enriches the fund of knowledge in understanding the variations in the physiology of early reproduction" (Ethics Committee of American Fertility Society 1986). Therefore, it is approved as a "clinical experiment." Another technology approved as a clinical experiment is surrogate gestational motherhood, that is, a woman carrying a genetically unrelated embryo transferred into her for the period of gestation. One committee member cites the potential for exploitation of women *in a page note*. But the committee as a whole highlights *in the text* its concern that women might abuse this "innovative reproductive technology" for selfish, nonmedical purposes such as vanity, convenience, or fear of pregnancy. However, the committee is willing to take the lesser risk that women might be exploited and the greater risk that women might exploit the technology because "there could be a role for surrogate gestation in reproductive medicine." The committee wants to ensure that the reproductive profession diversifies their portfolio as much as possible.

The committee is undisguised in its intentions: to set out guidelines by which the technologies *may be practiced*, not restricted.

> Professional guidelines must not casually accede to restrictions on reproductive technologies that offer enhanced options. Rather, as this report attempts to do, guidelines should be set out that detail *how the technologies may be offered* [emphasis mine] with safety and ethical appropriateness (Ethics Committee of the American Fertility Society 1986).

The committee distorts the overall success of the technologies, stating that the success rates vary but are as high as 25 percent per cycle of treatment. It expands the indications for treatment. Indications for IVF include low sperm concentrations, uterine disorders suffered from DES, other medically induced infertility and congenital causes, and also "unexplained" infertility. Whatever is risk-laden and ethically questionable is declared a "clinical experiment," and then approved. Research on embryos, which is generally abhorrent and ethically questionable, is justified in the following way. Through the first 14 days after fertilization, embryos are called "preembryos." Research on embryos is not yet ethically acceptable to the technologists; but research on preembryos becomes acceptable when they define preembryos not to be embryos. On the other hand, IVF is possible only because research on women's bodies is not abhorrent and is generally acceptable. Experimenting on women is disguised by collapsing women into "the couple" when there is talk about risk. And "egg donation" is treated as comparable to "sperm donation," even though there is substantial health risk to women from hormonal stimulation and general anaesthesia and none to men from sperm donation.

The committee is against compensation for eggs, sperm, and preembryos, while they ignore the breeder caste of women being created in the commercialization of surrogacy. The committee thinks that diagnostic and therapeutic procedures should not be patented. Again it would seem that crass commercialization offends their snobbish sensibilities. The committee is contradictory in discussion of the technologies' risks. It finds IVF generally "ethically acceptable" because the risks of IVF are no different than those "run by couples in their ordinary sexual lives." Yet, in the discussion on donor eggs, the committee does admit that the risks to the donor women of ovarian stimulation and general anaesthesia seem to outweigh the benefit of providing an egg for another couple. However, since the purposes of the report are to determine how the technologies "may be offered," the committee approves donor eggs in IVF—with its attendant risks to women—as a "clinical experiment." For best results, the committee recommends that the new reproductive technologies be practiced on people who are stable, reliable, medically docile, and genetically clean. Therefore, the technologies should be restricted generally to married, heterosexual people, people without hereditary diseases, people who will follow physicians' orders, and ethnic groups who are not overpopulating.

Scraping off the veneer of ethical and therapeutic concerns, we uncover the underside of this document. A profession of white, elite males trusts and licenses each other to carry out clinical experiments on women's bodies, on eggs, sperm, and preembryos. They do not trust women who might abuse surrogacy. They do not want to sully the profession with crass commercialization of egg, sperm, and preembryo selling, while they license the traffic in women arising from surrogacy. They want white, married, heterosexual couples as clients for babies, while the potential exploitation of Third World women as "surrogate gestational wombs" is an irrelevant ethical concern. They lie about success rates and share a "gentlemen's agreement" of secrecy about the failures of IVF. At least eleven women have died in IVF and a twelfth in surrogacy, while fewer than 5,000 babies have been born. Who knows and remembers the names of these women, while we all remember the names Steptoe and Edwards?[8]

These "technodocs" are white, male, and affluent; and they compare

---

8. Conversation, Gena Corea, December 21, 1988. Also see Corea (1986), footnote 2.

themselves to physicists on the Manhattan Project. They are the professional blood brothers of men who developed and prescribed DES to women without evidence of its efficacy. They are the colleagues of men like Dr Louis Keith, the professor of obstetrics who lied about his experiments with the Dalkon Shield in testifying on behalf of its safety as a consultant for the manufacturer, A. H. Robins Company (Shenon 1988). They are partners of medical entrepreneurs who will seek bankruptcy protection when technology failure is imminent. They are part of a notoriously tight-lipped profession, who will not blow the whistle on each other.

On the other hand, the women who undergo IVF feel that their bodies have cheated them and that they are failures. They experience strong social pressure, if they are married, to have children. If they fail to, they feel excluded from the social nexus of married couples with children. Many feel guilty, especially toward their husbands, and hope that the infertility is their problem and not their husband's. IVF takes over their lives; their hope for success is inflated by the false success rates published by the clinics and pandered to by the media. So they "consent" to as much medicalization of their lives as they can endure in order to assuage their guilt about being less than a woman (Crowe 1987). This is the social context in which IVF practitioners justify what they do by saying that "women want it."

IVF technology is a male-centered technical response to the social condition of women. IVF flourishes in a world in which women have little self-worth apart from bearing biological children. These women have so little self-worth that they will endure biomedical risks for a condition which is not life-threatening nor physically debilitating: risks that they would not ask of children or husbands. The less self-esteem women have, the more easily they will sign consent forms, and the more easily technodocs can practice risky and unproven procedures, called "clinical experiments," on them. IVF provides a few women with babies. But at least eleven women have died for those technical successes.

I should like to scan the world, as did Carson in the last chapter of *Silent Spring*, and to find alternatives to the "smooth superhighway" on which the new reproductive technologies are advancing so rapidly. Carson found "biological solutions, based on an understanding of the living organisms they seek to control." But if, in scanning the world, we find that the paths do not exist for women, as she found for nature, then must we not find or invent the tools with which to forge them?

International and US policy to regulate or guide the new reproductive technologies has centered on the fetus, the autonomy of IVF technologists, paternity, and "the couple," while the major health and welfare impacts of these technologies are on women. We urgently need a framework of analysis and public policy on the new reproductive technologies which is centered on women's right to dignity and bodily integrity.

1. Public Policy

Rachel Carson successfully argued that environmental regulation should be in the hands of environmental and public health scientists who have no ties to industry. A profound conflict of interest exists when the Ethics Committee of the American Fertility Society, the professional society of IVF technologists, makes public policy on the new reproductive technologies. Essentially, the biomedical profession is self-policing. Three examples have recently surfaced in consumer law-suits which should serve to illustrate the dangers of intraprofessional bias for the industry's own technology or product.

(a) Dalkon Shield. The A. H. Robins Company sold more than 2.5 million IUD devices, called the Dalkon Shield, between 1970 and 1974. About 200,000 users of the Dalkon Shield are pressing claims of injury, including uterine infection and sterility, against Robins in one of the largest mass injury cases in history. In early 1988 Dr Louis G. Keith, a Northwestern University professor of obstetrics who served as a key defense witness for Robins, was indicted for lying under oath that he had conducted experiments which demonstrated that the Dalkon Shield was not "unreasonably dangerous." Although a US Appeals Court found Dr Keith guilty of false testimony about the safety of the Dalkon Shield in 1985, he remained on the faculty at the Northwestern Medical School (Shenon 1988).

(b) Lead Paint Industry. Attorneys representing three lead-poisoned children contend that the lead industry has known since the thirties that lead poses serious hazards to young children, including the risk of permanent brain damage. They have charged the Lead Industries Association, the national trade association of the lead paint manufacturers, with a 50-year conspiracy to hide the poisonous qualities of lead paint from the public. The lawsuits claim that the manufacturing association engaged in a propaganda campaign to promote lead paint and to attack any medical findings which would impugn their product. Lead-paint poisoning was approached as a public relations problem, rather than a health problem. Association documents show that an article was published in a 1934 journal of the American Medical Association indicating that representatives of the lead association had talked with re-

searchers at Boston City Hospital that year about the danger of lead to small children. That same year lead association representatives lobbied in Massachusetts against proposed state lead regulations (Dumanoski 1987).

(c) Tobacco Industry. Lawyers in Newark, New Jersey, Federal District Court have found internal tobacco industry documents which show how some cigarette companies have developed strategies to mislead the public about the health risks of smoking. The Liggett Group did not reveal test results for seven years which showed that tars in Chesterfield and L&M cigarettes caused cancer in mice. When the results were disclosed, Liggett ensured that the results were not linked to Liggett or its brand of cigarette. The plaintiff attorney said that the tobacco industry and their trade association, the Tobacco Institute, used public health research funds on public relations strategies to polish their image. He discovered a Tobacco Institute strategy to create doubt in the public mind about the health charge that smoking causes cancer and other illnesses, without denying it. The strategy included advocating the public's right to smoke without actually urging the public to do so, and encouraging "objective" research as the only way to resolve the question of smoking's risks (Janson 1988).

All three cases offer compelling evidence that policy made to guide and regulate a new technology cannot issue from the industry or profession which stands to gain from the technology. The likelihood is too great that the policy will serve to justify and support the technology's development and use, as we saw with the American Fertility Society's report. This report protects the autonomy of the researchers and practitioners at the expense of women's health, which is so undervalued that it can be put at risk with "clinical experiments." Clinical experiment means that the colleagues of the biotechnologists review their work. Clearly, as the preceding cases demonstrate, people who stand to gain financially and professionally by silence and deceit should not be making regulatory policy. Finally, the genre of strategy developed by the tobacco industry—to advocate the public's right to smoke, without actually urging the public to do so—is being used by the American Fertility Society. The report argues that people have the moral and legal right to reproduce, including the freedom to use third parties where one or both members of a couple are physically incapable of reproducing by themselves. They state that this right might be stretched to mean that people are owed the means to reproduce from society, in the form of health insurance for IVF. The objective of this "right to reproduce" argument—the mirror image of the tobacco industry's "right to smoke"—is undisguised.

Policy and regulation on the new reproductive technologies should be made by those whose lives are affected by the technologies and by those who are specialized in analyzing the risks of the technologies for the sake of those affected by the technologies. This would include medical ethicists, reproductive toxicologists, and people who have worked with plaintiffs and victims of the technologies. The majority of policy-makers ought to be women experienced in advocacy for women's reproductive and health rights, because, overwhelmingly, the technologies are practiced on women. Analysis of the technologies must include an assessment of the causes of infertility, with emphasis on infertility which is preventable; a comprehensive risk assessment of the new reproductive technologies; a fair survey of current IVF clinic success rates; a detailed consideration of alternatives to solving the problem of infertility, including more appropriate technologies and social and political solutions; and consideration of other problems in which social protest has driven new solutions, e.g. how animal rights' activism has pushed the product research industry to develop alternatives to animal testing for product toxicology; and a strategy of legal recourse for women who are injured by the technologies.[9]

2. Government Funding of Reproductive Research

The final sentence of the American Fertility Society report recommends that the US Department of Health and Human Services revise its policies and fund "innovative" reproductive research proposals. We recommend that public funds for reproductive research be used where research is most neglected and scarce: to determine causes of infertility in women and men; and to identify how to eliminate and prevent drug-induced, doctor-induced, and chemical-induced causes of infertility. We recommend that OSHA workplace policies require industry to protect workers against exposure to chemicals which cause reproductive toxicity, rather than to keep women of childbearing age out of the workplace. We recommend that EPA require that all chemicals approved under FIFRA and TSCA be screened for reproductive toxicity prior to registration or reregistration.

---

9. Women who come forward as plaintiffs in reproductive injury cases are subject to the same kind of humiliating questions about their sexuality and sexual lives as women victims in rape cases have traditionally been. One tactic of the defense attorneys is to discourage women from pursuing lawsuits against the reproductive industry with the specter of the women's sexual lives being probed and picked apart in public.

3. Survey of IVF Clinic Success Rates

There should be an annual and unbiased survey of IVF success rates and IVF costs. The first unbiased US survey conducted by Gena Corea and Susan Ince found that half of the clinics which replied to their questionnaire never "produced" one test-tube baby. Yet many of those clinics reported high success rates. A more recent technology, gamete intrafallopian tube transfer, or GIFT, is being hailed in the media as much more successful than IVF, yet the same concerns about dubious definitions of success linger. The survey should disclose what new drugs, therapies, and technologies are being used at the clinics.

4. Health Insurance for IVF

IVF is not a successful treatment for infertility; it fails in most cases. Furthermore, it is being practiced on fertile women at an expanding rate; and the biomedical industry is virtually unregulated. To provide coverage under health insurance only gives the biomedical industry a guaranteed annual income, since private costs are so exorbitant and the federal government does not fund reproductive research. Health insurance coverage will help solidify this interventionist solution as the dominant one in solving infertility. We recommend that the new reproductive technologies not be provided coverage under private or public health insurance plans.

5. Appropriate Technologies

Women should not be the "site of technology" for problems of male sterility or "unexplained" infertility. If male sterility is to be remedied with any kind of technical or drug intervention, it should be done on men's bodies, not women's. Infertility technology should never be used on women who are not infertile. Ideally women should develop the analysis of female infertility: its causes, its consequences, its prevention, its solutions, and the controlling social mechanisms which make women need to have children. Our desire is to have our bodies work for us, not to control or replace our bodies' functions unnecessarily, as IVF does, nor to treat a condition which is not life-threatening with risky technologies. This difference should yield different solutions to infertility from the new reproductive technologies.

6. Technology Assessment

The new reproductive technologies must be evaluated for their total and long-term impacts on individual women, and women as a class.

While a few women get babies, most who enter IVF clinics do not. Using the statistics from France, 94 to 99 of 100 women who enter IVF clinics are experimental subjects for IVF researchers. They undergo hormonal stimulation with drugs whose full side-effects are not determined; they undergo general anesthesia and laparoscopy; their lives are encumbered, sometimes for years, for the sake of the 1 to 6 in 100 who leave with children. This rate of failure constitutes experimenting on women and jeopardizing women's health for the sake of a non-life-threatening condition. Risk assessment cannot be left in the hands of the biomedical industry. The American Fertility Society's Ethics Committee determined that IVF poses no greater risk "to the couple" than their own sex life does. This collapsing of the woman into "the couple" is dishonest since she, not he, of the couple undergoes general anesthesia, surgery, and drug treatments. It is inconsistent and deceptive because later the committee questions the ethics of egg donation for the physical risks it poses to the "egg donor." The committee's report is rife with conflict of interest, because when it says that these risks are worth taking, it means that they are worth taking for the researcher—for the sake of the IVF "fund of knowledge," that is, their publications and careers—not for women.

The technologies exploit women as a class, socialized to devalue themselves if they cannot have children, even when the cause is male sterility. The technologies' potential to encumber more and more women expands as the indications for which they are prescribed expand. This risk—of exploiting women's sense of being less than a full self without a child—is one of those nonquantifiable risks which cannot ever be calculated in the material way that the risks of general anesthesia, probing egg follicles, and synthetic hormones can. Yet it is at the core of why the biomedical profession can get away with treating women in ways which animal rights' activists have protested as inhumane when the same is done to animals.

A risk assessment, with women's rights and women's dignity at the center of it, would compellingly demonstrate that such invasive technologies used as the dominant solution to infertility—female and male, and increasingly used on fertile women—are unethical. Medically induced and environmentally induced infertility should be solved by prevention. Male infertility should be solved in men, not women. Technical solutions for a non-life-threatening condition should not pose more risk than the condition. Such risks are currently posed for women.

7. Surrogacy

Where surrogacy has been banned, it has been banned because "the sale of a child" is heinous. Where it has been permitted under regulation, the underlying objective of the regulation is to quality control the surrogate mother and to keep her from breaking the contract. Surrogacy is, foremost, the sale of women as breeders; it is objectifying and degrading to women. The profile of the surrogate industry in the United States is upper-middle-class men—lawyers and doctors as brokers for other men obsessed with having a child from their own sperm—using lower-middle-class women as breeders. It is easy to imagine that this industry will go the way of many US industries, who have gone to developing countries for cheap, female labor. Increasingly, surrogacy is being used in combination with in vitro technologies and cesarian sections. Surrogacy should be banned on the grounds that it exploits women, that it is a violation of women's person, dignity, and integrity (Raymond 1988a).

The biotechnology revolutions—in agriculture and in women's reproduction—are not fundamentally novel and momentous changes. They are technical turnkeys for essentially social and political problems, developed by biotechnologists who liken themselves to a new Manhattan Project. The flash of their biotechnical bombs blinds the biotechnologists, as it did the original atomic bomb physicists (Wyden 1984, p. 366).

Above all, we must not concede that these technologies are necessary and inevitable, even when they are dominant. We must find other paths—however remote, unused, and inaccessible—which, to paraphrase Rachel Carson, do not presume that women and nature exist for the use and convenience of men. Widened and deepened by feminism, these paths offer our last, our only, chance to reach a destination that assures the integrity of earth and ourselves.

REFERENCES

American Heritage Dictionary of the English Language 1981. Boston, Massachusetts: Houghton Mifflin.

Anderson, I. and Connor, S. 1987. US questions gene regulator's links with Porton. *New Scientist* 22 October, 24.

Andrews, J. 1986, Here a gene, there a gene. *Environmental Action*, November/December, 18.

Berry, W. 1987. *Home Economics*. San Francisco: North Point Press.

Brill, W. J. 1986. Biotechnology: its potential. *EPA Journal*, **12**(8), 6–7.

Carson, R. 1962. *Silent Spring*. Greenwich, Connecticut: Fawcett Publications.

Carson, R. 1962. Of man and the stream of time. *Scripps College Bulletin*, July, 5–10.

Corea, G. 1985. *The Mother Machine: Reproductive Technologies from Artificial Insemination to Artificial Wombs*. New York: Harper and Row.

Corea, G. 1986. The Reproductive Manhattan Project. Paper presented at High-Tech Baby-Making Conference, Women's Research Institute, Hartford College for Women, Connecticut, March.

Corea, G. and Ince, S. 1985. IVF a game for losers at half of U.S. clinics, *Medical Tribune*, **26**(9), 1.

Crawford, M. 1987. Document links NSF official to biotech firm. *Science* 238: 742.

Crowe, C. 1987. "Women want it": *in vitro* fertilization and women's motivations for participation. *Made to Order: The Myth of Reproductive and Genetic Progress*, P. Spallone and D. L. Steinberg (eds), pp. 84–93. Oxford and New York: Pergamon Press.

Dankelman, I. and Davidson, J. 1988. *Women and Environment in the Third World*. London: Earthscan Publications.

Developing confidence in biotechnology: an interview with John Moore. 1986 *EPA Journal*, **12**(8), 2.

Doyle, J. 1985. *Altered Harvest*. New York: Penguin.

Doyle, J. 1986. Biotechnology: its possible dangers. *EPA Journal*, **12**(8), 8–9.

Dumanoski, D. 1987. Industry sued in lead paint poisonings. *Boston Globe*, 18 November, 1.

Dunlap, T. R. 1981. *DDT: Scientists, Citizens, and Public Policy*. Princeton, New Jersey: Princeton University Press.

Ellington, A. 1988. The biotechnology revolution: for rich nations only? *The Valley Advocate*, 22 February, 17.

Ethics Committee of the American Fertility Society 1986. Ethical considerations of the new reproductive technologies. *Fertility and Sterility*, Supplement 1, **46**(3).

Janson, D. 1988. Data on smoking revealed at trial. *New York Times*, 13 March, 34.

Kingsbury, D. T. 1986. Regulating biotechnology: the White House policy. *EPA Journal*, **12**(8), 5.

Laborie, F. 1987. New reproductive technologies: news from France and elsewhere. Paper presented to Forum International sur les Nouvelles Technologies de la Production Humaine, organized by Conseil du Statut de la Femme, Gouvernement du Quebec, Montreal, 31 October.

MacKenzie, Debora. 1988. Science milked for all it's worth. *New Scientist*, 22 March, 28–29.

Matthiessen, C. and Kohn, H. 1985. Ice minus and beyond. *Science for the People*, **17**(3), 23–25.

Murphy, S. 1988. Scholar foresees end to hunger. *Boston Globe*, 15 February, 36.

Pacific War Research Society 1972. *The Day Man Lost*. Tokyo and New York: Kodansha.

Perrow, C. 1984. *Normal Accidents: Living with High Risk Technologies*. New York: Basic Books.

Presidential candidates' quiz. 1988. *Valley Advocate*, February 29, 3.

Raymond, J. 1988a. In the matter of Baby M–rejudged. *Reproductive and Genetic Engineering*, **1**(1), 175–181.

Raymond, J. 1988b. The spermatic market: surrogate stock and liquid assets. *Reproductive and Genetic Engineering*, **1**(1), 111–117.

Shenon, P. 1988. Professor is charged with lying for makers of birth control device. *New York Times*, 4 March 1988, 1.

Some possible uses for biotechnology. 1986. *EPA Journal*, **12**(8), 13.

Spallone, P. and Steinberg, D. (eds) 1987. *Made to Order: the Myth of Reproductive and Genetic Progress*. Oxford and New York: Pergamon Press.

World Commission on Environment and Development 1987. *Our Common Future*. Oxford and New York: Oxford University Press.

Wyden, P. 1984. *Day One: Before Hiroshima and After*. New York: Simon and Schuster.

Yesterday's miracle. 1988. *Parade Magazine, Boston Globe*, 28 February, 8.

Zwerdling, D. 1977. The pesticide treadmill. *The Environmental Journal*, September, 15–18.

INDEX

ABOUT THE AUTHOR

Pat Hynes is Founding Director of the Institute on Women and Technology. The purposes of the Institute are to assess the impacts of new and existing technologies on women; to bring a woman-centered perspective to public policy on specific technologies and technology-based issues; and to advocate for technology that empowers women intellectually, financially and politically and that sustains the natural world. An environmental engineer, she was Section Chief in the Hazardous Waste Division of the Environmental Protection Agency, Boston and Chief of Environmental Management at the Massachusetts Port Authority. In 1985 she won the annual Environmental Service Award of the Massachusetts Association of Conservation Commissions. She recently completed a comparative study of lead contamination and remedial action policy in the European Community and the United States, under the auspices of a German Marshall Fund Environmental Fellowship. Her current work is *Semiramis Reconstructing Babylon: Essays, Speeches and Testimony on Women and Technology, Volume 1.*

THE ATHENE SERIES
An International Collection of Feminist Books
General Editors: Gloria Bowles, Renate Klein, and Janice Raymond
Consulting Editor: Dale Spender
